Composing Questions

Linguistic Inquiry Monographs
Samuel Jay Keyser, general editor

A complete list of books published in the Linguistic Inquiry Monographs series appears at the back of this book.

Composing Questions

Hadas Kotek

The MIT Press
Cambridge, Massachusetts
London, England

This book was set in Nimbus by Westchester Publishing Services. Printed and bound in the United States of America.

Library of Congress Cataloging-in-Publication Data is available.

Names: Kotek, Hadas, author.
Title: Composing questions / Hadas Kotek.
Description: Cambridge, MA : The MIT Press [2019] | Series: Linguistic
    Inquiry Monographs; #80 | Includes bibliographical references and index.
Identifiers: LCCN 2018019331 | ISBN 9780262039291 (hardcover : alk. paper) |
    ISBN 9780262536547 (pbk. : alk. paper)
Subjects: LCSH: Grammar, Comparative and general--Interrogative. | Grammar,
    Comparative and general--Word order.
Classification: LCC P299.I57 K68 2019 | DDC 415--dc23 LC record available at
https://lccn.loc.gov/2018019331

10 9 8 7 6 5 4 3 2 1

Contents

Series Foreword

We are pleased to present the eightieth volume in the series *Linguistic Inquiry Monographs*. These monographs present new and original research beyond the scope of the article. We hope they will benefit our field by bringing to it perspectives that will stimulate further research and insight.

Originally published in limited edition, the *Linguistic Inquiry Monographs* are now more widely available. This change is due to the great interest engendered by the series and by the needs of a growing readership. The editors thank the readers for their support and welcome suggestions about future directions for the series.

Samuel Jay Keyser
for the Editorial Board

Acknowledgments

This book has benefited from the continued support and input of many friends and colleagues over several years. Some made passing observations; others provided detailed commentary. Many had to tolerate repeated queries for complex data and judgments. During its five-year development, from early drafts of my dissertation to its current book form, this work has gone through several versions and undergone quite a few revisions. If it is any closer to correct now than it was at the beginning, no doubt the following people deserve the credit: my MIT dissertation committee—David Pesetsky, Martin Hackl, Danny Fox, and Irene Heim; senior colleagues at Yale and NYU—especially Bob Frank, Raffaella Zanuttini, Lucas Champollion, Chris Collins, Stephanie Harves, and Anna Szabolsci; and my many MIT friends and colleagues who supported me throughout graduate school. Special thanks go to Chris Tancredi for detailed comments on an earlier draft of the book, and to Michael Yoshitaka Erlewine for all kinds of support and advice, as well as for detailed comments.

Parts of the dissertation and book manuscript were taught in seminars at McGill University (Fall 2014), Yale University (Fall 2016), and NYU (Fall 2017). Participants in all of these classes made invaluable contributions to my thinking and to the development of this work from dissertation-form to book-form. Parts of this work were also presented at various conferences and colloquia, whose audiences I would like to thank: LSA 87 in Boston (2012), NELS 44 at the University of Connecticut (2013), LSA 88 in Minneapolis (2013), LSA 89 in Portland (2014), DGfS 37 workshop in Leipzig (2015), SuB 20 in Tübingen (2015), IATL 31 at Bar-Ilan University (2015); the Tokyo Semantics Research Group (2012), Tel Aviv University (2014), McGill University (2014), University of Calgary (2014), University of Ottawa (2015), University of Arizona at Tucson (2015), Queen Mary University of London (2015), CUNY Graduate Center (2015), UC Irvine (2017), and the MIT panel on questions at Pesetsky@60 (2017).

This book is a modified and extended version of my dissertation, Kotek 2014a. Chapters 6 and 7 are revised versions of work that was reported in Kotek 2017a and Kotek 2016, respectively. Chapter 8 is an extended version of joint work reported in Kotek and Hackl 2013. The book's title, like the dissertation title, is a play on the title of Hagstrom's (1998) dissertation, "Decomposing Questions," which served as inspiration for this work. Parts of this work were supported by National Science Foundation Dissertation Improvement Grant 1251717 in 2013–2014 and by a Mellon Postdoctoral Fellowship in 2014–2016.

Notation

Semantic types

e	Individual
t	Truth value
s	World
σ, τ	Arbitrary semantic types
$\langle \sigma, \tau \rangle$	A function from D_σ to D_τ

Functions

$[\![\cdot]\!], [\![\cdot]\!]^o$	The ordinary semantic value function
$[\![\cdot]\!]^f$	The focus-semantic value function

Judgments

✓	Acceptable (presumed grammatical)
*	Unacceptable (presumed ungrammatical)
*PL	Lacking a pair-list reading

Examples and trees

italic	*Wh*-word
bold	Intervener
X_1	Element base-generated in a higher position
X_2	Element base-generated in a lower position
X t	Overt movement
X t	Covert movement
X 〰 t	Area of in-situ composition

Glosses

ACC	accusative
AGR	agreement
ASP	aspect
AUX	auxiliary
C	complementizer
CL	clitic
CONJ	conjunction
DAT	dative
DEF	definite
EMPH	emphatic
ERG	ergative
EXPL	expletive
F	feminine
M	masculine
NEG	negation
NOM	nominative
PREP	preposition
PRT	particle
PST	past
Q	question particle
REL.PRO	relative pronoun
SG	singular
TOP	topic
VM	verbal marker

1   Introduction

The main focus of this book concerns the syntax and semantics of *wh*-questions, bringing new data to bear on a central question in the study of interrogatives: given that overt *wh*-movement is crosslinguistically common but not ubiquitous, is syntactic movement a prerequisite for the interpretation of *wh*-phrases? A significant body of research has argued that all *wh*-phrases undergo movement to interrogative C even if this is not overtly visible, while an equally important body of research has proposed mechanisms of in-situ interpretation that do not require any movement at all. The book investigates the syntax and semantics of *wh*-in-situ in depth and argues for a proposal that I believe resolves the debate.

The core result of this work is that *wh*-in-situ *does* move covertly, but not necessarily to C. Instead, *wh*-in-situ undergoes a short movement step akin to *covert scrambling*. Longer-distance movement is possible, but occurs only under special circumstances. This makes the LF behavior of English parallel to the overt behavior of German, contributing to our understanding of the acquisition of questions and the crosslinguistic typology of interrogative constructions. I motivate this thesis through new diagnostics for the underlying structure of questions, using as a principal tool the distribution of *intervention effects*—a topic of much attention in recent work on questions—in both offline judgment data and online sentence processing.

Specifically, I present (a) a detailed investigation of the syntax of multiple *wh*-questions through the lens of intervention effects; (b) a series of self-paced reading experiments, alongside judgment data from German, to substantiate the idea of covert scrambling; and (c) a principled semantic mechanism that is able to derive the single-pair and pair-list readings of multiple *wh*-questions from this syntax, as well as deriving known and previously unobserved patterns of intervention effects. This system is able to model a variety of phenomena in the domain of interrogative syntax/semantics for which previous proposals have not given a unified account, including pied-piping, superiority effects, the presuppositions of the question, the crosslinguistically varied syntax of questions, and intervention effects. Central to this analysis is the ALTSHIFT operator, whose distribution can help us understand the variation in the syntax and possible interpretations of interrogatives crosslinguistically.

The book is split into three parts. Part I develops a theory of interrogative syntax/semantics, building on English and German data and then extending the discussion to *wh*-in-situ languages, partial *wh*-movement languages, and multiple *wh*-fronting languages. Part II studies the phenomenon of intervention effects in *wh*-questions. New data are introduced, leading to a new generalization concerning the nature of intervention as crucially tied to the availability of *wh*-movement in a question vs. the necessity to use a mode of in-situ composition for *wh*-in-situ. Finally, part III motivates the view that covert *wh*-movement should be modeled as a short scrambling operation instead of as an unbounded, successive-cyclic, and potentially long-distance movement operation. Evidence in favor of this account comes from considerations relating to intervention effects, as well as from online sentence processing.

In what follows, I briefly survey the central issues of this book.

1.1   Questions and Their Interpretation

As is well-known, D-linked English questions allow for both Superiority-obeying and Superiority-violating variants.

(1) *Superiority-obeying and Superiority-violating multiple* wh-*questions*
   a. *Which* student ___ read *which* book?
   b. *Which* book did *which* student read ___?

These multiple *wh*-questions can have single-pair and pair-list (or: multiple-pair) readings.[1] The single-pair reading of the question can be fruitfully modeled as a set of propositions that denote the possible complete answers to the question (Hamblin 1973; Karttunen 1977). Example (2) shows the denotation of the question assuming a domain with three students (Abby, Betty, and Cathy) and three books (*Moby-Dick, Jane Eyre*, and *Oliver Twist*).

(2) *A single-pair reading is modeled as a set of propositions*
$$\left\{ \begin{array}{l} \text{Abby read MD, Abby read JE, Abby read OT,} \\ \text{Betty read MD, Betty read JE, Betty read OT,} \\ \text{Cathy read MD, Cathy read JE, Cathy read OT} \end{array} \right\}$$

Adopting the presupposition that a question must have a unique maximally informative true answer (Dayal 1996; Fox 2012a,b), the structure in (2) will ensure a single-pair answer. This is because none of the propositions in (2) are stronger than any of the others—none are entailed from or entail any of the others. Hence, for there to be a unique maximally informative true member in the set, it must be the case that only one proposition is true, and all the others are false. This, then, ensures a single-pair interpretation.

A crucial component of the analysis developed in this book is the treatment of the pair-list reading of the question as a *family of questions*, sorted by the higher *wh*-phrase in the structure (Büring 2003; Fox 2012b; Hagstrom 1998; Krifka 2001; Nicolae 2013; Roberts 1996; Willis 2008). This will allow us to derive the exhaustivity and uniqueness presuppositions of the pair-list reading of the question (Dayal 1996) from an approach generalized from the presupposition of the single-pair reading. In a nutshell, we require there to be a unique maximally informative true member of each set of propositions (i.e., in each question) in the family of questions. Example denotations of pair-list readings of Superiority-obeying and -violating questions are given in (3)–(4).

(3) *Family-of-questions denotation for a Superiority-obeying question*
Which student read *which* book?

$$\left\{ \begin{Bmatrix} \text{Abby read MD} \\ \text{Abby read JE} \\ \text{Abby read OT} \end{Bmatrix}, \begin{Bmatrix} \text{Betty read MD} \\ \text{Betty read JE} \\ \text{Betty read OT} \end{Bmatrix}, \begin{Bmatrix} \text{Cathy read MD} \\ \text{Cathy read JE} \\ \text{Cathy read OT} \end{Bmatrix} \right\}$$

(4) *Family-of-questions denotation yields a pair-list reading*
Which book did *which* student read?

$$\left\{ \begin{Bmatrix} \text{Abby read MD} \\ \text{Betty read MD} \\ \text{Cathy read MD} \end{Bmatrix}, \begin{Bmatrix} \text{Abby read JE} \\ \text{Betty read JE} \\ \text{Cathy read JE} \end{Bmatrix}, \begin{Bmatrix} \text{Abby read OT} \\ \text{Betty read OT} \\ \text{Cathy read OT} \end{Bmatrix} \right\}$$

I propose that the semantic derivation of a question involves three interrogative components: the interrogative complementizer C, *wh*-words, and a question operator, ALTSHIFT.

The interrogative complementizer C triggers interrogative movement. In English, this complementizer has an EPP feature that requires at least one *wh*-phrase to occupy its specifier, and furthermore exactly one *wh*-phrase to be pronounced in this position. A central issue taken up in part II is whether the syntactic derivation of multiple *wh*-questions involves *covert* movement of the phonologically in-situ *wh*-phrase. The semantic theory developed in part I will be able to handle both structures in which covert movement has taken place and structures in which it has not. As we will see, both types of structures exist crosslinguistically and even within the same language.

The interrogative complementizer plays an important role in deriving the syntax of the question, but it plays no role in deriving its semantics—it simply passes up the denotation of its sister.

(5) *The semantics of the interrogative complementizer*
$$[\![C]\!] = \lambda P_\tau . P$$

Wh-words are elements that introduce alternatives into the derivation (Hamblin 1973). I assume that they do not have a defined ordinary semantic value (Beck 2006; Cable 2010; Ramchand 1997). For example, the semantics of *who* is given in (6).

(6) *The semantics of* who *as a set of alternative individuals*
  Ordinary value: $[\![who]\!]^o$ is undefined
  Alternative value: $[\![who]\!]^f = \{x_e : x \in \text{human}\}$

Finally, I introduce a new operator into the derivation of a question: the *ALTSHIFT operator*, which is the source of interrogative semantics. In English, this operator necessarily sits on the clausal spine above TP, but I will argue that in other languages its distribution may vary (see also Uegaki 2018), deriving some patterns of crosslinguistic variation both in the syntax and semantics of questions and in the use of *wh*-indeterminates in noninterrogative constructions such as *wh*-indefinites and disjunctions.

The ALTSHIFT operator takes a set of propositions (or a set of such sets, etc.) and returns the focus-semantic value of that set as its ordinary value; that is, it takes the set of alternatives denoted by its sister in the focus domain and shifts them into the ordinary domain.

(7) *The semantics of the ALTSHIFT operator*
  a. $[\![\text{ALTSHIFT } \alpha_\sigma]\!]^o = [\![\alpha_\sigma]\!]^f$
  b. $[\![\text{ALTSHIFT } \alpha_\sigma]\!]^f = \{[\![\text{ALTSHIFT } \alpha_\sigma]\!]^o\}$ $(\sigma \in \{\langle st, t \rangle, \langle\langle st, t \rangle, t \rangle, \dots \})$

This is a type-flexible version of the semantics for C proposed by Beck and Kim (2006) and Shimoyama (2001). This type-flexibility is crucial in allowing the pair-list reading of a multiple *wh*-question to be derived as a family-of-questions denotation. This will allow single-pair and pair-list readings to be derived in a principled way from minimally different LF structures (hereafter, *LFs*).

I lay out the proposal in more detail in chapter 3. There, I also show how the proposal explains the behavior of English and German multiple *wh*-questions. In chapter 4, I show how this proposal can be extended to model the crosslinguistically varied syntax of *wh*-questions in *wh*-in-situ languages, in partial *wh*-movement languages, and in multiple *wh*-fronting languages.

1.2   Intervention Effects and Covert Movement

A second issue central to this book is the behavior of multiple *wh*-questions with respect to *intervention effects*. The term *intervention effect* describes a situation in which a question is rendered ungrammatical because an in-situ wh-phrase is c-commanded by an offending *intervener*—certain quantifica-tional and negative elements, as well as focus-sensitive items—at LF.

Intervention effects are best observed in wh-in-situ languages such as Japanese and Korean. Although question formation in these languages gen-erally does not require wh-fronting, in-situ wh-phrases must scramble above interveners in order to avoid intervention effects. Example (8a) shows an in-situ question with a canonical word order. When an intervener (here: the negative polarity item *daremo* 'anyone') c-commands the in-situ wh-phrase, the result is degraded. This ungrammaticality can be avoided by scrambling the wh-phrase above the intervener, (8b).

(8) *Japanese: Intervention effects are avoided by scrambling (Tomioka 2007b:1, 2; adapted from (1), (4))*

    a. ✓ Hanako / ?***Dare-mo*** | *nani-o* | yom-ana-katta-no?
        Hanako   anyone   what-ACC read-NEG-PST-Q
        'What did Hanako/*no one read?'

    b. | *Nani-o* | **dare-mo** ___ yom-ana-katta-no?
        what-ACC anyone   read-NEG-PST-Q
        'What did no one read?'

A parallel effect is observed in German, for wh-in-situ in multiple wh-questions. Here, the negative quantifier *niemand* 'no one' is the intervener.

(9) *German: Intervention above* wh-*in-situ is avoided by scrambling (Beck 1996a:6; adapted from (10))*

    a. *Wer* hat ✓ Luise / ??**niemanden** | *wo* | angetroffen?
        who has Luise   no-one   where met
        'Who didn't meet Luise/*anybody where?'

    b. *Wer* hat | *wo* | **niemanden** ___ angetroffen?
        who has where no-one   met
        'Who didn't meet anybody where?'

Data like the above lead to the following descriptive characterization of the intervention effect: an intervener cannot c-command a wh-phrase (10a); to yield an interpretable structure, wh must move above the intervener (10b). A structure such as (10a) is judged by speakers to be degraded. Beck (2006) proposes that the relevant level of representation at which intervention is evaluated is LF.

(10) *The intervention configuration (Beck 2006:17; adapted from (54))*
      a. * [$_{CP}$ C ... [**intervener** [... wh ...]]]
      b.   [$_{CP}$ C ... [wh [**intervener** [... *t* ...]]]]

In English multiple *wh*-questions, a more complex pattern is observed, which supports the idea that the generalization in (10) is active at LF. Pesetsky (2000) shows that intervention effects correlate with superiority: an intervention effect is observed in *Superiority-violating* questions but not in *Superiority-obeying* ones. Three of Pesetsky's examples are reproduced below.

(11) *Intervention effects in English questions correlate with superiority*
     a.   *Which* book did **only Mary** give ___ to *which* student?
                                                           (Superiority-obeying)
     b. ?? *Which* student did **only Mary** give *which* book to ___?
                                                          (Superiority-violating)
          (Pesetsky 2000:61; adapted)

(12) a.   *Which* student **didn't** ___ read *which* book?   (Superiority-obeying)
     b. ?? *Which* book **didn't** *which* student read ___?   (Superiority-violating)
          (Pesetsky 2000:60; adapted)

(13) a.   *Which* picture did **very few children** want to show
           ___ to *which* teacher?   (Superiority-obeying)
     b. ?? *Which* teacher did **very few children** want to show
           which picture to ___?   (Superiority-violating)
          (Pesetsky 2000:61)

Pesetsky (2000) proposes that this grammaticality pattern is explained by a difference in the syntax of *wh*-questions: in Superiority-obeying questions the (surface) in-situ *wh*-phrase is able to covertly move to C at LF, whereas in Superiority-violating questions the in situ *wh*-phrase is truly in-situ at LF, and interpreted without movement.

(14) *English questions: The interaction of superiority and interveners at LF*
     a. Superiority-obeying: Covert *wh*-movement, no intervention
        [$_{CP}$ wh_1 wh_2 [C [$_{TP}$ … **intervener** … t_1 … t_2]]]

     b. Superiority-violating: *Wh* in situ at LF, intervention effects
        $*^{PL}$[$_{CP}$ wh_2 [C [$_{TP}$ … **intervener** … wh_1 … t_2]]]

Here and throughout, solid straight arrows indicate overt movement, dashed arrows indicate covert movement, and squiggly arrows indicate regions of Rooth-Hamblin alternatives composition. These arrows are used as a notational convenience only.

I adopt these syntactic assumptions as my starting point in parts I and II. In part II, I present novel data showing that this previously assumed strict correlation between intervention and superiority in English, as in (11)–(13), is incorrect. Instead, intervention strictly correlates with movement possibilities of the *wh*-phrases in the question. Whenever *wh*-phrases can move above an intervener, or alternatively the intervener can move out of the way, intervention effects are avoided. Conversely, when an intervener c-commands a *wh*-phrase at LF and this structure cannot be undone, an intervention effect is observed.

In particular, I show that whenever covert *wh*-movement in a derivation such as (14a) is restricted in some way—using islands, binding configurations, or other means—intervention effects are observed above the highest possible interpretable position of *wh*-in-situ. That is, intervention effects are observed in Superiority-obeying questions when covert movement is blocked. Conversely, intervention effects are absent from Superiority-violating questions whenever the intervention configuration (10a) can be avoided. Although covert *wh*-movement is not available to *wh*-in-situ expressions in these questions, if a *wh*-in-situ expression undergoes another type of movement, such as right-node raising or extraposition, or if the intervener is moved out of the way, intervention is avoided. This again reinforces the conclusion that the configuration in (10) is active at LF. This, in turn, will allow us to use intervention effects as a diagnostic for the position of *wh*-elements at LF in part III.

1.3   Covert *Wh*-Scrambling

Part III introduces a refinement of the covert movement proposal for *wh*-in-situ in English questions. I present arguments from offline judgments as well as from online sentence processing that the covert movement step of in-situ *wh*-phrases in Superiority-obeying questions is *QR (quantifier raising)-like*—that is, it can (and perhaps, on occasion, must) target positions other than interrogative C. I propose that any node with a propositional type is a possible target for this movement.

More specifically, I argue that this movement should be thought of as *covert scrambling* instead of the unbounded movement to interrogative C that is traditionally assumed. Movement targets a low position inside TP, where a *wh* is interpretable, and is only extended in extraordinary cases—for example, to avoid an intervention effect, or to allow for ellipsis resolution in cases of Antecedent-Contained Deletion. I take this movement to be scrambling-like in the sense that it parallels the behavior of overt scrambling in German.

(15) *A covert scrambling approach to question formation*
$$[_{CP} wh_1 [C [_{TP} \ldots wh_2 [_{vP} \ldots t_1 \ldots t_2]]]]$$

Although I remain agnostic about whether QR and scrambling are one and the same or two distinct operations, I conclude the book by briefly entertaining the idea that *wh*-expressions denote *sets of alternative quantificational interpretations*, which necessitate a short QR-like movement step for their interpretation, as a possible source of the short covert *wh*-scrambling I argue for in this part of the book. By merging the Hamblin set approach to *wh*-expressions with Karttunen-based approaches that view *wh*-expressions as quantifiers, I argue that we are able to combine the results developed throughout this book into a single coherent proposal.

The covert scrambling proposal makes the behavior of English parallel to that of German in terms of their LF representations: both languages form questions through overt (successive-cyclic) movement of one *wh*-phrase to interrogative C, alongside (short) scrambling of lower *wh*-phrases. This scrambling step may be overt (in German) or covert (in English). I argue that this is advantageous from the viewpoint of the acquisition of questions and of intervention effects, which—as will become apparent—are very complex and hence are best acquired via independent principles that do not require exposure to data specifically about the forms discussed in this book. My proposal also helps to account for the crosslinguistic typology of questions and intervention effects.

A THEORY OF *WH*-QUESTIONS

2   Background: *Wh*-Questions

In a language like English, the formation of a constituent question involves at least two steps. First, a structure is formed in which a *wh-phrase* is produced in its base position—for example, as an argument of a predicate, (1a).[1] Second, that *wh*-phrase is *overtly moved* to the left edge of the question, (1b). In a *multiple* wh-*question* only one *wh*-phrase is pronounced at the left edge of the question, while the remaining *wh*-phrase or *wh*-phrases are pronounced in situ, in what appears to be their base-generated positions, (1c).

(1) Wh-*in-situ in a* wh-*movement language*
   a. Mary gave *which* gift to Fred?
   b. *Which* gift did Mary give ___ to Fred?
   c. *Which* gift did Mary give ___ to *which* boy?

The question in (1c) exemplifies a *Superiority-obeying* structure, in which the base-generated *higher wh-phrase* is overtly fronted. In addition to such questions, English allows *Superiority-violating* structures, where the base-generated *lower wh*-phrase is fronted.

(2) *Superiority-obeying and Superiority-violating questions*
   a. *Which* gift did Mary give ___ to *which* boy?
   b. *Which* boy did Mary give *which* gift to ___?

An understanding of the structure and interpretation of these multiple *wh*-questions is a central goal of this book. In particular, an important question concerns the interpretation of in-situ *wh*-phrases in these multiple *wh*-questions: are they interpreted in their pronounced positions, or do (phonologically) in-situ *wh*-phrases undergo covert movement to a higher position in the question? The literature affords means of interpreting *wh*-phrases in situ or in moved positions, but fewer means of determining which syntax is correct in a given language and situation.

In part I of this book, I motivate a new syntax and semantics for *wh*-questions. My goal is to combine Pesetsky's (2000) syntactic theory of *wh*-movement and its extension to pied-piping by Cable (2007; 2010) with a simple semantics for questions, building on established ingredients in the literature. This proposal is able to derive the readings of multiple *wh*-questions in a principled way, while naturally fitting with existing analyses of the presuppositions of these questions (Dayal 1996) and with Beck's (2006) theory of intervention effects, which will become the focus of part II.

Before presenting the proposal, in this chapter I provide a brief introduction to interrogative syntax/semantics, concentrating on those data points and assumptions that will become crucial in the following chapters.

2.1 Two Types of Semantics for Questions

The literature offers two main approaches to the semantic denotation of questions. Under one, a question is modeled as a *partition* of the universe (i.e., the sets of worlds under consideration) into equivalence classes that agree with each other with respect to the answer to the question (Groenendijk and Stokhof 1984). Under the other, a question denotes sets of possible answers to the question (Hamblin 1973; Karttunen 1977). In this book, I will adopt the latter approach, but I briefly introduce both to give an idea of the ways scholars have approached the problem of the denotation of a question.

2.1.1 Questions as Partitions of Possible Worlds

I begin by briefly entertaining the idea that a question denotes *partitions* of the set of worlds under consideration into equivalence classes that agree with each other with respect to the answer to the question (Groenendijk and Stokhof 1984). Under this view, the intension of a question is a function from worlds to sets of worlds. This function maps every world to the set of worlds that are equivalent to it with respect to the property denoted by the question.

This semantics can be illustrated for a question such as *Who came?* with a domain consisting of just two individuals, Jane and Mary, (3b). The propositions that the question operates on are given in (3c), the meaning of the question is given in (3d), and the partition induced by the question is given in (3e).

(3) *Groenendijk and Stokhof's (1984) semantics for questions*
   a. *Who* came?
   b. Domain: {Jane, Mary}
   c. p_1 = Jane came, p_2 = Mary came
   d. $\lambda w' . \lambda w \, [(\lambda x . x \text{ came in } w) = (\lambda x . x \text{ came in } w')]$
   e.

$p_1 = 0, p_2 = 0$	$p_1 = 1, p_2 = 0$
$p_1 = 0, p_2 = 1$	$p_1 = 1, p_2 = 1$

The answer to the question is its extension in the world of evaluation w_0—that is, the set of propositions that coincide with w_0 in terms of who came. If both Jane and Mary came, then the true answer is the bottom right cell in the partition; if Jane came but Mary didn't, the answer is the top right cell in the partition; and so on.

More recently, Groenendijk and Stokhof, along with several colleagues at the University of Amsterdam, have put forth the *Inquisitive Semantics* framework for questions. Inquisitive Semantics is not meant to constitute a *theory* of any particular construction in any particular language. Instead, it is intended to provide the formal tools needed to express meanings in such theories. Either a partition-based account of questions, as introduced here, or an Alternative Semantics account of questions, as introduced immediately below, may be adapted into the Inquisitive Semantics framework. A detailed presentation of this framework goes beyond the scope of this book, but see for example Ciardelli, Groenendijk, and Roelofsen 2017, Groenendijk 2009, Groenendijk and Roelofsen 2009, and Roelofsen 2011, as well as the collected works featured at https://projects.illc.uva.nl/inquisitivesemantics/ for specifics.

2.1.2   Questions as Sets of Possible Answers

The other mainstream approach to question semantics is the Hamblin/ Karttunen approach (Hamblin 1973; Karttunen 1977), also dubbed Alternative Semantics, following Rooth (1985, 1992). Under this approach, a question denotes a set of propositions, which constitute the possible answers to the question. This is illustrated in (4) for the same domain consisting solely of Jane and Mary (4b), where (4c) shows the meaning of the question, and (4d) shows the set of possible answers to the question given our domain and the fact that *who* can denote either singular or plural individuals.

(4) *A Hamblin/Karttunen semantics for questions*
  a. *Who* came?
  b. Domain: {Jane, Mary}
  c. $\lambda p_{\langle s,t \rangle}. \, \exists x \, [x$ is a person in w_0 & $p = x$ came]
  d. {Jane came in w_0, Mary came in w_0, Jane and Mary came in w_0}

An important point of discussion within this literature that will not concern us here is whether the answer set should list all possible answers to the question, or only those answers that are true. This question is important for modeling question embeddings, but will not affect the theory that I will develop in subsequent chapters. See Karttunen 1977 for details and Uegaki 2015 for recent discussion.

In this book, I do not use a partition-based approach but instead adopt the Alternative Semantics approach. As Fox (2012a) and Heim (1994) show, it is possible to induce a partition over the set of propositions provided by Alternative Semantics for any analysis that might require these partitions. In particular, these authors show that we can define a function that takes a Hamblin/Karttunen denotation and yields an equivalence relation, or partition, on any set of possible worlds. However, it is not possible to define the reverse function: one that takes a partition and returns a Hamblin/Karttunen denotation.[2] For this and other reasons, in the remainder of the book I will be concerned with developing a syntax/semantics for questions based on Alternative Semantics.

2.2 Two Approaches to *Wh*-in-Situ

Turning our attention next to multiple *wh*-questions (e.g., *Which gift did Mary give to which boy?*), an important debate in the syntax/semantics literature concerns the interpretation of *in-situ wh*-phrases—*wh*-phrases that have not been overtly fronted—in these questions. The literature provides two major approaches to the interpretation of in-situ *wh*-phrases: *covert movement* and *in-situ interpretation*. Both approaches are commonly adopted and used. Moreover, some recent theories make use of both mechanisms within the same language and even in the derivation of the same question (e.g., Beck 2006; Cable 2010; Kotek 2014b; Pesetsky 2000).

2.2.1 The Covert Movement Approach

Covert movement is typically viewed as a language- or construction-specific variant of overt movement. In particular, many researchers have proposed that (phonologically) in-situ *wh*-phrases as in (1c) covertly move to C at LF in the same way that overt *wh*-movement is observed in (1b–c). Under this approach, *wh*-phrases must be at the CP edge in order to make their contribution to the meaning of the question. Consequently, no *wh*-phrase may remain in situ at LF; instead, all *wh*-phrases occur syntactically next to the complementizer, regardless of where they are pronounced (see Aoun, Hornstein, and Sportiche 1981; Beck 2006; Cable 2007, 2010; Hornstein 1995; Huang 1982a,b; Karttunen 1977; Lasnik and Saito 1992; Nishigauchi 1986; Pesetsky 2000; Richards 2001).[3]

The LF proposed under this approach for (1c) is schematized in (5). This LF adopts the notion of *tucking-in*—where the covertly moved *wh*-phrase targets a position *below* the overtly moved one—which I will discuss in more detail in section 2.3. For the moment, the important point is that all *wh*-phrases in the structure must occupy positions in the CP periphery at LF.

(5) *The covert movement approach to* wh-*in-situ*
   which gift [*which* boy [C [Mary gave ___ to ___]]]

Under this approach to *wh*-in-situ, then, the LF representation of *Who gave what to whom?* is as shown in (6b), where all three *wh*-phrases have undergone *wh*-movement. Overstrikes indicate the pronunciation pattern.

(6) *English multiple* wh-*question LF and pronunciation*
   a. *Who* gave *what* to *whom*?
   b. [who ~~what whom~~ [~~who~~ gave *what* to *whom*]]

Modeling English multiple *wh*-questions in this way is supported by the behavior of multiple *wh*-questions in Slavic languages (see, e.g., Lasnik and Saito 1984; Pesetsky 1987; Rudin 1985). In these languages, the covert instances of *wh*-movement posited for English can be observed overtly. That is, the proposed LF for English multiple *wh*-questions in (6b) differs from its Bulgarian counterpart in (7b) only in how its *wh*-chains are pronounced.

(7) *Bulgarian multiple* wh-*question LF and pronunciation*
   a. *Koj kakvo* na *kogo* dade?
      who what to whom gave
      'Who gave what to whom?'
   b. [koj kakvo na kogo [~~koj kakvo na kogo~~ dade]]

English and Bulgarian multiple *wh*-questions, then, have identical LFs under this approach. What distinguishes these two languages (and others that follow these same patterns, as discussed further in chapter 4) is the pronunciation rules that govern the PF representations of English, (8), and Bulgarian, (9), respectively (see Pesetsky 1998, 2000).

(8) *Pronunciation rule (English)*
   Pronounce the highest *wh*-phrase in Spec,CP in its high position; pronounce all other *wh*-phrases in their trace positions.

(9) *Pronunciation rule (Bulgarian)*
   Pronounce all *wh*-phrases in Spec,CP in their high position; leave them unpronounced in their trace positions.

The covert movement approach thus predicts pervasive covert movement in multiple *wh*-questions. Moreover, movement is always triggered for one and the same reason—the semantic needs of the *wh*-phrases themselves—and it always targets the same syntactic position at LF: C.

2.2.2 The In-Situ Approach

A second popular approach to *wh*-in-situ is the *in-situ approach*. Under this approach to questions, no (overt or covert) movement is required in order to assign interrogative meaning to a structure containing *wh*-elements (see Baker 1970; Cheng 1991; Chomsky 1995; É. Kiss 1986; Engdahl 1986; Hamblin 1973; Kratzer and Shimoyama 2002; Nishigauchi 1986, 1990; Reinhart 1997, 1998; Shimoyama 2006; Tsai 1994). The meaning of a question like (10) can be calculated through a mechanism that passes the meanings of *wh*-words up the structure until they reach C, where they can be interpreted.[4]

Rooth-Hamblin alternatives are a parallel mode of semantic composition, where an *alternative* (or *focus-semantic*) *value* is computed compositionally for each syntactic node, in parallel to its ordinary semantic value. This computation has been argued to supply operators such as focus operators and question complementizers with a relevant set of alternative denotations or propositions (e.g., Hamblin 1973; Rooth 1985, 1992). Consider the LF for the *wh*-in-situ pseudo-English question "Mary likes *who*?" in (10). Focus-semantic values are given for each node.

(10) *A toy LF of question interpretation via Rooth-Hamblin alternatives*

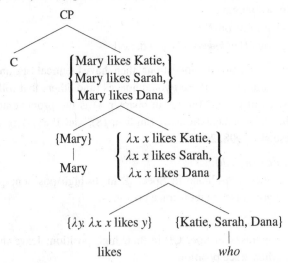

In (10), the *wh*-phrase *who* has a focus-semantic value corresponding to relevant individuals in its domain: Katie, Sarah, and Dana.[5] These alternatives compose pointwise at each nonterminal node, until they are finally interpreted by the interrogative C.[6] The complement of C thus contains a set of propositions as its focus-semantic value, corresponding to possible (weak) answers to the question. In this way, the alternatives introduced by the in-situ *wh*-phrase are interpreted by the interrogative C without establishing a syntactically local relationship between the two.

From this perspective, there is no reason to expect any instances of *wh*-movement that are caused by the semantic needs of the *wh*-words themselves. Even the fact that English questions require overt fronting of one *wh*-phrase is unexpected. To explain this fact, a purely syntactic mechanism must be invoked, unrelated to interrogative semantics—for example, an EPP feature requiring C to have a filled specifier (Chomsky 1981).

(11) *Movement happens for syntactic reasons such as an EPP requirement*
     which gift [C$_{+EPP}$ [Mary gave ___ to *which* boy]]

Finally, all *wh*-phrases are pronounced at the head of their respective chains; nothing special needs to be said about *wh*-in-situ.

2.3 Superiority Effects

Next, we observe that *wh*-phrases of different levels of complexity sometimes have varying degrees of freedom in the movement operations that may apply to them. In English, as we have already seen, questions with D-linked *wh*-phrases allow for both Superiority-obeying and Superiority-violating variants. However, Superiority-violating questions with simplex *wh*-phrases, like (12b), lead to ungrammaticality (Chomsky 1973).

(12) *Superiority effect (English)*
     a.   *Who* ___ bought *what*?
     b. * *What* did *who* buy ___ ?

An early description of this phenomenon is given by Kuno and Robinson (1972:474).

(13) *Kuno and Robinson's constraint*
     A *wh*-word cannot be preposed crossing over another *wh*.

Following this description, Superiority violations can be explained by locality principles such as Attract Closest, requiring an ordering of agreement and movement operations (Relativized Minimality: Frampton 1991; Rizzi 1990, 2001; Minimal Link Condition: Chomsky 1995, 2000). Here, I adopt a version of Attract Closest inspired by Pesetsky (2000) under which it is Agree, not Attract, that is subject to strict locality, (14).[7] This principle induces a strict ordering on Agree operations, such that higher targets must be agreed with before lower targets can be attended to. An Attract operation may be triggered immediately following an Agree operation (Chomsky 1998, 1999).

(14) *Definition: Agree with Closest*
A probe K can enter an Agree relation with a goal α only if there is no potential goal β that is closer to K than α is. (α is closer to K than β if and only if α asymmetrically c-commands β, and K c-commands both α and β.)

(15) *Definition: C-command*
Node A c-commands node B if and only if the first branching node that dominates A also dominates B, and A does not dominate B and B does not dominate A.

(16) *Definition: Asymmetric c-command*
Node A asymmetrically c-commands node B if and only if A c-commands B and B does not c-command A.

As we have seen, English questions with D-linked *wh*-phrases allow Superiority violations in cases where non-D-linked questions do not.

(17) *D-linked questions can violate Superiority*
a. *Which* person ___ bought *which* book?
b. *Which* book did *which* person buy ___?

The derivations of these Superiority-obeying and -violating questions that I adopt here rely on two principles: Agree with Closest, defined above, and tucking-in (Richards 1997). The notion of tucking-in follows from Agree with Closest and an additional principle such as Shortest Move (Chomsky 1995). Tucking-in requires crossing paths in multiple *wh*-questions instead of nested paths: this would allow for the shortest movement step of each *wh*-phrase in the question from its base-generated position to C. This explains the strict ordering of *wh*-phrases in Bulgarian, a multiple *wh*-fronting language, where *wh*-phrases appear in the same order in the specifiers of CP where they were base-generated.[8]

(18) *Tucking-in (Bulgarian, Pesetsky 2000:22)*
a. Crossing paths

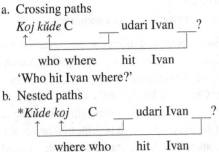

       who where   hit   Ivan
    'Who hit Ivan where?'
b. Nested paths
    *Kŭde koj   C   ___ udari Ivan ___?

       where who   hit   Ivan

I follow Pesetsky (2000) and Richards (1997), among others, in assuming that Agree with Closest and tucking-in also apply to *wh*-questions in English. I adopt standard assumptions concerning the interrogative probing system: an interrogative probe on C must (attempt to) agree with all *wh*-phrases in its c-command domain (Preminger 2011). Higher goals—as defined by c-command—must be agreed with before the probe can move on to lower goals, and the probe is not allowed to look back at previous goals after they have been agreed with. *Wh*-movement may (but need not) immediately follow an Agree operation. In this sense, *wh*-movement is parasitic on agreement. It follows, then, that higher goals will have the option to move before lower goals will. In the LFs given here, this means that wh_1 will always be the probe's first goal and will always have the option to move first, before the probe can attend to wh_2.

Pesetsky (2000) proposes that the difference in the ability of D-linked questions (17a–b) and non-D-linked questions (12a–b) to violate Superiority results from a difference in the movement options available to the *wh*-phrases in these questions. In non-D-linked questions, all *wh*-phrases must move to C at LF, after they have been agreed with by the interrogative probe. In D-linked questions, all *wh*-phrases must be agreed with, but it suffices that just one *wh*-phrase move to C (although it is possible for more than one *wh*-phrase to do so).

Hence, the Superiority-obeying (17a) can be derived from a structure in which both *wh*-phrases move to C at LF, and similarly for (12a): wh_1 is found by the probe first; it is agreed with and is moved to Spec,CP. The probe then agrees with wh_2, at which point wh_2 moves and tucks in below wh_1 in Spec,CP. The pronunciation rule introduced in (8) dictates that the highest *wh*-phrase in Spec,CP will be pronounced in its moved position, and all other *wh*-phrases will be pronounced in their base positions.

The Superiority-violating (17b) is derived from a structure in which both *wh*-phrases have been agreed with but only the lower one—wh_2—has undergone movement, leaving the higher *wh*-phrase in situ. This step—leaving the base-generated higher *wh*-phrase in situ in the Superiority-violating question— is crucial in order to yield the correct word order in this question, given the pronunciation rule in (8). Such a derivation is not available to non-D-linked questions in English because of the requirement that in such questions all *wh*-phrases must move to C, explaining the ungrammaticality of (12b).

The schematic description of Superiority-obeying questions and Superiority-violating D-linked questions is given in (19).

(19) *LFs of Superiority-obeying and Superiority-violating questions*
    a. $[_{CP} wh_1 \ wh_2 \ [C \ [_{TP} \ ... \ t_1 \ ... \ t_2]]]$ (Superiority-obeying)

b. [$_{CP}$ *wh$_2$* [C [$_{TP}$ ... *wh$_1$* ... *t$_2$*]]]   (Superiority-violating)

Pesetsky (2000) presents two arguments for the idea that Superiority-obeying and Superiority-violating multiple *wh*-questions in English involve different LF structures. I discuss one of these arguments—from Antecedent-Contained Deletion—in an appendix to this chapter. The other argument, from the behavior of intervention effects in multiple *wh*-questions, is a central topic of part II.

Other languages are reported not to exhibit superiority effects, even with simplex *wh*-phrases. In German, for example, both the Superiority-obeying question (20a) and the Superiority-violating question (20b) are grammatical, although several authors still report a preference for the superiority-obeying word order over the violating word order (e.g., Featherston 2005b).

(20) *Superiority effect (German)*
    a. *Wer* hat *was* gekauft?
       who has what bought
       'Who bought what?'
    b. *Was* hat *wer* gekauft?
       what has who bought
       'What did who buy?'

Pesetsky (2000) proposes that in German, only one *wh*-phrase can be hosted in Spec,CP, and all other *wh*-phrases must remain in situ at LF. A derivation proposed for English D-linked Superiority-violating questions, (19b), is used for all German questions. As we will see in part II, this proposal is able to explain differences in the behaviors of English and German with regard to intervention effects.

As a result of these syntactic considerations, it follows that we require a semantic mechanism for the interpretation of *wh*-questions that is able to handle diverse syntactic representations and still yield the same semantic meaning. This will be the goal of chapter 3, but before I delve into the proposal, there is one last bit of background to introduce.

2.4   Presuppositions and the Readings of Multiple Wh-Questions

The literature recognizes three distinct readings of multiple *wh*-questions: the single-pair, pair-list (or: multiple-pair), and echo question readings (Bolinger 1978; Comorovski 1989; Dayal 1996; Pope 1976; Wachowicz 1974). In this book, I concentrate on the first two reading, and do not discuss the third. To see the difference between the single-pair and pair-list answers to a question, consider two situations in which the multiple *wh*-question *Who ate what?* can occur and the answers it admits in those situations.

Suppose that we know that one person ate one dish, but we do not know who was doing the eating and what that person ate. In that case, we might ask (21a) in order to find out the identity of the single person-dish pair given in the context. This is the single-pair reading of the question, with the possible answer in (21b).

(21) *Single-pair answer to a multiple* wh-*question*
   a. *Who* ate *what*?
   b. Fred ate the beans.

We can model the single-pair reading of the question as a set of propositions that are the possible answers to the question (Hamblin 1973; Karttunen 1977). In a context with three guests (Fred, Mary, Dana) and three dishes (beans, soup, salad), we can spell out the full set of possible answers to (21a) as in (22).

(22) *A single-pair reading is modeled as a set of propositions*
$$\left\{ \begin{array}{l} \text{Fred ate the beans, Fred ate the soup, Fred ate the salad, Mary ate} \\ \text{the beans, Mary ate the soup, Mary ate the salad, Dana ate the} \\ \text{beans, Dana ate the soup, Dana ate the salad} \end{array} \right\}$$

Combined with the requirement that a question must have a unique maximally informative true answer, the denotation in (22) will ensure a single-pair answer (Dayal 1996). This is because each proposition in the set is independent of all the other propositions—no proposition entails or is entailed by any other proposition. Therefore, in order for a unique maximally informative true answer to exist, it must be the case that exactly one proposition in the set is true.

Next, suppose there are several dishes on the table and we know that several people have been eating them. We can then ask the question in (23a). In this case, we are interested in the proper pairing between two sets that are given in the discourse—the people and the dishes—and we are crucially presupposing that there are at least two pairs in the list. This is the pair-list reading of the question.

(23) *Pair-list answer to a multiple* wh-*question*
   a. *Who* ate *what*?
   b. Fred ate the beans, Mary ate the soup, and Dana ate the salad.

At this point, it is useful to note that we can ask questions about our context in which multiple people ate multiple things in one of two ways. As Jackendoff (1972:261) points out, "We presuppose … that there were a number of people and a number of different things to eat, and that various people ate various things. Speaker A in the discourse is asking questions of the form *Who ate what?"*

(24) *A discourse strategy for discussing* Who ate what?
    a. *What* did Fred eat?
    b. *What* did Mary eat?
    c. *What* did Dana eat?
         ⋮

Formally, the meaning of the questions in (24) can be described as a *family of questions* ordered by the higher *wh*-word in the question, *who*, therefore asking a question about each person in the context—namely, what that person ate.

In what follows, I consider the more complex question *Which guest ate which dish?*, which will allow us to compare Superiority-obeying and Superiority-violating word orders. Here again, the discourse is structured in such a way that we ask a question about each guest in the context, namely, what that person ate. In our context with three guests (Fred, Mary, Dana) and three dishes (beans, soup, salad), we can spell out the full denotation of each subquestion in the family of questions as follows:

(25) *Family-of-questions denotation for a Superiority-obeying question*
    Which guest ate *which* dish?

$$\left\{ \left\{ \begin{matrix} \text{F ate the beans} \\ \text{F ate the soup} \\ \text{F ate the salad} \end{matrix} \right\}, \left\{ \begin{matrix} \text{M ate the beans} \\ \text{M ate the soup} \\ \text{M ate the salad} \end{matrix} \right\}, \left\{ \begin{matrix} \text{D ate the beans} \\ \text{D ate the soup} \\ \text{D ate the salad} \end{matrix} \right\} \right\}$$

More formally, we can describe this family of questions as in (26):

(26) *Family-of-questions denotation keyed on* guests
    $[\![which$ guest ate *which* $dish]\!] = \{\{x \text{ ate } y : y \in dish\} : x \in guest\}$
    $\approx$ {What did Fred eat? What did Mary eat? What did Dana eat?}

Büring (2003) develops a theory of question-answer congruence that explains the pitch associated with the answer to such questions. Concentrating on just one such subquestion in the discourse above, we might provide the answer that Fred ate the beans. Here, *Fred* is the (contrastive) *topic* and *the beans* is the *focus*. This corresponds to the pronunciation scheme described in (27), also known as "Rise-Fall-Rise."[9]

(27) *Subquestion keyed on* Fred *(Büring 2003:511)*
    Q: Well, what about FRED? What did HE eat?
    A: FRED$_{CT}$ ate the BEANS$_F$

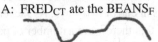

There is, in addition, a second questioning strategy that we could develop given the discourse above.

(28) *Another discourse strategy for discussing* Who ate what?
    a. *Which guest* ate the beans?
    b. *Which guest* ate the soup?
    c. *Which guest* ate the salad?
           ⋮

The family of questions described by (28) is now ordered by the base-generated lower *wh*-phrase. That is, we now ask a question for each dish in the context—namely, who ate it. Following Dayal (1996), I assume that this denotation describes a Superiority-violating question.

(29) *Family-of-questions denotation for a Superiority-violating question*
    Which dish did *which* guest eat?

$$\left\{ \left\{ \begin{array}{l} \text{F ate the beans} \\ \text{M ate the beans} \\ \text{D ate the beans} \end{array} \right\}, \left\{ \begin{array}{l} \text{F ate the soup} \\ \text{M ate the soup} \\ \text{D ate the soup} \end{array} \right\}, \left\{ \begin{array}{l} \text{F ate the salad} \\ \text{M ate the salad} \\ \text{D ate the salad} \end{array} \right\} \right\}$$

More formally, we can describe this family of questions as in (30). Compare with (26) to observe that the order in which the *wh*-phrases appear in the structure is reversed, corresponding to the surface syntax of the respective Superiority-obeying and Superiority-violating questions.

(30) *Family-of-questions denotation keyed on* dish
    $[\![$*which* dish did *which* guest eat$]\!] = \{\{x \text{ ate } y : x \in guest\} : y \in dish\}$
    $\approx \{$Who ate the beans? Who ate the soup? Who ate the salad?$\}$

Focusing on just one subquestion again, we notice that although we can provide the same string as the answer to the question, the pitch associated with the answer is different. Here, *Fred* is the *focus* and *the beans* is the (contrastive) *topic*. This corresponds to the pronunciation scheme described in (31).

(31) *Subquestion keyed on* the beans *(Büring 2003:512)*
    Q: Well, what about the BEANS? Who ate THEM?
    A: FRED$_F$ ate the BEANS$_{CT}$

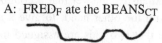

Dayal (1996) shows that pair-list readings of multiple *wh*-questions have two presuppositions, both crucially zeroing in on the status of the higher *wh*-phrase in the question.[10]

(32) *Presuppositions of multiple* wh-*questions*
    a. Exhaustivity
       Every member of the set quantified over by the overtly moved *wh* is
       paired with a member of the set quantified over by the in-situ *wh*.
    b. Pointwise uniqueness (functionhood)
       Every member of the set quantified over by the overtly moved *wh* is
       paired with no more than one member of the set quantified over by the
       in-situ *wh*.

Within the family-of-questions analysis of multiple questions, we predict *exhaustivity* to apply to members of the outer set in cases like (26), and *uniqueness* to apply to the inner set. Together, these two presuppositions impose the following requirement: for each member of the overtly moved *wh*-phrase's denotation, there is *exactly one* member in the denotation of the in-situ *wh*-phrase that is paired with it. Notice that this leaves open the possibility that some members of the set denoted by the in-situ *wh*-phrase are *not* paired with any member of the moved *wh*-phrase's denotation.

The exhaustivity and uniqueness presuppositions are illustrated in examples (33)–(34).

(33) *Exhaustivity presupposition*
    a. Guess *which* one of these 3 kids will sit on *which* of these 4 chairs.
       Good with a single-pair answer and with a pair-list answer.
    b. Guess *which* one of these 4 kids will sit on *which* of these 3 chairs.
       Only good with a single-pair answer.

(34) *Uniqueness presupposition*
    The Jones family (3 boys) will not sit down for dinner before the boys do
    all of the chores.
    a. I wonder *which* one of the 3 boys will do *which* one of the 3 chores.
    b. # I wonder *which* one of the 3 boys will do *which* one of the 4 chores.
       Suggests that the boys will not do all of the chores.

The context in (33a) allows for a pair-list answer (as well as a single-pair answer) because it is possible to give an exhaustive answer that accounts for each of the kids. In the context in (33b), on the other hand, to give a pair-list answer we would be forced to assume that two kids are assigned to the same chair, making this reading deviant. Hence, only a single-pair answer is felicitous in this context. The context in (34a) allows for a unique chore to be assigned to each boy, but in the context in (34b) either one chore is not assigned to any boy or else the 1:1 pairing is lost. Hence, only a single-pair answer is felicitous in this context.

Finally, note the importance of using singular *which*-phrases, to ensure that we are dealing with a pair-list reading. If a plural *which*-phrase is used (e.g., *Which boys will do which chores?*), it is possible to give a single-pair answer where each member of the pair is a plurality: *John, Tom, and Bill will set the table, sweep the floor, and do the dishes (respectively).*

2.5 Appendix: *Wh*-in-Situ and Antecedent-Contained Deletion

The existing literature provides some evidence for covert *wh*-movement of in-situ *wh*-phrases in English multiple *wh*-questions. The arguments come from the licensing of Antecedent-Contained Deletion (ACD) and the licensing of parasitic gaps. Here, I reproduce Pesetsky's (2000) argument based on ACD, which shows that in-situ *wh*-phrases in English undergo covert movement in Superiority-obeying questions but not in Superiority-violating ones. For arguments from parasitic gaps, see Nissenbaum 2000.[11]

An example of ACD is given in (35) (Bouton 1970; Larson and May 1990; May 1985; Sag 1976).

(35) *Antecedent-Contained Deletion*
      Sue [$_{VP}$ read [$_{DP}$ every book that Mary did [$_{VP}$ $\triangle$]]].

Example (35) is interpreted by speakers as in (36), where the missing VP is interpreted as the expression *read t*.

(36) *Interpretation of the ellipsis in (35)*
      Sue [$_{VP}$ read [$_{DP}$ every book that Mary did [$_{VP}$ ~~read t~~]]].

For VP-ellipsis to be licensed, a pronounced antecedent VP must exist that is identical to the missing VP. The fact that the elided VP in (36) is resolved to the VP *read t* shows that the linguistic context must contain an antecedent of the form *read t*. However, if the analysis of (35) does not involve covert movement, there is no instance of the VP *read t* in the structure to serve as the antecedent for the ellipsis. In fact, the only VP in the structure appears to be *read every book that Mary did*, which itself contains the ellipsis site. If we were to choose this VP as the antecedent for the purposes of ellipsis resolution, we would run into the "infinite regress" problem, and we would not arrive at the correct meaning of the sentence: *John read every book that Mary read every book that Mary read every book that Mary ....*

This apparent contradiction is resolved if we assume covert movement of the object, hosting the relative clause, to a VP-external position. This movement leaves behind a trace, creating a VP of the form *read t* and thereby, supplying the appropriate antecedent for the elided VP.

(37) *Resolution of ACD using covert movement*
   [DP every book that Mary did [VP ~~read *t*~~]] [Sue [VP read *t*]]

If covert *wh*-movement happens in a manner similar to overt movement, it should be able to resolve ACD that occurs inside a (phonologically) in-situ *wh*-phrase. This prediction will be a driving factor behind the investigation in part III. Pesetsky (2000) presents data showing that *wh*-phrases in Superiority-obeying questions, but not in Superiority-violating questions, can host ACD. Consequently, Pesetsky argues that *wh*-phrases in Superiority-obeying questions, but not those in Superiority-violating questions, undergo covert *wh*-movement.

(38) *ACD licensed by* wh-*in-situ in Superiority-obeying questions (Pesetsky 2000:6)*
   a. *Which* girl invited [*which* student that John did [VP △]]?
   b. I need to know *who* can speak [*which* languages that Ken Hale can [VP △]].

These examples show that ACD can be hosted inside an in-situ *wh*-phrase in Superiority-obeying questions. To create a test sentence to check whether the same is possible with in-situ *wh*-phrases in Superiority-violating questions, we require a more complex structure. We can obtain this by attaching a modifier that contains ACD to an otherwise grammatical Superiority-violating question. The resulting examples are quite complex, but nonetheless appear to give rise to crisp judgments.

Before arriving at the crucial test case, we construct a similarly more complex Superiority-obeying question, (39a). This example contains three relevant DP positions: the subject of *order*, the object of *order*, and the object of *congratulate*. The gap indicates the base position of the overtly moved *wh*-phrase. The intended interpretation of (39a) is given in (39b).

(39) *ACD licensed by* wh-*in-situ in a question with 3 DPs (Pesetsky 2000:30)*
   a. I need to know *which* girl ___ ordered [*which* boy that Mary (also) did △] to congratulate Sarah.
   b. Paraphrase: I need to know for which girl *x* and for which boy *y* such that Mary ordered *y* to congratulate Sarah], *x* also ordered *y* to congratulate Sarah. [i.e., I need to know the girl-boy pairs such that both the girl and Mary ordered the boy to congratulate Sarah]

Next, we compare (39) with a Superiority-violating counterpart, (40). Again, the same three DPs are being manipulated, and the gap indicates the base position of the overtly moved *wh*-phrase. The intended interpretation of (40a) is given in (40b). However, despite its similarity to the Superiority-obeying baseline (39a) and even though it is a semantically felicitous question, (40a) is judged by speakers to be markedly worse than (39a); it appears that ACD cannot be licensed by the in-situ *wh*-phrase in a Superiority-violating question.

(40) *ACD not licensed by* wh-*in-situ in a Superiority-violating question (Pesetsky 2000:31)*
   a. * I need to know *which* girl Sue ordered [*which* boy that Mary (also) did △] to congratulate ___ .
   b. Paraphrase: I need to know for which girl *x* and [which boy *y* such that Mary ordered *y* to congratulate *x*], Sue also ordered *y* to congratulate *x*. [i.e., I need to know the girl-boy pairs such that both Sue and Mary ordered the boy to congratulate the girl]

This contrast between (39) and (40) is explained if the in-situ *wh*-phrase in a Superiority-obeying question undergoes covert movement, but the in-situ *wh*-phrase in a Superiority-violating question is truly LF-in-situ.[12] Because the in-situ *wh*-phrase in a Superiority-obeying question undergoes covert movement, it occupies a position at LF that allows for the construction of an appropriate antecedent for the ellipsis. A parallel derivation is not available to the Superiority-violating question: the in-situ *wh*-phrase is in fact in situ at LF; it is therefore contained inside the elided material, and as a result it is impossible to find a constituent that is parallel to the elided constituent and could serve as the antecedent for the ellipsis.

This contrast should also be supported by additional baseline examples that are not provided by Pesetsky (2000), but that appear to support the contrast. In particular, it is important to verify that the ungrammaticality of the configuration in (40a) is due to the presence of the in-situ *wh*-phrase and not to some extraneous factor—for example, the fact that the *wh*-phrase in this example is extracted across an object relative clause. That is, a minimally different example, one containing a DP that we expect to be able to undergo QR at LF, should again be grammatical. Here, I illustrate this with a definite DP.

Example (41a) provides a baseline that does not contain ellipsis. Example (41b) is a slight variation on (41a), using the same predicate (*ordered*) in the matrix and embedded clauses, and it remains grammatical.[13] Example (41c) replaces the predicate *ordered* in the embedded clause with an ellipsis marker, and it still remains grammatical. Finally, in (41d) the definite description heading the relative clause, *the boy*, is replaced with a *wh*-phrase, *which boy*. This step leads to ungrammaticality, showing that (40a) is indeed ungrammatical because ACD cannot be licensed by the in-situ *wh*-phrase in that question.[14]

(41) *ACD licensed in questions with a definite article, but not with* wh-*in-situ*
   a.   I need to know *which* girl Sue ordered [the boy that Mary was dancing with *t*] to congratulate ___.
   b.   I need to know *which* girl Sue ordered [the boy that Mary$_F$ (also) ordered △] to congratulate ___.
   c.   I need to know *which* girl Sue ordered [the boy that Mary$_F$ (also) did △] to congratulate ___.
   d. * I need to know *which* girl Sue ordered [*which* boy that Mary$_F$ (also) did △] to congratulate ___.   (= (55a))

Finally, one might ask whether, adopting Fox and Nissenbaum's (1999) theory of ACD resolution under which it always involves late merger (extraposition) of the relative clause, the contrast between (39) and (40) could be accounted for by an appeal to the impossibility of rightward movement of an element that has a gap in it (*to congratulate t*). To test this, below I compare examples with and without extraposition of the relative clause. Examples (42a–b) are based on a suggestion by Danny Fox (pers. comm.); (42a) is similar in structure to (40a), while (42b) contains an extraposed relative clause.

(42) *Extraposition does not improve Superiority-violating questions with ACD*
   a. ** I need to know *which* book Sue ordered [*which* boy that Mary (also) did △] to read ___.
   b. * I need to know *which* book Sue ordered *which* boy to read ___ [that Mary also did △].

Example (42b) is improved over (42a), but both are judged ungrammatical. I propose that (42b) removes a center-embedding confound found in (42a) and (40a), but it illustrates that ACD hosted by the in-situ *wh*-phrase in a Superiority-violating question remains impossible even when this confound is eliminated.

3 The Syntax and Semantics of *Wh*-Questions

In this chapter, I present my formal proposal for the syntax and semantics of *wh*-questions. I begin with a brief reminder of the syntactic assumptions that I make and the denotations of multiple *wh*-questions that I assume here. I then sketch the proposal and spell out in more detail how it can model simplex and multiple *wh*-questions in English. I show how the single-pair and pair-list readings of multiple *wh*-questions are derived and how their presuppositions are explained. In chapter 4, I will show how this proposal extends to model the cross linguistically varied syntax of *wh*-questions in *wh*-in-situ languages, partial *wh*-movement languages, and multiple *wh*-fronting languages.

3.1 The Desiderata

I begin by surveying the facts that this chapter aims to derive. As we have seen, D-linked English questions can either obey or violate Superiority.

(1) *Superiority-obeying and Superiority-violating multiple* wh-*questions*
   a. *Which* student read *which* book?   (Superiority-obeying)
   b. *Which* book did *which* student read?   (Superiority-violating)

I adopt a standard probing model, under which an interrogative probe on C must (attempt to) agree with all *wh*-phrases in its c-command domain. Higher goals—as defined by c-command—must be agreed with before the probe can move on to lower goals, and the probe is not allowed to look back at previous goals after they have been agreed with. Immediately following agreement, *wh*-movement may be triggered.

I assume different LF structures for Superiority-obeying and superiority-violating *wh*-multiple questions in English: in Superiority-obeying questions, the in-situ *wh*-phrase(s) undergo covert *wh*-movement to C at LF. In Superiority-violating questions, the in situ *wh*-phrases must remain truly in situ at LF.[1]

(2) *Different syntactic assumptions for Superiority-obeying and -violating questions*

    a. *Which* student *which* book C ___ read ___ ?

    b. *Which* book C did *which* student read ___ ?

These multiple *wh*-questions can have single-pair and pair-list readings. Here, I model the pair-list reading of the question as a family of questions, keyed on the higher *wh*-phrase (Dayal 1996). The denotations of the pair-list readings of the questions in (1) are given in (3)–(4), respectively, for a domain with three students Abby, Betty, Cathy and three books (*Moby Dick*, Jane Eyre, *Oliver Twist*.

(3) *Family-of-questions denotation for a Superiority-obeying question*
    Which student read *which* book?

$$\left\{ \begin{Bmatrix} \text{Abby read MD} \\ \text{Abby read JE} \\ \text{Abby read OT} \end{Bmatrix}, \begin{Bmatrix} \text{Betty read MD} \\ \text{Betty read JE} \\ \text{Betty read OT} \end{Bmatrix}, \begin{Bmatrix} \text{Cathy read MD} \\ \text{Cathy read JE} \\ \text{Cathy read OT} \end{Bmatrix} \right\}$$

(4) *Family-of-questions denotation for a Superiority-violating question*
    Which book did *which* student read?

$$\left\{ \begin{Bmatrix} \text{Abby read MD} \\ \text{Betty read MD} \\ \text{Cathy read MD} \end{Bmatrix}, \begin{Bmatrix} \text{Abby read JE} \\ \text{Betty read JE} \\ \text{Cathy read JE} \end{Bmatrix}, \begin{Bmatrix} \text{Abby read OT} \\ \text{Betty read OT} \\ \text{Cathy read OT} \end{Bmatrix} \right\}$$

I model the single-pair reading of the question as a set of propositions that are possible answers to the question, as in (5).

(5) *A single-pair reading is modeled as a set of propositions*

$$\left\{ \begin{array}{l} \text{Abby read MD, Abby read JE, Abby read OT, Betty read MD,} \\ \text{Betty read JE, Betty read OT, Cathy read MD, Cathy read JE,} \\ \text{Cathy read OT} \end{array} \right\}$$

I take these semantic differences in answer patterns to correspond to differences in the syntax of the question, and my goal will be to provide a compositional analysis that derives these readings.[2]

3.2 The Proposal

In this section, I turn to the semantics of multiple *wh*-questions. I propose that the derivation of an interrogative sentence involves three basic ingredients: the interrogative complementizer, C; *wh*-words; and a new operator, the question operator ALTSHIFT. In what follows, I discuss each of these ingredients in turn.

The interrogative complementizer, C, triggers interrogative movement. In English, this complementizer has an EPP feature that requires at least one *wh*-phrase to occupy its specifier, and furthermore exactly one *wh*-phrase to be pronounced in this position. I propose that this interrogative complementizer plays no role in the semantics of the question, and simply passes up the denotation of its sister. Thus, in (6) C is modeled as a type-flexible identity function.

(6) *The semantics of the complementizer*
$$[\![C]\!] = \lambda P_\tau . P$$

Following Beck (2006), Beck and Kim (2006), Cable (2010), and Ramchand (1997), I propose that *wh*-words denote Hamblin sets, corresponding to the answer to the short question denoted by the *wh*-word. Here, I use the implementation in Beck and Kim 2006. Crucially, *wh*-words have an alternative (or focus-semantic) value, but no ordinary value. The ordinary and alternative values of *what* and *who* are given in (7a–b). The alternative value of a *which*-NP phrase is equivalent to its NP extension, and its ordinary value is undefined.

(7) *The semantics of* who *and* what *as sets of alternatives*
   a. Ordinary value: $[\![who]\!]^o$ is undefined
      Alternative value: $[\![who]\!]^f = \{x_e : x \in \text{human}\}$
   b. Ordinary value: $[\![what]\!]^o$ is undefined
      Alternative value: $[\![what]\!]^f = \{x_e : x \notin \text{human}\}^3$

(8) *The denotation of a* which-*phrase is equivalent to its NP extension*
   $[\![which\ \text{student}]\!]^f = [\![\text{student}]\!]^o = \{\text{Jane, Mary, Katie, Dana, ...}\}$

These *wh*-words, like F-marked elements in the derivation, are interpreted using Alternative Semantics, the standard approach to focus semantics originally proposed by Rooth (1985, 1992). F-marked constituents introduce a set of alternatives to the syntactic object's ordinary denotation. Non-F-Marked constituents have an alternative value consisting of the singleton set of their ordinary value. These elements compose point-wise with one another, using the recursive definition in (9).[4]

(9) *A recursive definition for the computation of alternative values*
   a. Terminal nodes (TN)
   $$[\![\alpha_\tau]\!]^f = \begin{cases} \{[\![\alpha_\tau]\!]\} \text{ or lexically listed} & \text{if } \alpha \text{ is not F-marked} \\ \text{a subset of } D_\tau & \text{if } \alpha \text{ is F-marked} \end{cases}$$

   b. Function application (FA)
   $$\left[\!\!\left[\begin{array}{c} \alpha_\tau \\ \overbrace{} \\ \beta_{\langle\sigma,\tau\rangle} \quad \gamma_\sigma \end{array} \right]\!\!\right]^f = $$
   $$\begin{cases} \{b(g) \mid b \in [\![\beta]\!]^f, g \in [\![\gamma]\!]^f\} & \text{if } \alpha \text{ is not F-marked} \\ \text{a contextually determined subset of } D_\tau & \text{if } \alpha \text{ is F-marked} \end{cases}$$

I adopt the interpretability condition proposed by Beck (2006) and Beck and Kim (2006).

(10) *Principle of Interpretability (Beck 2006:16)*
   An LF must have an ordinary semantic interpretation.

Since the *wh*-word itself has an alternative value but no defined ordinary value, any containing expression whose semantic value is composed entirely of ordinary semantic values will likewise have an undefined ordinary value. I propose that such a structure must be interpreted using a special question operator, *ALTSHIFT*, which assigns to its mother node as an ordinary value the alternative value of its sister node. As a methodological point, I note that I refrain from using the perhaps more common operator Q for this purpose, as it has been invoked elsewhere to model pied-piping, as well as for quantifiers and quantifier phrases. Likewise, since it is important for my proposal to separate interrogative syntax from interrogative semantics, I do not use the head C for this purpose.[5]

The ALTSHIFT operator is the source of interrogative semantics. In English, ALTSHIFT occupies a position on the clausal spine. It takes a set of propositions (or a set of such sets ...) as its argument and returns the alternative value of that set as the ordinary value of the question; that is, it takes the alternatives introduced by its sister in the focus domain and shifts them into the ordinary domain.[6] As we will see in chapter 4, variation in the syntactic positions this operator may occupy will help explain variation in the syntax and semantics of questions and related constructions built from *wh*-indeterminates cross linguistically (see Kuroda 1965).

(11) *The semantics of the* ALTSHIFT *operator*
   a. $[\![\text{ALTSHIFT } \alpha_\sigma]\!]^o = [\![\alpha_\sigma]\!]^f$
   b. $[\![\text{ALTSHIFT } \alpha_\sigma]\!]^f = \{ [\![\text{ALTSHIFT } \alpha_\sigma]\!]^o \}$ $(\sigma \in \{ \langle st, t \rangle, \langle \langle st, t \rangle, t \rangle, \dots \})$

Note that this is a type-flexible version of the semantics for the interrogative complementizer in Beck and Kim 2006 and Shimoyama 2001. This type-flexibility will be crucial in order to allow for the family-of-question derivations for the pair-list readings of multiple *wh*–questions.[7]

3.3 Simplex *wh*-Questions

With the ingredients of the proposal in place, let us consider the derivation of a simplex question, *Which book did Abby read?* A simplified LF for this question is given in (12).[8] The *wh*-phrase *which book* moves from its position as the complement of *read* to Spec,CP, and the question operator ALTSHIFT (abbreviated as **AS** in trees) merges with this structure at this point. I represent

λ-binders as nodes in the tree, and I indicate the element that they are abstracting over with indices. The binder and the index alike are used here as notational conveniences only.

(12) *A (simplified) LF for a simplex* wh-*question*

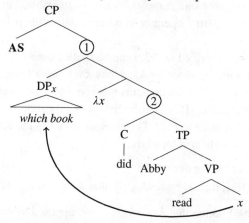

The derivation of (12) is given in (13). Up to the node labeled ②, the derivation proceeds in the ordinary domain, using standard composition rules as in Heim and Kratzer 1998. Nothing interesting happens in the focus domain, where singleton sets are combined. The denotation of this node is the open proposition "that Abby read x," (13b) (recall that C simply passes up the value of its sister and does not contribute to the semantics any further). The free variable x is then abstracted over, and the resulting derived predicate composes pointwise with the denotation of the *wh*-phrase *which book*, which is the set of books in the context, (13c). Notice that at this point the denotation of node ① can only be composed in the focus dimension. The ordinary value of this node is undefined, because the meaning of the *wh*-phrase in it is undefined, (13d). The ALTSHIFT operator takes the alternatives introduced by $[\![①]\!]^f$ and shifts them into the ordinary dimension, yielding the desired interpretation of the question, (13e). The meaning of the question is a set of propositions that are possible answers to the question—a Hamblin/Karttunen set.[9]

(13) *The derivation of a simplex* wh-*question*[10]

   a. $[\![TP]\!]^o = \lambda w$. Abby read x in w
   b. $[\![②]\!]^o = \lambda w$. Abby read x in w
   c. $[\![DP_x]\!]^o$ is undefined
       $[\![DP_x]\!]^f = \{x_e : x \in \text{book}\}$
   d. $[\![①]\!]^o$ is undefined
       $[\![①]\!]^f = \{\lambda w$. Abby read x in $w : x \in \text{book}\}$
   e. $[\![CP]\!]^o = [\![①]\!]^f = \{\lambda w$. Abby read x in $w : x \in \text{book}\}$

Importantly, here the contribution of C is separated from that of ALTSHIFT. C is syntactically *below* the *wh*-phrase and is responsible for interrogative syntax. ALTSHIFT is syntactically *above* the *wh*-phrase and is responsible for interrogative semantics. This distinction will become crucial in the case of multiple *wh*-questions, where only one complementizer is available, but we will require more than one ALTSHIFT operator in order to derive the pair-list reading of the question.

The Hamblin/Karttunen set described in (13e) can be spelled out as in (14), assuming a simple context with just three books: *Moby-Dick*, *Jane Eyre*, and *Oliver Twist* (as in section 3.1). This set contains answers only for singular individuals, without any pluralities. This is enforced by the meaning of the singular *which*-phrase that was used in (12). Let us assume that in the actual world, Abby read *Moby-Dick*, indicated by a box.

(14) *A set of possible answers to the question*
$$\left\{ \boxed{\text{that Abby read}_{w_0}\ \text{MD}}\ , \text{that Abby read}_{w_0}\ \text{JE, that Abby read}_{w_0}\ \text{OT} \right\}$$

Here, I adopt Dayal (1996) notion that a question is presupposed to have a unique maximally informative true answer. This requirement can be enforced by an answer operator, as in (15).[11]

(15) *The ANS operator as Max$_{inf}$ (Dayal 1996, cf. Fox 2012:b)*[12]
$\llbracket \text{ANS} \rrbracket (P) = \text{Max}_{inf}(P)$
$\text{Max}_{inf}(P)(w) = \iota p \in P, \text{ such that } w \in p \text{ and } \forall q \in P\ (w \in q \rightarrow p \subseteq q)$

The ANS operator takes as input a set as in (14) and is defined if and only if there is exactly one true proposition in the set that entails all other true propositions in the set. Here, there is a single proposition that is true in the set, and the ANS operator will return this proposition. Notice that the propositions in (14) are logically independent of one another. Therefore, if more than one proposition were true, ANS would be unable to return a unique value, and the result would therefore be undefined.[13] This is the desired result.

3.4 Superiority-Obeying Multiple *Wh*-Questions

With this background in mind, I next show that the proposal put forth here can correctly model multiple *wh*-questions. I first show how the single-pair reading of such a question is derived without any additions or changes to the theory. I then show that one addition to the theory allows us to account for the pair-list reading, deriving the two readings from minimally different LFs, building on principled and well-argued-for syntactic assumptions regarding English questions.

3.4.1 The Single-Pair Reading

The tree in (17) illustrates the LF I assume for Superiority-obeying *wh*-questions in English. Following Beck (2006), Cable (2007, 2010), and Pesetsky (2000), among others, I assume the following derivation:

(16) *Syntactic derivation of a Superiority-obeying English* wh-*question*
  a. An interrogative probe on C probes its c-command domain. The principle Agree with Closest dictates that DP_x will be the probe's first target, since it is closer to C than DP_y.
  b. C agrees with DP_x and attracts it to its specifier.
  c. C continues probing its c-command domain. Its next goal is DP_y.
  d. C agrees with DP_y and attracts it to a lower Spec,CP, where DP_y tucks in below DP_x.

A pronunciation rule then dictates that the highest phrase in Spec,CP—here, DP_x—is pronounced at the head of its chain, and all remaining *wh*-phrases are pronounced at the tail of their respective chains. As with (12), I assume that ALTSHIFT merges with this structure and interprets the question.

(17) *LF of a Superiority-obeying* wh-*question with a single-pair reading*

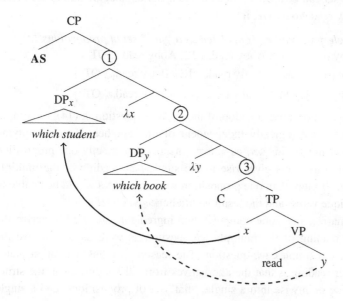

As with simplex *wh*-questions, the derivation of the structure up to node ③ is uneventful. At node ③, we have an open proposition "that x read y," (18a). The contained free variables are bound, and the alternative values of the resulting derived predicates compose pointwise with the denotations of the *wh*-phrases *which book* and *which student* at nodes ② and ①, respectively, (18b–c). This yields a set of propositions as the alternative value of node ①, whose ordinary value is undefined. ALTSHIFT takes this alternative value in $[\![①]\!]^f$ and returns it as the ordinary value of the question, yielding the desired interpretation (18d).

(18) *Key parts of the derivation of (17)*

　　a. $[\![③]\!]^o = \lambda w \,.\, x$ read y in w

　　　　$[\![③]\!]^f = \{\,[\![③]\!]^o\,\} = \{\lambda w \,.\, x$ read y in $w\}$

　　b. $[\![②]\!]^o$ is undefined

　　　　$[\![②]\!]^f = \{\lambda w \,.\, x$ read y in $w : y \in$ book$\}$

　　c. $[\![①]\!]^o$ is undefined

　　　　$[\![①]\!]^f = \{\lambda w \,.\, x$ read y in $w : y \in$ book, $x \in$ student$\}$

　　d. $[\![CP]\!]^o = [\![①]\!]^f = \{\lambda w \,.\, x$ read y in $w : y \in$ book, $x \in$ student$\}$

The resulting meaning is a "flat" set of propositions, corresponding to the possible answers to the question. In a simple context with three individuals—Abby, Betty, and Cathy—and three books—*Moby-Dick*, *Jane Eyre*, and *Oliver Twist*—this set can be spelled out as in (19). Let us imagine that in the actual world, Betty read *Jane Eyre*, indicated by a box.

(19) *A single-pair reading is modeled as a "flat" set of propositions*

$$\left\{ \begin{array}{l} \text{Abby read}_{w_0} \text{ MD, Abby read}_{w_0} \text{ JE, Abby read}_{w_0} \text{ OT,} \\ \text{Betty read}_{w_0} \text{ MD, } \boxed{\text{Betty read}_{w_0} \text{ JE}} \text{, Betty read}_{w_0} \text{ OT,} \\ \text{Cathy read}_{w_0} \text{ MD, Cathy read}_{w_0} \text{ JE, Cathy read}_{w_0} \text{ OT} \end{array} \right\}$$

As in the case of the denotation of the simplex question in (14), the propositions in (19) are logically independent of one another. Hence, applying the ANS operator to this set, as above, ensures that exactly one proposition in this set is true. This gives rise to the single-pair reading of the multiple *wh*-question. If more than one proposition were true, ANS would be unable to return a unique value, and the result would hence be undefined.[14]

To summarize, the same compositional ingredients are used to derive the single-pair reading of the multiple *wh*-question as were used to derive the meaning of the simplex *wh*-question. The reason why this derivation yields a single-pair reading is that the alternatives from all *wh*-phrases in the structure compose pointwise into a single, "flat" set of propositions, and a single ALTSHIFT operator then returns the resulting set as the meaning of the question. As we will see next, matters change if we allow more than one ALTSHIFT operator to occur in the structure.

3.4.2 The Pair-List Reading

Consider next the pair-list reading of a Superiority-obeying multiple *wh*-question. I assume here a syntactic derivation identical to the one illustrated in section 3.4.1 for the single-pair reading of the question, with just one modification: I introduce a second ALTSHIFT operator into the derivation. This allows each *wh*-phrase in the structure to be interpreted by a separate ALTSHIFT operator. As we will see, this yields the desired family-of-questions denotation for the question.

(20) *LF of Superiority-obeying question with a pair-list reading (cf. (17))*

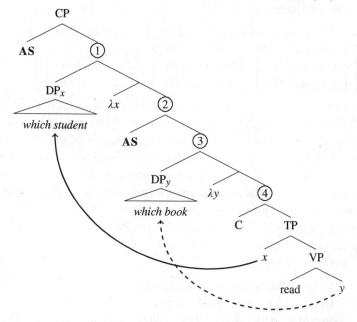

The derivation proceeds as in (18) up to node ③: the result is the set of open propositions $\{\lambda w \, . \, x \text{ read } y \text{ in } w : y \in book\}$, (21a). Crucially, at this point, an ALTSHIFT operator takes this set of alternative propositions and returns it as the ordinary value of node ②, (21b). As with other typical nonfocused nodes, I assume that the alternative value of ② is identical to the singleton set of its ordinary value, (21c) (Rooth 1985, 1992). This node then composes pointwise with the meaning of *which student*, yielding as the meaning of ① the set of sets of alternative propositions: $\{\{\lambda w \, . \, x \text{ read } y \text{ in } w : y \in book\} : x \in student\}$, (21d). Finally, the higher ALTSHIFT operator takes this set of alternative propositions and returns it as the ordinary value of the question, (21e). The result, then, is a set of *questions*, or a family-of-questions denotation.

(21) *Key parts of the derivation of (20)*

   a. $[\![③]\!]^{f} = \{\lambda w \,.\, x \text{ read } y \text{ in } w : y \in \text{book}\}$

   b. $[\![②]\!]^{o} = [\![③]\!]^{f} = \{\lambda w \,.\, x \text{ read } y \text{ in } w : y \in \text{book}\}$

   c. $[\![②]\!]^{f} = \{\{\lambda w \,.\, x \text{ read } y \text{ in } w : y \in \text{book}\}\}$

   d. $[\![①]\!]^{f} = \{\{\lambda w \,.\, x \text{ read } y \text{ in } w : y \in \textit{book}\} : x \in \textit{student}\}$

   e. $[\![\text{CP}]\!]^{o} = [\![①]\!]^{f} = \{\{\lambda w \,.\, x \text{ read } y \text{ in } w : y \in \textit{book}\} : x \in \textit{student}\}$

The resulting family-of-questions denotation in (21e) is sorted by the higher *wh*-phrase: *student*. Spelling this out for our small context, the result is (22), identical to our desideratum in (3).

(22) *A family of questions sorted by* student *yields a pair-list reading*

$$\left\{ \begin{Bmatrix} \text{Abby read MD} \\ \text{Abby read JE} \\ \text{Abby read OT} \end{Bmatrix}, \begin{Bmatrix} \text{Betty read MD} \\ \text{Betty read JE} \\ \text{Betty read OT} \end{Bmatrix}, \begin{Bmatrix} \text{Cathy read MD} \\ \text{Cathy read JE} \\ \text{Cathy read OT} \end{Bmatrix} \right\}$$

Notice that Dayal's (1996) ANS operator in (15) is unable to apply to families of questions as in (22), because it is a set of sets instead of a set of propositions. ANS will seek the maximally informative proposition in the set, but fail to find one because the set contains no propositions. In (23), I define a recursive ANS operator that is able to apply to sets of propositions, or to sets of such sets, and so on.[15] This proposal amounts to a recursive application of the requirement that each question—that is, each set of propositions in a family-of-questions denotation—have a unique maximally informative true answer. This guarantees exhaustivity over the first element in the pair and pointwise uniqueness for the second element.[16]

(23) *A recursive definition for generalized* ANS

   a. $[\![\text{ANS}]\!] \left(P_{\langle st,t \rangle} \right) = \lambda w \,.\, \text{Max}_{\text{inf}}(P)(w)$
       where $\text{Max}_{\text{inf}}(P)(w) = \iota p \in P$, such that $w \in p$ and
       $$\forall q \in P \,(w \in q \rightarrow p \subseteq q)$$

   b. $[\![\text{ANS}]\!] \left(K_{\langle \sigma,t \rangle} \right) = \lambda w \,.\, \cap P_{\sigma} \in K \left([\![\text{ANS}]\!] \,(P)(w) \right)$
       $[\text{i.e., } \lambda w \,.\, \lambda w' \,.\, \forall P_{\sigma} \in K([\![\text{ANS}]\!] \,(P)(w)(w'))]$
       $(\sigma \in \{ \langle st,t \rangle, \langle \langle st,t \rangle, t \rangle, \,\ldots\, \})$

The ANS operator in (23) takes a question denotation and returns the maximally informative true member in the set. If the input to ANS is a set of propositions (of type $\langle st, t \rangle$), ANS behaves like the operator in (15): it requires there to be a true proposition in the question denotation that is maximally informative. That is, there must be a single true answer to the question. This will derive the correct presupposition for both a simplex *wh*-question and for a single-pair multiple question. If, on the other hand, the input to ANS is a family of questions, ANS applies recursively to each question in the family of questions and requires there to be a maximally informative true answer to each question in the set.

In our case, if (22) (of type $\langle\langle st, t\rangle, t\rangle$) is the input to ANS, the operator will recursively apply to each question (of type $\langle st, t\rangle$) in the set, using the second line of the definition, of ANS, (23b). For each question, the first line in the definition, (23a), can now apply and return the true maximally informative answer to the question. We thus exhaustify over the set of questions, ordered by the higher wh_1, essentially asking the question *For each student, what did she read?* We now require uniqueness: namely, that there be a unique true answer to each question. Thus, the question is defined only if there is exactly one answer to each question. Note, however, that there is allowed to be a book that no one read; that is, the set of books corresponding to the lower wh_2 is not exhaustified here.

This recursive definition of ANS is thus able to explain the presuppositions of both the single-pair and the pair-list readings of multiple *wh*-questions. In addition, we may wish to add an operator to our semantic lexicon that is able to act as a filter on question meanings. This operator will take the meaning of the question as input, check that this question is well-defined—that is, that it has a maximally informative true answer (or the equivalent of this requirement for a family of questions)—and return the same set as output. This set can then be used by operators in the performative layer, as needed. Such an operator, which I will call *answerable* here, can be defined using ANS (see also Nicolae's (2013:175) ID operator).[17]

(24) *A recursively defined filter on question meanings using ANS*
$$[\![\text{ANSWERABLE}]\!]\left(P_{\langle st,t\rangle}\right) = \exists q : [\![\text{ANS}]\!]\,(P) = q \,.\, P$$
$$[\![\text{ANSWERABLE}]\!]\left(K_{\langle\sigma,t\rangle}\right) = \forall P_\sigma \in K\left(\exists q : [\![\text{ANS}]\!]\,(P) = q\right) \,.\, K$$
$$(\sigma \in \{\langle st, t\rangle, \langle\langle st, t\rangle, t\rangle, \ \dots \ \})$$

3.5 Superiority-Violating Multiple *Wh*-Questions

Next, I turn to Superiority-violating multiple *wh*-questions. I focus first on the single-pair reading of such questions, and then on the pair-list reading.

3.5.1 The Single-Pair Reading

Consider first the derivation of the single-pair reading of a Superiority-violating *wh*-question.[18] Following Beck (2006), Cable (2007, 2010), and Pesetsky (2000), among others. I assume that the syntax of such a question differs from that of Superiority-obeying questions in one important way, namely, the syntactic position of *wh*-in-situ. The derivation begins like that of a Superiority-obeying question.

(25) *Syntactic derivation of a Superiority-violating English* wh-*question*
    a. An interrogative probe on C probes its c-command domain. Agree with Closest dictates that DP_x will be the probe's first target, since it is closer to C than DP_y.
    b. C agrees with DP_x, but—unlike in Superiority-obeying *wh*-questions—does not attract DP_x to its specifier; instead, it leaves it in situ.
    c. C continues probing its c-command domain and finds its next goal, DP_y.
    d. C agrees with DP_y and attracts it to its specifier.

DP_y is hence the only (and consequently, the highest) *wh*-phrase in Spec,CP. Following the pronunciation rule from above, DP_y will be pronounced in its moved position, and the in-situ *wh*-phrase DP_x will be pronounced in its base position, yielding the Superiority-violating word order.[19]

(26) *LF of a Superiority-violating* wh-*question with a single-pair reading*

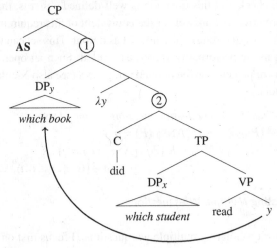

Here, it is important to note that there would be no way to derive a Superiority-violating word order if the higher DP_x were attracted to Spec,CP. In that case, the pronunciation rule would dictate that DP_x would be pronounced in its moved position and DP_y would be pronounced in its base position, leading to a Superiority-obeying word order instead of the desired Superiority-violating one. In order to achieve a Superiority-violating word order, DP_x must be left in situ at LF, to allow DP_y to be attracted over it to the highest spec, CP.

The derivation of the meaning of this structure is given in (27). Note that since TP contains an element that has an alternative value but no ordinary semantic value—DP_x *which student*—TP too has an alternative value but no ordinary value. C passes up the value of TP at node ②. We then abstract over the resulting open proposition, and at node ① we compose this set point-wise with the meaning of the moved *wh*-phrase—here, the set of books in the context. Finally, ALTSHIFT takes this set of propositions and returns it as the ordinary meaning of CP.

(27) *Key parts of the derivation of (26)*

a. $[\![②]\!]^o = [\![TP]\!]^o$ is undefined

$[\![②]\!]^f = [\![TP]\!]^f = \{\lambda w \, . \, x \text{ read } y \text{ in } w : x \in \text{student}\}$

b. $[\![①]\!]^o$ is undefined

$[\![①]\!]^f = \{\lambda w \, . \, x \text{ read } y \text{ in } w : x \in \text{student}, y \in \text{book}\}$

c. $[\![CP]\!]^o = [\![①]\!]^f = \{\lambda w \, . \, x \text{ read } y \text{ in } w : y \in \text{book}, x \in \text{student}\}$

The resulting meaning is again a "flat" set of propositions, correspond-ing to the possible answers to the question. In our simple context with three individuals—Abby, Betty, and Cathy—and three books—*Moby-Dick, Jane Eyre*, and *Oliver Twist*—this resulting set is identical to the one spelled out for the Superiority-obeying question in (19). Again, these propositions are logi-cally independent of one another. Hence, applying the ANS operator to this set, as above, ensures that exactly one proposition in this set is true, giving rise to a single-pair reading of the superiority-violating multiple *wh*-question.

The difference between the LF for this Superiority-violating question and the one for the Superiority-obeying question lies in the fact that in the for-mer, nontrivial focus alternatives are computed across a larger portion of the structure, resulting from the fact that a *wh*-phrase was left in situ at LF in that structure, whereas the derivation of the latter involved covert movement of *wh*-in-situ. The fact that the base-generated higher *wh*-phrase *which student* is left in situ in this LF makes predictions for the sensitivity of this structure to intervention effects, as we will see in part II.

3.5.2 The Pair-List Reading

Finally, I turn to the derivation of the pair-list reading of a Superiority-violating question. An LF for such a question is illustrated in (28). Again, the LF I pro-pose for this reading differs from the LF I propose for the single-pair reading in only one way: two ALTSHIFT operators are introduced into the structure, one above *which student* and another above *which book*. This will yield a family-of-questions denotation keyed on *books*, as desired.

(28) *LF of a Superiority-violating question with a pair-list reading*

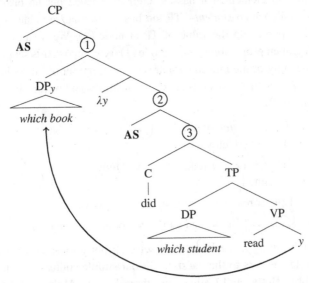

As with the parallel Superiority-obeying question, the pair-list reading is derived via a nested set structure, created by interpreting each *wh*-phrase with a separate ALTSHIFT operator. The crucial difference between the derivation in (28) that yields the pair-list reading of the question and the derivation in (27) that yields the single-pair reading lies in step (b) of the derivation: at node ②, the alternative value of the structure is returned as its ordinary value, using the lower ALTSHIFT operator. As the derivation continues and the resulting set composes with the meaning of the *wh*-phrase *which book*, we now have a family-of-questions denotation instead of a "flat" set of propositions.

(29) *Key parts of the derivation of (28)*
   a. $[\![③]\!]^f = \{\lambda w \,.\, x \text{ read } y \text{ in } w : x \in student\}$
   b. $[\![②]\!]^o = [\![③]\!]^f = \{\lambda w \,.\, x \text{ read } y \text{ in } w : x \in student\}$
   c. $[\![②]\!]^f = \{\{\lambda w \,.\, x \text{ read } y \text{ in } w : x \in student\}\}$
   d. $[\![①]\!]^f = \{\{\lambda w \,.\, x \text{ read } y \text{ in } w : x \in student\} : y \in book\}$
   e. $[\![CP]\!]^o = [\![①]\!]^f = \{\{\lambda w \,.\, x \text{ read } y \text{ in } w : x \in student\} : y \in book\}$

This yields a family-of-questions denotation sorted by the higher *wh*-phrase at LF, *which book*. Spelling this out for our small context, the result is (30), identical to the desideratum in (4). Moreover, applying the generalized ANS operator in (23) to this family of questions results in the requirement that each question in the set have one unique maximally informative true answer, correctly modeling the presuppositions of this question. That is, this derivation yields a pairlist reading of the multiple *wh*-question, where for each book in the context, we must specify the single student who read it.

(30) *A family of questions sorted by* book *yields a pair-list reading*

$$\left\{ \left\{ \begin{array}{l} \text{Abby read MD} \\ \text{Betty read MD} \\ \text{Cathy read MD} \end{array} \right\}, \left\{ \begin{array}{l} \text{Abby read JE} \\ \text{Betty read JE} \\ \text{Cathy read JE} \end{array} \right\}, \left\{ \begin{array}{l} \text{Abby read OT} \\ \text{Betty read OT} \\ \text{Cathy read OT} \end{array} \right\} \right\}$$

3.6 Quiz-Master Questions and Nested *Which*-Phrases

In this section, I show that the proposal developed here is able to explain restrictions on the possible readings of "quiz-master" questions and of questions with nested *which*-phrases. Example (31) illustrates a quiz-master question. Such questions exceptionally require *wh* to remain in situ and often require a unique intonation that gives the question its name. They have been argued to allow only a single-pair answer, not a pair-list answer.

(31) *Quiz-master questions have only single-pair answers*
   [TP Elvis Presley introduced *which* actress to *which* director]?

Similarly, nested *wh*-phrases have been argued to systematically lack a pair-list reading (Elliott 2015). This can be illustrated using the strongly distributive predicate *list*. Examples (32a–b) show that *list* may only embed a multiple *wh*-question with a pair-list answer.

(32) List *may only embed a question with a pair-list answer*
   Context: There are two girls.
   a.   Mary listed *which* girl hit *which* boy.
   b. # Mary listed *which* one hit *which* one first.

Examples (33a–b) now show that nested *wh*-phrases cannot be embedded under *list*. This incompatibility of *list* and its embedding is explained if nested *wh*-questions can only have a single-pair reading, making them unsuitable complements to the predicate *list*.

(33) "List" *cannot a nested* wh-*question*
   a.   Mary listed *which* book she had borrowed from *which* library.
   b. # Mary listed [DP *which* book by *which* author] she had read.

The two structures in (31) and (33b), though unusual, have one property in common: *in both cases, the two* wh-*phrases in the structure will necessarily compose pointwise with one another before an* ALTSHIFT *operator is encountered.* In the case of quiz-master questions, the *wh*-phrases are both inside the same vP. In the case of nested *wh*-questions, the *wh*-phrases are contained inside a single DP. In contrast, the ALTSHIFT operator must occupy a position in the CP layer. Hence, all the *wh*-phrases in these questions necessarily occur below the lowest position that the operator may occupy.

This syntactic restriction on the position of ALTSHIFT limits the available interpretations for these multiple *wh*-questions in a principled manner. In particular, because all the *wh*-phrases in the structure will necessarily compose pointwise with one another into a "flat" set before any ALTSHIFT operator is encountered, we correctly predict that only single-pair readings are available for these questions. There is no way to interleave the *wh*-phrases and ALTSHIFT operators in these structures, as is required for the derivation of pair-list readings.

A question I leave open at this point is whether a context can be constructed for a quiz-master question that allows a pair-list interpretation. This idea has been suggested to me, but the data are complicated and I have not been able to verify the availability of this reading, perhaps because the unusual context of these questions tends to favor the single-pair reading. If such readings are available, this would provide important evidence concerning the distribution of ALTSHIFT. I return to a discussion of the crosslinguistic distribution of ALTSHIFT in chapter 4. For the purposes of this chapter, it suffices to allow ALTSHIFT to take scope above and near interrogative C, and to remain agnostic about its ability to occur in other positions of the right type.

3.7 Appendix 1: ALTSHIFT and Declarative Sentences

A question arises about ALTSHIFT's ability to apply to declarative sentences.[20]

We have adopted the two-dimensional Alternative Semantics framework of Rooth (1985, 1992), where each syntactic node α is associated with an ordinary semantic value $[\![\alpha]\!]^o$ and a set of alternatives $[\![\alpha]\!]^f$, which by default is the singleton set of its ordinary value, $\{[\![\alpha]\!]^o\}$. Following Beck (2006), Beck and Kim (2006), and Ramchand (1997), *wh*-phrases have no ordinary value defined, but take their domain as their alternative set. Through pointwise composition, *Sarah read what?* has the denotation in (34). (*What did Sarah reads* would be the same.) Because the *wh*-phrase does not have a well-defined ordinary value, the same is true of A.

(34) A = Sarah read *what*?

  a. $[\![A]\!]^o$ undefined

  b. $[\![A]\!]^f = \left\{ \begin{array}{l} \lambda w \text{ . Sarah read } \textit{Moby-Dick} \text{ in } w, \\ \lambda w \text{ . Sarah read } \textit{Jane Eyre} \text{ in } w, \ \ldots \end{array} \right\}$

We have additionally defined the ALTSHIFT operator in (35) (= (11)), which takes the set of alternatives constructed in the alternative dimension and returns it as an ordinary value, resulting in a Hamblin denotation for the question (cf. "Q" in Beck and Kim 2006: 177).

(35) *The semantics of the ALTSHIFT operator*

  a. $[\![\text{ALTSHIFT } \alpha]\!]^o = [\![\alpha]\!]^f$

  b. $[\![\text{ALTSHIFT } \alpha]\!]^f = \{[\![\text{ALTSHIFT } \alpha]\!]^o\} = \{[\![\alpha]\!]^f\}$

(36) $[\![\text{ALTSHIFT A}]\!]^o = \begin{Bmatrix} \lambda w \text{ . Sarah read } \textit{Moby-Dick in } w, \\ \lambda w \text{ . Sarah read } \textit{Jane Eyre in } w, \text{ ...} \end{Bmatrix}$

As will be discussed in chapter 4, the use of ALTSHIFT is not constrained to interrogative clause-types. Uegaki (2018) adopts this meaning for the Japanese Q-particle *ka*, which forms *wh*-question meanings when at the clause edge, but which also adjoins to certain subclausal constituents to yield *wh*-indefinites.

Now consider the interpretation of focus, the original motivation for Rooth's Alternative Semantics framework. A focused phrase has a contextually determined, nonsingleton set of alternatives, which includes the ordinary value: the prejacent. With pointwise composition (9), the clause *Sarah read [*MOBY DICK*]*$_F$ with narrow focus on *Moby-Dick* has the denotation in (37).

(37) B = Sarah read [*MOBY-DICK*]$_F$.

  a. $[\![\text{B}]\!]^o = \lambda w.\text{Sarah read } \textit{Moby-Dick in } w$

  b. $[\![\text{B}]\!]^f = \begin{Bmatrix} \lambda w \text{ . Sarah read } \textit{Moby-Dick in } w, \\ \lambda w \text{ . Sarah read } \textit{Jane Eyre in } w, \text{ ...} \end{Bmatrix}$

The application of ALTSHIFT to B would yield the same denotation as for [ALTSHIFT A] in (36). Hence, *Sarah read [*MOBY DICK*]*$_F$ is predicted to have a possible interpretation as a constituent question equivalent to *What did Sarah read?*, contrary to fact. This appears to be a linguistic universal.

(38) *A generalization about interrogative syntax*
  Narrow focus is never interpreted as a constituent question ranging over its contextual alternatives.

To explain this, I propose to adopt a generalized version of Buccola and Spector's (2016) 'Pragmatic Economy Constraint'[21] on the use of numerals. According to this constraint, the use of a numeral is blocked if the numeral does no semantic work—that is, if replacing the numeral with another numeral would yield the same result.

(39) *Pragmatic Economy Constraint (Buccola and Spector 2016:165)*
An LF ϕ containing a numeral n is infelicitous if, for some m distinct from n, ϕ is truth-conditionally equivalent to $\phi[n \rightarrow m]$ (the result of substituting m for n in ϕ).

This economy-driven logic can be extended beyond the domain of numerals, as in (40).

(40) *Generalized Pragmatic Economy Constraint*
An LF ϕ containing a focused expression A is infelicitous if, for some B distinct from A, ϕ is truth-conditionally equivalent to $\phi[A \rightarrow B]$ (the result of substituting B for A in ϕ).

In the case of (37), notice that replacing the focused [*Moby-Dick*]$_F$ with any other focused nominal would yield the same result illustrated in (37b). Consequently, the use of such focused phrases to introduce alternatives that will be used interrogatively is blocked here. Instead, only *wh*-expressions can be used, as in (34).[22]

This proposal is also able to account for more complex cases of questions with focus. Consider questions such as (41), which combine free focus with a *wh*-expression. Such structures pose a problem for traditional Hamblin approaches to questions, since alternatives generated from the focused constituent (here, *Moby-Dick*) and alternatives generated by the *wh*-expression are predicted to compose pointwise and give a denotation of a multiple *wh*-question parallel to (42), contrary to fact.[23]

(41) C = *Who* read [*Moby-Dick*]$_F$?

(42) D = *Who* read what?

(43) a. $[\![C]\!]^o = [\![D]\!]^o$ undefined

b. $[\![C]\!]^f = [\![D]\!]^f = \left\{ \begin{array}{l} \lambda w \,.\, \text{Sarah read } \textit{Moby-Dick} \text{ in } w, \\ \lambda w \,.\, \text{Katie read } \textit{Moby-Dick} \text{ in } w, \\ \lambda w \,.\, \text{Sarah read } \textit{Jane Eyre} \text{ in } w, \\ \lambda w \,.\, \text{Katie read } \textit{Jane Eyre} \text{ in } w, \,... \end{array} \right\}$

As with B in (37), we are able to rule out the possibility of D receiving a multiple *wh*-question interpretation by adopting the economy principle in (40): focused phrases cannot be used to introduce alternatives that will be used interrogatively—instead, *wh*-expressions must be used for this purpose.

3.8   Appendix 2: Wiltschko's Observation

Wiltschko (1997) points out a correlation between superiority and the possible readings of German multiple *wh*-questions. While Superiority-obeying questions can have both single-pair and pair-list answers, Superiority-violating questions can only receive pair-list interpretations. Thus, when a question is asked in a context that establishes that there could only be one pair in the answer set, the Superiority-violating variant of the question is ungrammatical.

(44) *Ungrammaticality caused by blocking of the pair-list reading (German)*
Context: Peter is walking his stubborn dog on a leash. The dog is dragging really hard in the direction of his favorite tree.
  a. *Wer₁* führt denn hier *wen₂* an der Leine?
      who leads PRT here whom on the leash
      'Who is leading whom here on the leash?'
  b. **Wen₂* führt denn hier *wer₁* an der Leine?

In Kotek 2012, 2014b, I have shown that the same observation holds for Hebrew multiple *wh*-questions. Here, I argue that a similar effect is observed in English. The situation in English is complicated by the fact that Superiority violations are only possible with D-linked *wh*-phrases, leading to more elaborate examples than are necessary for German and Hebrew. However, consider examples (45)–(46). In the given contexts, only the Superiority-obeying questions are possible, (45a) and (46a), the Superiority-violating variants are ungrammatical, (45b) and (46b).[24]

(45) *Superiority-violating question has only a pair-list reading (English)*
Context: Scientists have discovered a new star system, consisting of just two stars. They appear to be interacting with one another because of their gravitational fields. Researchers are now asking:
  a. *Which* one ___ revolves around *which* one?
  b. * *Which* one does *which* one revolve around ___?

(46) Context: The Jones family has two sons who always fight with one another. They're even fighting right now. I wonder:
  a. *Which* one ___ hit *which* one first, this time?
  b. * *Which* one did *which* one hit ___ first, this time?

This effect is also found in matrix questions (Chris Tancredi, pers. comm.).

(47) A: Those two people just walked into the bar in rapid succession.
    B1: Oh yeah? *Which* one ___ followed *which* one in?
    B2: Oh yeah? #*Which* one did *which* one follow in ___?

Note that these same questions can have felicitous pair-list readings, given an appropriate context; only the single-pair reading is unavailable here.[25]

Here, I propose to explain this fact as a Scope Economy effect (Fox 2000), following proposals by Fox (2012c) and Golan (1993): a Superiority-violating question is possible only when its meaning differs from that of its Superiority-obeying counterpart. That is, economy principles like Shortest Move are relativized to interpretation: one convergent derivation blocks another if it has shorter links and results in an interpretively equivalent LF representation. Derivations resulting in nonequivalent LFs are not compared and hence cannot block each other. This is explained by Fox's (2012c) cross-derivational Semantically Sensitive version of Shortest Move (SSSM).

(48) *Semantically Sensitive version of Shortest Move*
C must attract the closest *wh*-phrase it can to derive a designated semantic interpretation.

Given SSSM, we predict that Superiority-violating questions should allow pair-list readings, because overtly raising wh_2 above wh_1 yields a different meaning than overtly raising wh_1 above wh_2. Recall that the *exhaustivity* and *uniqueness* presuppositions of the pair-list reading of the multiple *wh*-question apply to the *higher wh*-phrase in the structure, resulting in distinct meanings of Superiority-obeying and -violating questions.

In (49)–(50), the member of the pair that is subject to exhaustivity is marked in bold, and the italicized member is subject to uniqueness. I illustrate in addition the single-pair reading of the question.

(49) *Superiority-obeying question*
Which student cooked *which* dish?
a. Pair-list
   ⟨**student 1**, *dish a*⟩
   ⟨**student 2**, *dish b*⟩
   ⟨**student 3**, *dish c*⟩
   ⋮
b. Single-pair
   ⟨**student 1**, *dish a*⟩

(50) *Superiority-violating question*
Which dish did *which* student cook?
a. Pair-list
   ⟨**dish a**, *student 1*⟩
   ⟨**dish b**, *student 2*⟩
   ⟨**dish c**, *student 3*⟩
   ⋮
b. Single-pair
   ⟨**dish a**, *student 1*⟩

For the Superiority-obeying question in (49a), exhaustivity applies to the students and uniqueness applies to the dishes. The answer must pair each contextually relevant student with exactly one dish (but some dishes may not be mentioned at all). For the Superiority-violating question in (50a), exhaustivity applies to the dishes and uniqueness to the students. The answer must therefore pair each dish with exactly one student (but some students may not be mentioned at all). Hence, these two answers are distinct from one another.

However, SSSM predicts that Superiority-violating questions should not allow single-pair readings. This is so because the single-pair reading is identical under the Superiority-obeying and Superiority-violating word orders. In other words, the single-pair answers to (49) and (50) necessarily pick out the same pair. Consequently, given SSSM, the availability of the single-pair answer to the more economical Superiority-obeying question (49b) blocks that same answer from being available to the less economical Superiority-violating question (50b).[26]

Given the above discussion, I submit that although the grammar can generate both single-pair and pair-list readings of both Superiority-obeying and Superiority-violating questions, other considerations may intervene to block certain interpretations in certain cases. Here, the single-pair reading of the Superiority-violating question is blocked by economy considerations—namely, by the availability of an identical meaning provided by the more economical Superiority-obeying question.

4 Crosslinguistic Variation in Interrogative Syntax

The preceding chapters concentrated on English data and showed how the framework I develop in this book can account for the behavior of simplex and multiple *wh*-questions. In this chapter, I turn to the crosslinguistic variation attested in interrogative syntax.

In particular, I discuss German, a *wh*-fronting language in which covert *wh*-movement is generally believed not to be available; Japanese, Mandarin Chinese, and Bùlì, representing *wh*-in-situ languages—where all *wh*-phrases are pronounced in situ, although they may not all be interpreted in situ at LF; Bulgarian, Russian, Serbo-Croatian, and Hungarian, representing different types of multiple *wh*-fronting languages; French and Defaka, languages that employ both a movement strategy and an in-situ strategy for the formation of *wh*-questions; and Malay, which uses both of those strategies for question formation, in addition to a partial movement strategy. Additionally, I discuss pied-piping in questions, concentrating on Cable's (2007, 2010) theory of pied-piping. I show how to combine this theory with the proposal I develop here.

As it is beyond the scope of this book to provide full descriptions of the syntax and semantics of each language surveyed here, my goal is quite modest: I aim to show examples of the major syntactic strategies associated with questioning across a broad selection of languages and to sketch how my proposal accounts for the observed variation. An important component in accounting for variation in interrogatives, I will argue, can be attributed to the syntactic distribution of the ALTSHIFT operator crosslinguistically.

4.1 *Wh*-Fronting Languages without Covert Movement

On the surface, question formation in German is quite similar to question formation in English. Simplex *wh*-questions involve fronting of a *wh*-word, whereas multiple *wh*-questions again involve the fronting of just one *wh*-word, with all other *wh*-words remaining in situ.

(1) *Simplex and multiple* wh-*questions in German*
   a. *Wer* ist gekommen?
      who has come
      'Who came?'
   b. *Wer* hat *was* gekauft?
      who has what bought
      'Who bought what?'

Unlike English, German has been argued not to exhibit superiority effects, even with simplex *wh*-phrases (although several authors (e.g., Featherston 2005b) nonetheless report a preference for a Superiority-obeying word order over a superiority-violating one).

(2) *D-linked* wh-*multiple questions in German allow Superiority violations (Wiltschko 1997:114)*
   a. *Welcher* Lehrer hat *welches* Buch empfohlen?
      which   teacher has which   book recommended
      'Which teacher recommended which book?'
   b. *Welches* Buch hat *welcher* Lehrer empfohlen?
      which   book has which   teacher recommended
      'Which book did which teacher recommend?'

(3) *Non-D-linked multiple* wh-*questions in German also allow Superiority violations (Wiltschko 1997:107)*
   a. *Wer* hat *was* behauptet?
      who has what claimed
      'Who claimed what?'
   b. *Was* hat *wer* behauptet?
      what has who claimed
      'What did who claim?'

The absence of superiority effects, in addition to German's behavior with regard to intervention effects (to be discussed in part II), has led researchers to argue that unlike English, German does not have a covert *wh*-movement option available in the construction of *wh*-questions. Instead, *wh*-phrases are interpreted in their pronounced positions, and they may be moved only through scrambling, not through covert movement. This has been spelled out in different ways by Cable (2010) and Pesetsky (2000) in their attempts to model the syntax of German questions. Here, I sketch the syntactic assumptions shared by these and other recent theorists—crucially, the fact that the non-moved *wh*-phrase remains in situ at LF, both in Superiority-obeying and in

Superiority-violating questions (here I use pseudo-English examples, based on the data in (3)).

(4) *Syntactic assumptions for Superiority-obeying and -violating German questions*

    a. *Who* C has ____ *what* claimed?

    b. *What* C has *who* claimed ____ ?

Within the framework developed here, structures like those in (4) will be assigned a derivation parallel to the one shown for English Superiority-violating questions in section 3.5.2. Such a derivation involves overt movement of one *wh*-phrase to Spec,CP and in-situ composition of any other *wh*-phrases in the structure without covert movement. (Here, I simplify and do not represent assumptions about the syntax of German that are not essential for present purposes, such as successive-cyclic movement and T-to-C movement.)

(5) *LF of a Superiority-obeying German question with a single-pair reading*

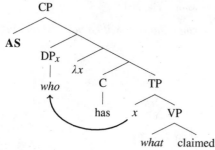

(6) *LF of a Superiority-violating German question with a single-pair reading*

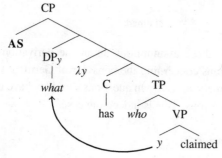

In both derivations, only one *wh*-phrase moves; the other *wh*-phrase remains in situ at LF. Furthermore, only one ALTSHIFT operator is merged into the structure, above all *wh*-phrases. The result is a flat set of propositions, yielding a single-pair reading of the question.

The LFs I posit for the pair-list readings of these questions differ minimally: the only divergence from the syntax of the single-pair reading is that a second ALTSHIFT operator is added between the two *wh*-phrases. The result is a nested structure—a family-of-questions denotation—modeling the pair-list readings of the questions.

(7) *LF of a Superiority-obeying German question with a pair-list reading*

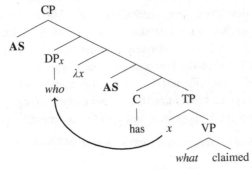

(8) *LF of a Superiority-violating German question with a pair-list reading*

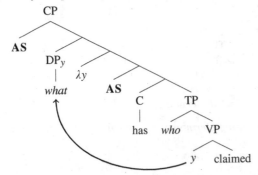

As we will see in chapter 5, these assumptions about the derivation of German questions make predictions concerning the behavior of German with regard to intervention effects: namely, all German questions should behave like English Superiority-violating questions. This is indeed the case.

4.2 Multiple *Wh*-Fronting Languages

Question formation in Slavic languages such as Russian, Bulgarian, and Serbo-Croatian famously involves fronting all the *wh*-phrases in the question to the left periphery. Beyond this similarity, however, an interesting diversity emerges: multiple *wh*-fronting languages vary in whether or not they allow

Superiority violations, as well as in the possible readings of the resulting questions. I argue that these two facts are correlated, and are related to differences in the distribution of the ALTSHIFT operator in these languages.

4.2.1   Superiority and Readings of Multiple *Wh*-Questions

Multiple *wh*-fronting languages such as Bulgarian, Russian, and Serbo-Croatian have been argued to be divided into two categories: those that do not allow superiority violations in multiple *wh*-questions, such as Bulgarian,[1] and those that do, such as Russian and Serbo-Croatian.

(9)   *Variability in Superiority violations in multiple* wh-*fronting languages (Bošković 2007:159)*

    a.   *Koj kogo* običa?

       who whom loves

       'Who loves whom?'

    b. * *Kogo koj* običa?   (Bulgarian)

(10) a.   *Ko koga* voli?

       who whom loves

       'Who loves whom?'

    b.   *Koga ko* voli?   (Serbo-Croatian)

(11) a.   *Kto kogo* ljubit?

       who whom loves

       'Who loves whom?'

    b.   *Kogo kto* ljubit?   (Russian)

This property of multiple *wh*-fronting languages has been argued to correlate as well with possible readings of the question: whether the language allows for a single-pair reading of the question or for a pair-list reading. Languages such as Bulgarian are argued to require a pair-list reading, while languages such as Russian are said to allow a single-pair reading as well (see Bošković 2003 et seq.).[2] Following Rudin (1988) and Bošković (2002) et seq., these properties are said to follow from the syntax of the question. In Bulgarian, all moved *wh*-phrases target Spec,CP. In languages like Serbo-Croatian and Russian, on the other hand, some *wh*-fronted elements have not undergone *wh*-movement to Spec,CP; rather, they have undergone noninterrogative (focus) movement to a lower position, often assumed to be FocP.[3] In these languages, Spec,CP does not have to be filled.

Interestingly, some multiple *wh*-fronting languages have also been shown to allow exceptional *wh*-in-situ, in which case the question must receive a single-pair reading. Such a state of affairs has been described in Hungarian (all Hungarian data below are from É. Kiss 2002).[4]

(12) *Hungarian multiple* wh-*questions with a single-pair reading*
　　a. *Ki*　verekedett *ki-vel*?
　　　who fought　　who-with
　　　'Who fought with whom?
　　b. *Kivel* verekedett *ki*?

In all other cases, all *wh*-phrases must occur in the left periphery, with possible Superiority violations. The resulting questions require a pair-list interpretation and cannot receive a single-pair response.

(13) *Hungarian multiple* wh-*questions with a pair-list reading*
　　a. *Ki*　*melyik* ajándék-ot　választotta?
　　　who which present-ACC chose
　　　'Who chose which present?'
　　b. *Melyik* ajándékot *ki* választotta?

Along similar lines to the arguments made by Bošković for Slavic languages, É. Kiss (2002) proposes that fronting of *wh*-elements in Hungarian targets two different positions. The higher *wh*-phrase moves to a position she calls DistP (DistributiveP), explaining the strong distributivity requirements on the elements denoted by the domain of this *wh*-phrase (akin to the presuppositions described by Dayal (1996); see chapter 2). Lower *wh*-phrases move to a focus projection, FocP. Superiority violations are then allowed because any of the *wh*-phrases in the question may be targeted for *wh*-movement to Spec,DistP or for focus movement to Spec,FocP.

(14) *LF of a Superiority-obeying question in Hungarian*

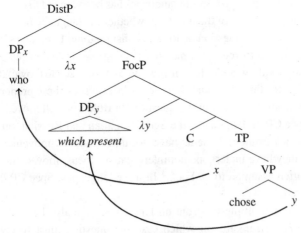

Another important fact concerning Hungarian questions is that when only one *wh*-phrase fronts, it moves to Spec,FocP. We know this is so because *wh*-phrases compete with other focused elements for fronting to this same focus position;[5] crucially, if both a *wh*-phrase and an *only*-phrase occur in the same structure, the former fronts and the latter remains in situ.[6]

(15) *Normally,* only-*phrases front to the focus projection*
  a. * János be-mutatta   csak Péter-t   Mari-nak.
     John VM-introduced only Peter-ACC Mary-DAT
     'John introduced only Peter to Mary.'
  b.   János csak Pétert mutatta be Marinak.

(16) Wh-*phrases also appear to front to the same position*
  a. * János be-mutatott   *kit*   Mari-nak?
     John VM-introduced whom Mary-DAT
     'Whom did John introduce to Mary?'
  b.   János *kit* mutatott be Marinak?

(17) Wh-*phrase fronts,* only *remains in situ, if both are present in the question*
  a.   *Ki*   látta csak Péter-t?
     who saw only Peter-ACC
     'Who saw only Peter?'
  b. * Csak Pétert látta *ki*?

4.2.2 The Distribution of ALTSHIFT

I propose to model this observed variation as the result of crosslinguistic variation in the possible adjunction sites of the ALTSHIFT operator. In particular, I propose that in Hungarian, FocP is the lowest position in the tree at which an ALTSHIFT operator may adjoin.[7] Moreover, I propose that *some* alternative-interpreting operator must always occur above FocP, as the position that traditionally hosts focus-fronted elements in Hungarian. This may also explain other focus-related effects in the language, such as the exact interpretation of numerals that occur in FocP, conditionals' strengthened interpretation as biconditionals, as well as the obligatory pair-list interpretation of questions, which is our main interest here. See É. Kiss 2002 and Szabolcsi 1981, among others, for additional discussion of the Hungarian focus position.[8]

Assuming that ALTSHIFT cannot occur below FocP, we immediately obtain the correct results for Hungarian. In (18), I sketch an LF for a question with a single-pair interpretation. As noted, the moved *wh*-phrase targets Spec,FocP, which is assumed to have an obligatory ALTSHIFT operator above it.[9] Other *wh*-phrases remain in TP.

(18) *LF for a Hungarian multiple* wh-*question with a single-pair interpretation*
  a. $[\textbf{AS} \ [_{\text{FocP}} \ wh_{1/2} \ \ldots \ [_{\text{TP}} \ \ldots \ wh_{2/1} \ \ldots \ ]]]$
  b. * $[\textbf{AS} \ [_{\text{FocP}} \ wh_{1/2} \ \ldots \ [\textbf{AS} \ \ldots \ [_{\text{TP}} \ \ldots \ wh_{2/1} \ \ldots \ ]]]]$

Since FocP is the lowest position at which ALTSHIFT may adjoin, the resulting derivation will necessarily first involve the pointwise composition of the alternatives projected from all *wh*-phrases into a "flat" structure. Then, as a second step, the resulting set of propositions will be converted by ALTSHIFT into the ordinary meaning of the question, as in (18a). Following the discussion in chapter 3, the requirement that a question have a unique maximally informative true answer will result in a single-pair reading of the question. See section 3.4.1 for a detailed derivation that is parallel to the one proposed here. The alternative LF (18b) which contains a second ALTSHIFT operator below FocP, which would be required in order to obtain a pair-list reading, is ruled out because ALTSHIFT cannot adjoin in such a low position.

In (19), I show the LF for a question with a pair-list interpretation. Here, following É. Kiss 2002, I assume that the lower *wh*-phrase moves to Spec,FocP and the higher *wh*-phrase moves to Spec,DistP. Again, following our previous assumptions (see note 9), one ALTSHIFT operator must occur above FocP. In addition, a second ALTSHIFT operator must occur above DistP in order to return an ordinary value of the whole question.[10] The derivation in (19b) is ruled out because it lacks an ordinary semantic value. More interestingly, the derivation in (19c), which would yield a single-pair interpretation of a question, is ruled out by the requirement that a focus-sensitive operator—in the case of questions, an ALTSHIFT operator—occur above FocP.

(19) *LF for a Hungarian multiple* wh-*question with a pair-list interpretation*
  a. [**AS** [$_{DistP}$ $wh_{1/2}$ [**AS** [$_{FocP}$ $wh_{2/1}$ ... [$_{TP}$ ...]]]]]
  b. * [$_{DistP}$ $wh_{1/2}$ [**AS** [$_{FocP}$ $wh_{2/1}$ ... [$_{TP}$ ...]]]]
  c. * [**AS** [$_{DistP}$ $wh_{1/2}$ [$_{FocP}$ $wh_{2/1}$ ... [$_{TP}$ ...]]]]

Let us turn back now to the variation found in Russian and Bulgarian, where the former allows both single-pair and pair-list interpretations of a multiple *wh*-question while the latter allows only a pair-list interpretation. I propose to capture this by requiring that each CP projection have its own adjoined ALTSHIFT operator.[11] Lower projections that can host *wh*-phrases may but need not host ALTSHIFT in these languages. These assumptions are sufficient to capture the data we have seen so far.

In Bulgarian, following Bošković (2002) et seq. I assume that all fronted *wh*-phrases undergo interrogative *wh*-movement, which targets Spec,CP. Recall that this explains the lack of Superiority violations in the language, given Attract Closest, ruling out derivations such as (20b–c), where wh_2 is fronted over wh_1 to a specifier either of CP or of FocP. If a separate ALTSHIFT must adjoin to each spec,CP, the resulting structure will then necessarily have a pair-list interpretation. A single-pair interpretation, which the LFs in (20d–e) would yield, is ruled out.

(20) *LF for a Bulgarian multiple question must have a pair-list interpretation*
  a. [**AS** [$_{CP}$ wh_1 [**AS** [$_{CP}$ wh_2 ... [$_{TP}$ ...]]]]]   (Superiority-obeying-PL)
  b. * [**AS** [$_{CP}$ wh_2 [**AS** [$_{FocP}$ wh_1 ... [$_{TP}$ ...]]]]]   (Superiority-violating-PL)
  c. * [**AS** [$_{CP}$ wh_2 [**AS** [$_{CP}$ wh_1 ... [$_{TP}$ ...]]]]]   (Superiority-violating-PL)
  d. * [**AS** [$_{CP}$ wh_1 [$_{FocP}$ wh_2 ... [$_{TP}$ ...]]]]   (Superiority-obeying-SP)
  e. * [**AS** [$_{CP}$ wh_1 [$_{CP}$ wh_2 ... [$_{TP}$ ...]]]]   (Superiority-obeying-SP)

In Russian, on the other hand, we allow *wh*-phrases to be fronted to positions lower than Spec,CP through focus movement. We again require ALTSHIFT to be adjoined to each CP—or alternatively, above the highest FocP—to yield an ordinary meaning for the question.[12] We crucially allow, but do not require, each FocP to be adjoined by an ALTSHIFT operator. As a result, more question LFs are possible in Russian than in Bulgarian, including ones that would yield a single-pair reading and others that would yield a pair-list reading.

(21) *LFs for Russian multiple* wh-*questions may have single-pair or pair-list interpretations*
  a. [**AS** [$_{CP/FocP}$ wh_1 [**AS** [$_{FocP}$ wh_2 ... [$_{TP}$ ...]]]]]
      (Superiority-obeying-PL)
  b. [**AS** [$_{CP}$ wh_2 [**AS** [$_{FocP}$ wh_1 ... [$_{TP}$ ...]]]]]   (Superiority-violating-PL)
  c. [**AS** [$_{CP/FocP}$ wh_1 [$_{FocP}$ wh_2 ... [$_{TP}$ ...]]]]   (Superiority-obeying-SP)
  d. [**AS** [$_{CP}$ wh_2 [$_{FocP}$ wh_1 ... [$_{TP}$ ...]]]]   (Superiority-violating-SP)

To summarize this section: I propose two sources of variation that explain the distribution of structures and corresponding meanings observed in multiple *wh*-fronting languages.

The first point of variation, following much previous work, is that *wh*-fronting can vary in terms of the triggers of movement and, correspondingly, in the target positions of movement: it can be the result of *wh*-movement or of focus movement, and it can target at least Spec,CP (or Spec,DistP) and Spec,FocP. *Wh*-phrases that are hosted in these different projections may be subject to different restrictions, and they do not compete with one another for the purposes of economy conditions such as Attract Closest.

The second point of variation concerns the availability and possible adjunction sites of ALTSHIFT. Following the Principle of Interpretability, we know that there must be at least one ALTSHIFT operator hosted above the highest *wh*-phrase in the structure, to return a convergent ordinary semantic value for the question. In addition to that, I have proposed that in Hungarian, every FocP must host *some* focus-sensitive operator—an ALTSHIFT in the case of questions but perhaps other operators in the case of focus movement. I showed how this models the distribution of single-pair and pair-list readings of questions in this language. In Bulgarian and Russian, I proposed that ALTSHIFT may but need not be hosted in Spec,FocP and that every CP must have its own ALT-SHIFT. Combined with other facts about *wh*-movement in these languages, specifically with regard to the nature of the movement (*wh*-movement vs. focus movement) and the landing site of the movement (Spec,CP vs. Spec,FocP), this derives the fact that Bulgarian multiple *wh*-questions must have pair-list interpretations while Russian allows both single-pair and pair-list interpretations.[13]

A third point of variation, independent of the position of ALTSHIFT, concerns the landing site of *wh*-movement. As noted above, some languages allow *wh*-fronting to positions other than interrogative C. This has been argued for Hungarian (e.g., Brody 1990; É. Kiss 1987, 2002;, Horvath 1986), where at least some *wh*-phrases front to a focus projection. Similarly, Farsi, an otherwise *wh*-in-situ language, has been argued to allow movement of *wh*-expressions to a focus projection immediately below C, visible in sluicing constructions (e.g., Toosarvandani 2008, 2009). Finally, Bangla, another (ostensibly) *wh*-in-situ language, has been argued to in fact involve *overt wh*-fronting to a position immediately below the subject, with other elements moving over this *wh*-expression to give the (surface) impression of a *wh*-in-situ language (see Simpson and Bhattacharya 2003 for details). When movement does not target a position that can host an ALTSHIFT operator (i.e., clause-peripheral FocP or CP), we expect an alternative mode of composition—namely, the projection of focus alternatives—to be used between the landing site of *wh* and the edge of the clause.

4.3 *Wh*-in-Situ Languages

Not all languages utilize *wh*-fronting in the process of question formation. In many languages, *wh*-phrases may (or must) remain in situ when a question is formed. Question formation may then be indicated by prosody or by the presence of dedicated morphemes that adjoin to the *wh*-phrase or to the clausal spine. In this section, I survey some facts concerning the syntax of interrogative constructions in Japanese, Mandarin Chinese, and Bùlì (a Gur language spoken in Ghana). In all three languages, *wh*-phrases are pronounced in their base-generated positions (unless scrambled), but they have been argued to have different underlying structures, as we will see. I show that the proposal developed in chapter 3 can easily account for this attested variation.

4.3.1　Surface In-Situ Does Not Necessarily Mean LF-in-Situ

In many languages, including Japanese, Mandarin Chinese, and Bùlì, which I will concentrate on here, question formation does not require *wh*-fronting. Below are simple *wh*-questions in the three languages, all perfectly acceptable without any *wh*-movement.

(22)　*Questions with* wh-*in-situ*

　　a.　John-ga　　*nani*-o　　kaimasita ka?
　　　　John-NOM what-ACC bought　　Q
　　　　'What did John buy?'　　　　　　　　　　(Japanese; Hagstrom 1998:15)

　　b.　Ni　kanjian-le *shei*?
　　　　you see-ASP　who
　　　　'Who did you see?'　　　　　(Mandarin Chinese; Huang 1982a:253)

　　c.　Bí:ká　　dìg　　ká *b^wā:?*
　　　　child.DEF cook.PST Q　what
　　　　'What did the child cook?'　　　　　　　　　　(Bùlì; Sulemana 2017:2)

Questions may also be embedded, again without movement of the *wh*-element to the matrix, despite receiving a matrix question interpretation.

(23)　*Embedded* wh-*phrases can take matrix scope*

　　a.　John-ga　[Mary-ga　*nani*-o　　katta　to] omotteiru no?
　　　　John-NOM Mary-NOM what-ACC bought that thinks　　Q
　　　　'What does John think that Mary bought?'
　　　　　　　　　　　　　　　　　　　　　(Japanese; Hagstrom 1998:17)

　　b.　Zhangsan xiangxin [*shei* mai-le　shu]?
　　　　Zhangsan believe　who buy-ASP book
　　　　'Who does Zhangsan believe bought books?'
　　　　　　　　　　　　　　　(Mandarin Chinese; Huang 1982a:253)

　　c.　Fì　wè:nì　　āyīn ká *wānā* ālī dìg　　lāmmú:?
　　　　2SG say.PST C　Q who　ALI cook.PST meat.DEF
　　　　'Who did you say cooked the meat?'　　　(Bùlì; Sulemana 2017:3)

Despite these similarities, these three languages have been argued to differ with respect to their underlying syntax: on the basis of island diagnostics, Japanese is argued to be truly *wh*-in-situ at LF; Bùlì is argued to involve covert *wh*-movement of the surface in-situ *wh*-phrase; and Mandarin Chinese exhibits a split, such that questions with argument *wh*-words are in situ, but adjunct *wh*-words undergo covert movement.

(24)　*No complex NP or adjunct island sensitivity in Japanese*

　　a.　Taro-wa　[[*dare*-ga　katta] mochi]-o　　tabemasita ka?
　　　　Taro-TOP who-NOM bought rice.cake-ACC ate　　　Q
　　　　'Who$_x$ did Taro eat rice cakes that x bought?'

b. Taro-wa [*dare*-ga kita-kara]   kaerimasita ka?
   Taro-TOP who-NOM came-because left   Q
   'Who$_x$ did Taro leave because x came?'

(25) Wh-*adjuncts but not* wh-*arguments are island-sensitive in Mandarin*

a.   [$_{RC}$ *Shei* xie   *t*] de shu   zui youqu?
        who write   DE books most interesting

     'Books that *who* wrote are the most interesting?'

b. * [$_{RC}$ Ta *weishenme* xie   *t*] de shu   zui   youqu?
        he why   write   DE books most interesting

     'Books that he wrote *why* are the most interesting?'

c. * [$_{RC}$ Ta *zenme* xie   *t*] de shu   zui   youqu?
        he how   write   DE books most interesting

     'Books that he wrote *how* are the most interesting?'

(26) *Island sensitivity in Bùlì questions*[14]

a. * Fí á-yáalí   [núrpók wāi   ālì dà   ká $b^w\bar{a}$ lá:?]
     2SG IMPV-love woman REL.PRO C buy.PST Q what PRT

     'You love the woman who bought what?'

b. * Azuma dà   [gbáŋ ālī   ká $b^w\bar{a}$:?]
     Azuma buy.PST book CONJ Q what

     'Azuma bought a book and what?'

This variation is easily captured within the interrogative framework developed in chapter 3: the system allows for a question to be constructed either using (covert) movement or by means of in-situ composition using focus alternatives, both yielding the same meaning of the question.[15]

(27) *(Simplified) LF of a* wh-*in-situ question that is truly LF-in-situ*

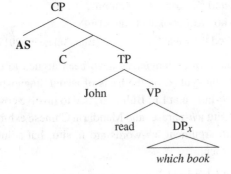

(28) *(Simplified) LF of a* wh-*in-situ question with covert* wh-*movement*

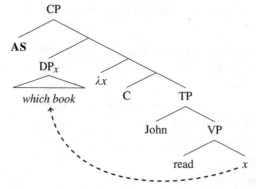

Two main differences between the LFs in (27) and (28) are predicted. First, structures with covert movement should be island- sensitive, unlike structures with in-situ composition. This leads to the prediction that a structure like (27) is correct for Japanese and for Mandarin Chinese wh-argument questions, while a structure like (28) is correct for Bùlì and for Mandarin Chinese wh-adjunct questions. The second prediction, which I will elaborate on in part II and which will ultimately be borne out, is that the former type of structure, with in-situ composition, but not the latter, with movement, should be sensitive to intervention effects.

These two differences notwithstanding, the predicted meaning of the question is the same regardless of whether movement is assumed or not—in both cases, we eventually calculate a set of propositions that are alternative answers to the question, and those are converted by the ALTSHIFT operator into the ordinary meaning of the question.

4.3.2 *Wh*-Indeterminates

In addition to their use in questions, wh-words are often used in other constructions involving the generation of alternatives and movement. Cross-linguistically, wh-words are found in relative clauses and free relatives, free choice items, negative polarity items, wh-quantification, wh-indefinites, and disjunctions. This has led Kuroda (1965) to coin the term wh-indeterminates in his seminal study of Japanese in-situ quantificational expressions composed of wh-words, which he proposes to describe as "nouns that behave like a logical variable" (p. 43).

In Japanese, wh-words can be used not only in questions but also, notably, in wh-indefinite constructions. In such cases, and in disjunctions, the sentence will also contain the morpheme -KA, which I have glossed in examples above as 'Q'. In (29)–(30) I show examples of the distribution of *wh*-indeterminates and -KA in Japanese, remaining agnostic about the meaning of -KA. I return to this issue immediately below.

(29) *Uses of* wh-*indeterminates and* -KA *in Japanese (Uegaki 2018:2)*
 a. [DP *Dare*-**ka**]-ga   hashitta.
  who-KA NOM ran
  'Someone ran.'   (*wh*-indefinite existential statement)
 b. [CP *Dare*-ga   hashitta-**ka**] (oshiete)?
  who-NOM ran-KA   tell
  '(Tell me) who ran?'   (*wh*-question)

(30) *Uses of* -KA *in Japanese disjunctions (Uegaki 2018:3)*
 a. [DP Hanako-**ka** Jiro-**ka**]-ga   hashitta.
  Hanako-KA Jiro-KA NOM ran
  'Hanako or Jiro ran.'   (declarative disjunction)
 b. [CP [Hanako-ga   hashitta-**ka**] [Jiro-ga   hashitta-**ka**]] oshiete.
  Hanako-NOM ran-KA   Jiro-NOM ran-KA   tell
  'Tell me which is true: It seems that Hanako ran or it seems that Jiro ran.'   (alternative question)

Uegaki (2018) shows that adopting the assumption that Japanese -KA is an overt instantiation of the ALTSHIFT operator and allowing it to attach at either the CP or DP level can derive the observed distribution of this operator in Japanese. In what follows, I show short LFs and derivations for the *wh*-indeterminate examples in (29). For brevity, I give a combined illustration of the LF and the derivation. Thus, the top line of nonterminal nodes in the tree illustrates the ordinary value of the node, and the bottom line, the alternative value of the node.

(31) *LF and short derivation of a* wh-*question (29b)*

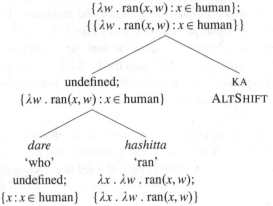

The result of this LF and derivation is a set of propositions of the form "that x ran in w" for any human x. In other words, the result is the set of possible answers to the question *Who ran?*—the Hamblin set, as desired. This parallels all other derivations shown so far in this book. The important point is that alternatives initiated by the *wh*-word project up the structure, compose pointwise with other elements in TP, and are finally converted into the ordinary meaning of the question by ALTSHIFT at the CP level. Below we see that if alternatives are closed off at the DP level, we are able to obtain an indefinite construction.[16]

(32) *LF and short derivation of a* wh-*indefinite-containing statement (29a)*

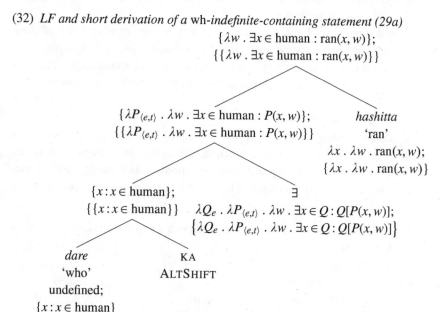

In this derivation, we allow ALTSHIFT to close off the alternatives generated by *wh* immediately after they are introduced into the structure, and then allow the resulting set of individuals to be existentially quantified over. As a result, we obtain an existential statement of the form "there is a human x such that x came," or in other words, "someone came." This minimal change to the syntax and resulting derivation yields the desired existential interpretation.

I refer the reader to Uegaki (2018) for motivation and additional details concerning the above derivations and for an illustration of how this proposal then further extends to declarative disjunctions and to alternative questions. At its core, the idea is that-KA is able to handle any alternative-generating construction, and allowing for crosslinguistic variation in its distribution may allow for a principled explanation of its behavior in Japanese and in other languages that make similar use of *wh*-indeterminates in noninterrogative contexts.

4.4   Combined Strategies for Question Formation

A main goal of this book is to develop a framework that allows for the modeling of questions with diverse syntactic configurations, including *wh*-movement and *wh*-in-situ. Going beyond the phonological form of the question, we have seen that the syntax of the question may differ from its pronunciation. This is often detected through island diagnostics, and has led to the conclusion that at least two different modes of composition are required for interrogative syntax/semantics: (overt or covert) *wh*-movement, and Rooth-Hamblin alternatives computation.

In this section, I discuss languages that overtly employ both of these strategies in their question formation. I additionally discuss languages where *wh*-movement need not target the interrogative complementizer, but may instead target intermediate CP projections along the path of movement.

4.4.1   Optional *Wh*-Fronting

In addition to languages that appear to employ just one question formation strategy in the formation of a given question—either movement or in-situ composition—we find languages that can employ either strategy, with reportedly no changes to meaning. This is the case in French, as illustrated in (33).[17]

(33) Wh-*in-situ and* wh-*movement in French question formation (Mathieu 2002:34)*
   a. Tu fais *quoi* ce soir?
      you do   what this evening
   b. *Qu$_i$*'est-ce que tu   fais *t$_i$* ce   soir?
      what   that you do   this evening
      'What are you doing tonight?'

At first glance, it may appear that English, too, allows both movement and in-situ strategies in question formation, but that is not the case. In particular, questions with in-situ *wh*-phrases in English are interpreted as echo questions. This can be diagnosed by the fact that such questions cannot be embedded under question-embedding predicates.

(34) Wh-*in-situ in English is an echo question, not a true question*
   a. I know *what* you did this evening.
   b. * I know you did *what* this evening.

Mathieu (2002) discusses at length restrictions on embedding of *wh*-in-situ, but provides the following grammatical example in colloquial French:

(35) *An embedded* wh-*in-situ question in French (Mathieu 2002:136)*

Je me   demande c'est *quoi.*

I myself wonder it is what

'I wonder what it is.'

A similar distribution of *wh*-in-situ and fronting strategies has been reported for some African languages. In Defaka (Ijoid; Southern Nigeria), questions can be formed through a focus-fronting strategy, using the markers *kò* (for subjects) and *ndò … kè* (for non-subjects), or through an in-situ strategy (Bennett 2009; Bennett, Akinlabi, and Connell 2012).

(36) *Fronting and in-situ question formation strategies in Defaka (Bennett 2009:10)*

    a. Boma *ndia*   ngi ete?

       Boma how.many axe have

       'How many axes does Boma have?'

    b. [*Ndia*   ngi] ndo Boma ete-ke?

       how.many axe NDO Boma have-KE

       'How many axes does Boma have?'

(37) a. Amanya *ndeka* lee   iya?

       Amaya which place go

       'Where did Amaya go?'

    b. [*Ndeka* lee] ndo Amanya iya-ke?

       which place NDO Amaya go-KE

       'Where did Amaya go?'

(38) a. Boma *taa*   koko ese?

       Boma what all   see

       'What did Boma see all of?'

    b. [*Taa* koko] ndo Boma ese-ke?

       what all   NDO Boma see-KE

       'What did Boma see all of?'

Likewise in Asante Twi (Kwa language of Ghana), we find two ways of forming *wh*-questions: a movement strategy, marked with *na*, and an in-situ strategy (Kobele and Torrence 2006).[18]

(39) *Two ways of forming questions in Asante Twi*

    a. Kofi bɔɔ   *hena*?

       Kofi hit.PST who

       'Who did Kofi hit?'

    b. *Hena* na Kofi bɔɔ   (no)?

       who   NA Kofi hit.PST 3SG

       'Who is it that Kofi hit?'

Here again we find restrictions on subject questions: such questions are not able to use the in-situ strategy and must use movement instead.[19]

(40) *Subject question must use the movement strategy*

    a. * *Hena* bɔɔ   Ama?

       who hit.PST Ama

       'Who hit Ama?'

    b. *Hena* na o-bɔɔ   Ama?

       who NA 3SG-hit.PST Ama

       'Who is it that hit Ama?'

In all cases, the restrictions on *wh*-in-situ do not seem to stem from the semantics; rather, they should be attributed to restrictions on the syntax of the question. These questions can be straightforwardly captured by the framework put forth here: we assume that questions involving *wh*-fronting receive derivations like the one in (12) in section 3.3, while questions involving *wh*-in-situ receive derivations like those in (27)/(31) in this chapter. As a result, we make predictions concerning the distribution of intervention effects: they should be observed in questions that use the in-situ strategy, but not in questions that use a movement strategy. These predictions are confirmed for French and for Asante Twi in the works cited above. See the discussion in part II of the book.

4.4.2 Partial *Wh*-Fronting

Finally, I briefly discuss languages that allow not only *wh*-in-situ and *wh*-fronting, but also a third, related strategy of question formation: *partial wh*-fronting. One such language is Malay (Austronesian), as discussed by Cole and Hermon (1998): questions can be formed by leaving a *wh*-phrase fully in situ, by moving it to its scope position, or by moving it to the edge of an embedded CP.

(41) Wh-*fronting in Malay (Cole and Hermon 1998:224)*

    a. *Siapa$_i$* (yang) [Bill harap [yang t_i akan membeli baju   untuknya]]?

       who   that   Bill hope that   will buy   clothes for. him

       'Who does Bill hope will buy clothes for him?'

    b. *Kenapa$_i$* [awak fikir [dia pergi t_i]]

       why   you   think he leave

       'Why do you think he left?'

(42) Wh-*in-situ in Malay (Cole and Hermon 1998:224)*[20]

    a. Ali memberitahu kamu tadi   [Fatimah baca *apa*]?

       Ali informed   you   just now Fatima   read what

       'What did Ali tell you Fatimah was reading?'

b. Bill harap [guru   itu akan mendenda *siapa*]?
    Bill hope teacher that will punish   who
    'Who does Bill hope that the teacher will punish?'

(43) *Partially moved* wh-*phrase in Malay (Cole and Hermon 1998:225)*
   a. Ali memberitahu kamu tadi   [CP *apai*$_i$ (yang) [IP Fatimah
      Ali told   you just.now   what that   Fatimah
      baca t_i]]?
      read
      'Ali told you just now, what was Fatimah reading?'
   b. Kamu percaya [CP ke *mana* (yang) [IP Mary pergi t_i]]?
      you believe   to where that   Mary go
      'Where do you believe (that) Mary went?'

Cole and Hermon (1998) report that the *wh*-in-situ strategy is immune from island effects, but both the partial movement strategy and the full movement strategy exhibit these effects—suggesting that both partial and full *wh*-movement are established through a movement relation. A similar data pattern has been described for Kîîtharaka (Abels 2012), while Zentz (2016) shows that in Shona (Bantu), partial *wh*-movement is not island-sensitive, suggesting that it is established using an in-situ mode of composition instead.

4.5 Pied-Piping

In addition to variation in the syntax of interrogative constructions, a related point of variation in *wh*-fronting languages concerns the *size* of the moved constituent—that is, to the availability of pied-piping in the language (Ross 1967).

In this section, I briefly review some data and a leading theory that accounts for the data, Cable's (2007; 2010) Q-particle theory. In short, cable's idea that the driving force behind movement stems from probing and movement not of the *wh*-element itself, but of another interrogative element that syntactically marks the scope of movement—a Q-particle. I will illustrate how the proposal presented in this book can be combined with Cable's theory; that is, I propose to adopt Cable's syntax for Q-particles, but propose a modified, simpler semantics that is compatible with the ALTSHIFT framework.

4.5.1 The Syntax of Q-Particles

Q-particles have been argued to be central to the analysis of *wh*-in-situ languages as well as *wh*-fronting languages (e.g., (Cable 2007, 2010; Hagstrom 1998; Kishimoto 2005; Miyagawa 2001). Here, I concentrate on Cable's

(2007;2010) theory of Q-particles, where movement of *wh*-elements and pied-piping are recast as instances of Q-movement.

Under Q-theory, *wh*-in-situ languages and *wh*-fronting languages share a very similar structure: in all languages, *wh*-words are rendered interpretable through the help of a Q-particle, which must move to the interrogative complementizer, C, in time for interpretation. The Q-particle can attach directly to a *wh*-word or to a larger structure that contains a *wh*-word—a *wh-phrase*.

The presence of Q-particles driving interrogative movement and pied-piping is apparent in Tlingit (Na-Dene; Alaska, British Columbia, Yukon), the object of Cable's study. In (44), we have several examples of questions in Tlingit. Questions may involve the fronting of a bare *wh*-word, (44a), or pied-piping of additional material of different sizes, (44b–d). Each fronted phrase contains a *sá* particle at its right edge. Cable argues that this is a Q-particle, which projects a further phrasal layer, a QP. In a multiple question, each *wh*-phrase occurs with its own Q-particle, (44e). The QPs in the question are all attracted to the CP layer by the interrogative probe, which probes for Q-features.

(44) Wh-*movement and pied-piping in Tlingit (Cable 2010:3, 8, 31, 32, 40)*

    a. [*Daa* **sá**] i   éesh al'óon?
       what **Q**   your father he.hunts.it
       'What is your father hunting?'

    b. [*Daakw* keitl **sá**] asháa?
       which   dog **Q** it.barks
       'Which dog is barking?'

    c. [*Goodéi* **sá**] kkwagóot?
       where.to **Q** I.will.go
       'Where will I go to?'

    d. [*Goodéi* wugootx **sá**] has oowajée i   shagóonich?
       where.to he.went **Q** they.think   your parents.ERG
       'Where do your parents think that he went?'

    e. [*Aadóo* **sá**]$_1$ [*daa* **sá**]$_2$ [$_{TP}$ t_1 yéi oowajée [t_2 du   jee
       who   **Q**   what **Q**   they.think   their hand.at
       yéi teeyí]]?
       it.is.there
       'Who thinks they have what?'

The possible adjunction sites of the Q-particle are subject to crosslinguistic variation. As (44) illustrates, in Tlingit it is possible to front large constituents, including verbal and clausal material. We find similar effects in other languages such as Basque and Imbabura Quechua, where pied-piping can be as large as CP-size, as long as the *wh*-word inside the pied-piping constituent is fronted to the edge of the moved constituent through secondary *wh*-fronting.

(45) *Pied-piping of subordinate CPs in Basque and Imbabura Quechua (Heck 2008:106–107)*

a.Basque

    i.   [$_{CP}$ *Nor*$_1$ [$_{IP}$ joango dela t$_1$]]$_2$ esan du   Jonek t$_2$?

        who   go   AUX   said AUX John

       'Who did John say will go?'

    ii. * [$_{CP}$ [$_{IP}$ Joango dela *nor*]]$_2$ esan du   Jonek t$_2$?

        go   AUX who   said AUX John

b.Imbabura Quechua

    i.   [$_{CP}$ *Imata*$_1$ [$_{IP}$ wawa t$_1$ mikuchun]]$_2$ -taj Maria t$_2$ munan?

        what   child   eat   Q   Maria   want

       'What does Maria want the child to eat?'

    ii. * [$_{CP}$ [$_{IP}$ Wawa *imata* mikuchun]]$_2$ -taj Maria t$_2$ munan?

        child what eat   Q   Maria   want

This general effect is described by the Edge Generalization:[21]

(46) *Edge Generalization (Heck 2008:88)*

If a *wh*-phrase α pied-pipes a constituent β, then α has to be at the edge of β.

We find effects of this Edge Generalization in English as well. Consider, for example, the difference between (47a) and (47b). Both examples contain a complex *wh*-phrase, but the former is much better than the latter. Similarly, we find obligatory secondary fronting in English how-many questions, (48).

(47) *The Edge Generalization in English*

    a.   *Whose* mother's friend did you see?

    b. * A friend of *whose* mother did you see?

(48) *Secondary fronting in English*

    a.   *How* expensive a car did you buy?

    b. * A *how* expensive car did you buy?

Despite these similarities, the overall availability and distribution of pied-piping in languages like English and German is more constrained than in Tlingit, Basque, or Imbabure Quechua. Cable refers to the former languages as "limited pied-piping" languages. In such languages, the placement of Q is regulated via a locality-sensitive Agree operation between the Q-particle and the *wh*-word.

(49) *Limited pied-piping languages (Cable 2010:147)*

If the Q-particle must Agree with the *wh*-word it c-commands, then a *wh*-word cannot be dominated in the sister of Q by islands or lexical categories. [Lexical categories here include NP, AP, and VP.] Thus limited pied-piping languages are those where Q/*wh*-Agreement must occur.

This explains the limited distribution of pied-piping in English, illustrated in (50)

(50) *Complements of lexical heads cannot pied-pipe (Cable 2010:151)*
    a.   I wonder [[DP *whose* [NP pictures]] John bought].
    b. * I wonder [[NP pictures of *whom*] John bought].
    c. * I wonder [[AP proud of *whom*] John was].
    d. * I wonder [[VP eaten *what*] John has].

Wh-in-situ languages and *wh*-fronting languages differ in the way Q-particles project after they have been merged into the derivation. In *wh*-in-situ languages, Q adjoins to XP and XP projects, (51a). In *wh*-movement languages, on the other hand, Q adjoins to XP and projects a QP layer, (51b).

(51) *Possible QP structures in Cable 2010:146–147 (adapted from (12)–(13))*
    a. *Wh*-in-situ languages   b. *Wh*-fronting languages

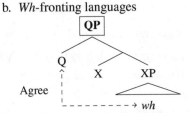

The difference in observed *wh*-movement in *wh*-in-situ languages and *wh*-fronting languages is explained in terms of Q-movement. In *wh*-in-situ languages, Q does not project any further structure after it is merged into the derivation. Consequently, we derive a language in which Q alone moves (overtly or covertly) to C, (52)—a *wh*-in-situ language.

(52) *Q-movement in* wh-*in-situ languages: Q-adjunction (Sinhala, Japanese, …)*

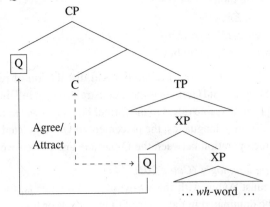

In *wh*-fronting languages, Q projects a QP layer following its merger with XP. Consequently, the whole QP—Q along with its sister—is attracted to C following interrogative probing, (53). The result is movement of a structure containing a *wh*-word and potential additional structure, commonly referred to as pied-piping.

(53) *Q-movement in* wh-*fronting languages: Q-projection (English, German, …)*

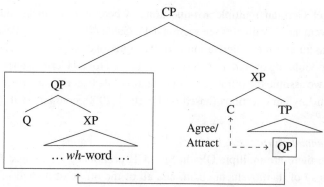

Q-theory provides an explanation for pied-piping that does not rely on feature percolation: the target of interrogative probing and movement is always a QP. QP necessarily contains a *wh*-word and may contain some additional material, leading to pied-piping.

Superiority-obeying questions in English are derived from structures where a QP is projected around each *wh*-word in the question. By the end of the derivation, all QPs move to Spec,CP in a structure-preserving order (obeying 'Attract Closest').[22] Once the QPs are at the CP edge, the question is interpreted using a semantics equivalent to Karttunen (1977) semantics for questions (see below).

In the derivation of Superiority-violating questions, the higher *wh*-word in the question is not merged with a Q-particle. Only one QP is constructed, by merging a Q-particle with the lower *wh*-word. Since interrogative probing targets the Q-feature, not a *wh*-feature, the higher *wh*-phrase is invisible to the probe and remains in situ. The QP containing the lower *wh*-phrase is found by the probe and attracted to Spec,CP. The in-situ *wh* is subsequently interpreted by a special C head (see below), using Rooth-Hamblin alternatives computation. The resulting LFs are sketched in (54a–b).

(54) *Structure of Superiority-obeying and Superiority-violating questions*
 a. Superiority-obeying

  [CP [QP₁ Q [wh₁]] [QP₂ Q [wh₂]] [C [TP ... t_1 ... t_2]]]

 b. Superiority-violating

  [CP [QP₂ Q [wh₂]] [C [TP ... [wh₁] ... t_2]]]

To model German multiple *wh*-questions, where it is assumed that no covert movement is available (see section 4.1), Cable (2010) follows Pesetsky (2000) in assuming that a derivation parallel to the one proposed for English Superiority-violating questions is the one that is used for all German questions.

Finally, we assume the following pronunciation rule to derive the word order observed in English questions (based on Pesetsky 2000; compare with (8) in chapter 2):

(55) *Pronunciation rule (English)*
 When there are multiple QPs in Spec,CP, pronounce the highest QP at the head of its movement chain, and all of the others at the tail of their respective chains.

This syntax for the Q-particle developed in Cable's work is paired with the semantics that I briefly describe next. For Cable, the Q-particle Q_i denotes a choice function, (56a).

(56) *The semantics of Q (Cable 2010:67)*
 a. $[\![Q_i]\!] = g(i) \in D_{cf}$
 b. $[\![Q_i\ XP]\!] = [\![Q_i]\!]\left([\![XP]\!]^f\right)$

Simplex *wh*-questions that contain just one QP are interpreted using the interrogative complementizer in (57). C contributes exactly one existential quantifier to the meaning of the question, which binds the choice function variable introduced by Q.

(57) *The semantics of simplex C (Cable 2010:78)*
 $[\![C\ XP]\!]^g = \lambda p\ [\exists f\ .\ p = [\![XP]\!]^{g(i/f)}]$

To interpret Superiority-obeying questions with two *wh*-phrases, Cable (2010) introduces an additional complementizer, C_2, which can yield a multiple question meaning and at the same time bind both of the Q-particles in the *wh*-question.[23] It does this by binding the choice function variables introduced by the two Q-particles. Under the assumption that there are at least as many choice functions over a certain set as there are elements in that set, the resulting meaning of the question is equivalent to the standard interrogative semantics assigned to *wh*-questions in a Hamblin/Karttunen framework.

(58) C_2 *in the semantics of superiority-obeying questions (Cable 2010:129)*
$$[\![C_{2ij} \text{ XP}]\!]^g = \lambda p \, [\exists f \, . \, \exists h \, . \, p = [\![\text{XP}]\!]^{g(i/f)(j/h)}]$$

To derive a suitable question-meaning for a Superiority-violating question with a *wh*-word in-situ—and all German questions—Cable assumes a C+ head that can give a *wh*-in situ an appropriate interrogative meaning without attracting it to its specifier. This is an operator that will yield a multiple *wh*-question meaning but can only bind one Q-particle; the other *wh*-word in the question must not be merged with a Q-particle and hence must be left in situ. The *wh*-in-situ is interpreted using the mechanism of Rooth-Hamblin alternatives.

(59) *C+ in the semantics of superiority-violating questions (Cable 2010:129)*
$$[\![C+_i \text{ XP}]\!]^g = \lambda p \, [\exists f \, . \, \exists h \, . \, p = h \, (\, [\![\text{XP}]\!]^{F \, g(i/f)})]$$

4.5.2 Q-particles and the semantics of ALTSHIFT

Q-theory can be straightforwardly combined with the semantic framework developed here in chapter 3. In particular, it is possible to adopt Q-theory's syntax wholesale, but we require a different semantics for Q and C than proposed by Cable, to make the resulting structure interpretable by ALTSHIFT. This result can easily be achieved by assuming that—like the interrogative complementizer—the Q-particle itself does not contribute meaningfully to the semantics of interrogative constructions. Instead—like the interrogative complementizer—Q is semantically inert.

(60) *The semantics of Cable's Q-particle*
$$[\![Q]\!] = \lambda P_\tau \, . \, P$$

This means that the semantic machinery developed in chapter 3 can apply to syntactic structures containing Q-particles just as it would to structures not containing these particles. In other words, Q-particles regulate interrogative movement and pied-piping, but they should not be responsible for interpreting question meanings. As a result, the derivations sketched in chapters 3–4 for interrogative constructions crosslinguistically do not require any substantive alterations. We can add Q-particles to regulate movement and pied-piping where needed, but otherwise not alter the resulting semantic derivations.

This proposal has two main advantages. First, it allows for the precise modeling of pied-piping within the framework I have developed here, where single-pair and pair-list readings are interpreted on a principled basis from minimally differing LFs.[24]

Second this proposal allows for the streamlining of the complementizer system, compared with Cable's (2010) original system. As shown above, Cable's system must assume a different C head with a different semantic content for each type of interrogative syntax found crosslinguistically: a C head that binds no QPs and delivers a simplex question interpretation; one that binds one QP and delivers the same interpretation; one that binds one QP, interprets one *wh* in-situ, and delivers a single-pair interpretation; one that binds two QPs and returns the same semantic interpretation; one that binds no QPs but has two in-situ *wh*-phrases and again returns the same interpretation; and likewise for questions with three *wh*-phrases, containing between zero and three QPs in them, and so on—and multiplied over again to also yield the pair-list readings of all these questions. The system proliferates quickly and must represent the syntactic structure of the question as part of its semantics. This is undesirable, and is replaced in my proposal by the principled iteration of ALTSHIFT operators with a single (recursive) meaning and with a single meaning for each of C and Q.

A detailed integration of the Q-particle proposal into the theory developed here is provided in kotek 2014a. As I showed above, Q-particles can be straightforwardly added to the interrogative system proposed in chapter 3 without any changes to the system, as long as the semantics for Q-particles that proposed in (60) is used. In what follows, I abstract away from these details, as they are incidental to the issues discussed there.

II   *WH*-INTERVENTION EFFECTS

5 Intervention Effects: The State of the Art

Part II of this book is concerned with the phenomenon of "focus" intervention effects (also sometimes called Beck effects).[1] I discuss the current understanding of intervention in the literature and then introduce new observations concerning intervention effects. These will lead to a new characterization of these effects, lending further support to the core syntactic and semantic assumptions put forth in part I.

Over the course of this investigation, I introduce a new view of covert movement in English, where it is not a long-distance successive-cyclic operation, but instead is better modeled as covert scrambling, parallel to its overt instantiation in German. This last argument will then be further supported in part III with new experimental evidence.

5.1 Some Basic Data

The study of intervention effects has received growing attention in the syntax/semantics literature over the past several decades. Going back to Hoji 1985, it has been observed that the syntax of Japanese questions is constrained in an interesting way: a certain class of "interveners," which include at least certain negative quantifiers, universals, and focus-sensitive operators, cannot precede an in-situ wh-phrase. The canonical word order of the question in (1a) is unavailable with a negative polarity item (NPI) subject, and the structure is rescued by scrambling the wh-phrase above the intervener as in (1b).

(1) *Japanese: Intervention effects are avoided by scrambling (Tomioka 2007b:1571–1572)*
   a. Hanako / ?***Dare-mo** $\boxed{nani\text{-}o}$ yom-ana-katta-no?
      Hanako anyone what-ACC read-NEG-PST-Q
      'What did Hanako/*no one read?'

b. [*Nani-o*] **dare-mo** ___ yom-ana-katta-no?
what-ACC anyone   read-NEG-PST-Q
'What did no one read?'

Parallel data for Tibetan are shown in (2). Similar data patterns have also been reported in other *wh*-in-situ languages, including Korean, Mandarin Chinese, Hindi/Urdu, Turkish, and Malayalam (e.g., Beck 2006; Hoji 1985; Kim 2002a,b; Li and Law 2014a,b, 2016; Tomioka 2007a,b; Yang 2008).[2]

(2) *Tibetan: Intervention effects are avoided by scrambling (Erlewine and Kotek 2016:162)*

  a. Tenzen-khi [*thep-kanghi*] lok-song(-pe)?
      Tenzen-ERG book-which   read-AUX-Q
      'Which book did Tenzen read?'

  b. * **Suchiye** [*thep-kanghi*] lok-me?
      anyone book-which   read-NEG

  c. [*Thep-kanghi*] **suchiye** ___ lok-me?
      book-which   anyone   read-NEG
      'Which book did no one read?'

In the 1990s and more recently in the last decade or so, intervention effects in *wh*-movement languages, and in particular in English and German, have received increased attention. An effect parallel to the one described for Japanese and Tibetan can be observed in German, for *wh*-in-situ in multiple *wh*-questions. Here, the negative quantifier *niemand* 'no one' is the intervener.

(3) *German: Intervention above* wh-*in-situ is avoided by scrambling (Beck 1996a:6)*

  a. *Wer* hat ✓Luise / ??**niemanden** [*wo*] angetroffen?
      who has Luise   no.one   where met
      'Who didn't meet Luise/*anybody where?'

  b. *Wer* hat [*wo*] **niemanden** ___ angetroffen?
      who has where no.one   met
      'Who didn't meet anybody where?'

Beck (2006) reports similar data patterns in Dutch, Passamaquoddy, and Thai. Likewise, some recent literature has shown that languages that use both a movement and an in-situ strategy for question formation exhibit a sensitivity to intervention effects only with the in-situ strategy, not with the movement strategy. For example, in Asante Twi the movement strategy for question formation must be used in questions with negation and with 'only' and 'even' phrases (cf. section 4.4.1).

(4) *Asante Twi: Negative questions require movement (Kobele and Torrence 2006:166)*

    a. * Kofi a-**m**-bɔ   ‖ *hena* ‖?

        Kofi PST-NEG-hit who

        'Who didn't Kofi hit?'   (neg > *wh*)

    b. ‖ *Hena* ‖ na Kofi a-**m**-bɔ   (no)?

        who   NA Kofi PST-NEG-hit   3SG

        'Who is it that Kofi didn't hit?'   (*wh* > neg)

        (≈ 'Which person is such that Kofi did not hit that person?')

(5) *Asante Twi: 'Only' and 'even' require movement (Kobele and Torrence 2006:167, 168)*

    a. * Kofi **nko-ara**   / **mpo** bɔɔ   ‖ *hena* ‖?

        Kofi only-EMPH / even hit.PST who

        'Who did only/even Kofi hit?'

    b. ‖ *Hena* ‖ na Kofi **nko-ara**   / **mpo** bɔɔ   (no)?

        who   NA Kofi only-EMPH / even hit.PST   3SG

        'Who is it that only/even Kofi hit?'

Similar data patterns have been reported in French, another language with optional *wh*-in-situ. Here I show data with a universal quantifier. See Bošković 2000, Chang 1997, Mathieu 1999, and Pesetsky 2000 for data with additional interveners, including sentential negation, 'always', 'each', and 'no one'.

(6) *French: Questions with quantifiers require movement (Chang 1997: 17, 65)*

    a. * **Tous** les étudiants ont rencontré ‖ *qui* ‖?

        all   the students have met   who

    b. ‖ *Qui* ‖ est-ce que **tous** les étudiants ont rencontré ___ ?

        who is-it that all   the students have met

        'Who did all the students meet?'

In English, matters appear to be more complex. Pesetsky (2000), providing the most comprehensive study of intervention effects in English, reports a correlation between superiority and intervention effects in multiple questions with D-linked *wh*-phrases, building on earlier observations by É. Kiss (1986) for English and Rizzi (1990) for German. Motivating examples are given in (7): (7a–b) show that English generally allows both Superiority-obeying questions and Superiority-violating questions with D-linked *wh*-phrases. Examples (7c–d) show that when certain interveners—here, negation—occur above the (phonologically) in-situ *wh*-phrase, only the Superiority-obeying structure is grammatical.

(7) *English: Intervention correlates with superiority*

    a.   Superiority-obeying, no intervener
           Which student ___ read *which* book?

    b.   Superiority-violating, no intervener
           Which book did *which* student read ___?

    c.   Superiority-obeying, intervener
           Which student did**n't** ___ read *which* book?

    d. *PL Superiority-violating, intervener
           Which book did**n't** *which* student read ___?

Pesetsky reports that at least in some cases of intervention effects in multiple *wh*-questions, many speakers judge that the question is ungrammatical while others report that its single-pair reading is maintained but its pair-list reading is lost. See Butler 2001, Kotek 2014a, and Pesetsky 2000 for a discussion of the judgments, and Beck 1996a for a similar observation in German.[3] I return to this point in section 5.4.

Note the importance of using singular *which*-phrases, to ensure that we are dealing with a pair-list reading. If plural *which*-phrases are used (e.g., *Which students read which books?*), it is possible to give a single-pair answer where each member of the pair is a plurality. For example, the question *Which students read which books?* could receive the answer *Jane, Mary, and Sue read* War and Peace, Moby-Dick, *and* Oliver Twist, *(respectively)*—that is, a single pair with multiple exponents.

Other operators that give rise to intervention effects in English include *only*, *very few*, *never*, and *no one*, as shown in (8)–(11). These examples all follow the same pattern: only the Superiority-violating question is affected by the presence of the intervener, losing at least its pair-list reading.[4]

(8) *Intervention effect with* only *only affects Superiority-violating questions (Pesetsky 2000:80)*

    a.   *Which* girl did **only** Mary introduce ___ to *which* boy?

    b. *PL *Which* boy did **only** Mary introduce *which* girl to ___?

(9) *Intervention effect with* very few *only affects Superiority-violating questions (Pesetsky 2000:80)*

    a.   *Which* picture did **very few** children want to show ___ to *which* teacher?

b. *[PL] *Which* teacher did **very few** children want to show *which* picture to ___?

(10) *Intervention effect with* never *only affects Superiority-violating questions (Pesetsky 2000:80)*

a.   *Which* student did he **never** claim ___ would talk about *which* topic?

b. *[PL] *Which* topic did he **never** claim *which* student would talk about ___?

(11) *Intervention effect with* no one *only affects Superiority-violating questions (Pesetsky 2000:80)*

a.   *Which* book did **no one** give to *which* student?

b. *[PL] *Which* student did **no one** give *which* book to ___?

How to characterize the set of interveners has been a topic of debate. Beck (2006) and Beck and Kim (2006) identify a number of focus-sensitive operators—including *only, also, even,* sentential negation, negative quantifiers such as *no one, never,* and *few,* and their counterparts in other languages—as a crosslinguistically stable set of interveners.[5] In addition, universal quantifiers such as *every, all,* and *each* and quantificational adverbs such as *often* and *always* (and their counterparts) act as interveners. Mayr (2010, 2014) proposes describing the set of interveners as nonadditive quantifiers.

Several competing theories have been proposed to explain intervention effects (cf. Beck 1996a, 2006; Beck and Kim 1997; Cable 2010; Kim 2002a,b; Kotek 2017b; Li and Law 2014a,b, 2016; Mayr 2014; Pesetsky 2000; Tomioka 2007a,b; see also Hagstrom 1998; Hoji 1985; Rizzi 1990; Soh 2005). These theories attribute intervention to a variety of sources, most prominently related to quantification, focus, topic-hood, and prosody. Other authors attribute intervention effects to a formal structural problem, such as a type mismatch or other semantic undefinedness.

Authors also differ in whether they offer a unified theory of these effects across languages, or propose an analysis that is language-specific. Although many of the effects in *wh*-in-situ languages and *wh*-movement languages are quite similar, some differences also exist. For example, theories that are prosody-based and apply to *wh*-in-situ languages such as Branan's (2017b) and Tomioka's (2007b) are not easily extended to the data found in *wh*-movement languages. See also Yang 2011 on whether a unification of all "intervention" phenomena is desirable.

In what follows, I provide a more detailed characterization of intervention effects based on Beck's (2006) influential theory, as a way of formalizing the observed effects. This theory crucially relies on the distinction between movement and focus alternatives as two modes of composition of (phonologically) in-situ *wh*-phrases. The broader point, going beyond the details of this theory, is this: *wh*-in-situ must be interpretable by at least two mechanisms—one sensitive to intervention effects (used, e.g., in German questions and English Superiority-violating questions) and one immune from intervention effects (used, e.g., in English Superiority-obeying questions). Beck's (2006) theory provides an entry point by contrasting movement with focus alternatives.

Researchers who opt to use choice functions or unselective binding instead of focus alternatives as their in-situ mode of composition will have to develop an alternative theory of intervention.[6] As, to my knowledge, no such theory currently exists, I leave this for future work and adopt instead the existing theory based on focus alternatives. The theory in part I was developed to be consistent with Beck's assumptions, as the reader can verify below. An additional, independent main advantage of this choice—the focus of part I—is the ability to model single-pair and pair-list readings of questions compositionally, on the basis of principled and minimally different LFs.

5.2 Intervention: An Informal Description

As we have seen, Pesetsky (2000) proposes that Superiority-obeying questions and Superiority-violating questions are derived from different structures. Of particular importance is the location of the (phonologically) in-situ *wh*-phrase: it covertly moves to C at LF in an English Superiority-obeying question, but remains in its base-generated position in a Superiority-violating question. The resulting structures for English are schematized in (12a–b). In German, all (phonologically) in-situ *wh*-phrases remain in situ at LF, yielding the schema in (12b) for all German multiple *wh*-questions.

(12) *LFs of Superiority-obeying and Superiority-violating questions*

    a. $[_{CP}\ wh_1\ wh_2\ [C\ [_{TP} \ldots t_1 \ldots t_2]]]$ (Superiority-obeying)

    b. $[_{CP}\ wh_2\ [C\ [_{TP} \ldots wh_1 \ldots t_2]]]$ (Superiority-violating)

Beck (2006) proposes that when the (phonologically) in-situ *wh*-phrase does not undergo covert movement (*wh*$_1$ in (12b)), it is interpreted via Rooth-Hamblin alternatives computation.

(13) *Two ways to interpret in-situ* wh-*phrases*
    a. Covert movement   b. Rooth-Hamblin alternatives

Beck then argues that the Rooth-Hamblin alternatives computation strategy of interpreting wh-in-situ is subject to intervention effects.

(14) *Description of an intervention effect.*
When a focus-sensitive operator occurs between an LF-in-situ wh-phrase and its associated complementizer, the operator disrupts the projection of alternatives from the wh. As a result, C cannot operate over the wh-containing-phrase, and the derivation crashes.

This logic stems from the fact that Rooth-Hamblin alternatives computation is *unselective*; that is, the semantic contribution of a constituent having nontrivial alternatives in its alternative interpretation is not visible only to the focus-sensitive operator that should interpret it. Instead, the first focus-sensitive operator c-commanding an alternative-generating element will interpret the alternatives projected by this element. In other words, one focus-sensitive operator can *intervene* and block alternatives from reaching a higher focus-sensitive operator that is meant to operate over them. This is schematized in (15), which Beck calls the *General Minimality Effect*.

(15) *The focus intervention schema (Beck 2006:17)*
$$*Op_1 \ \ldots Op_2 \ \ldots \mathrm{XP}_F$$

One instantiation of this illicit configuration—which affects the interpretation of multiple wh-questions—is schematized in (16b). The problem here is one of *Minimality*: the alternatives projected from the wh-word must be operated on by ALTSHIFT, in the C domain. However, focus-sensitive operators also interpret alternatives in their scope (Rooth 1985, 1992). When a focus-sensitive operator (represented as **intervener**) occurs between the in-situ wh-word and C, the alternatives projected by the wh-word will be interpreted by the intervener instead of by ALTSHIFT, disrupting the question interpretation.[7] The covert movement strategy of interpreting wh-phrases, on the other hand, is immune from intervention effects: intervention only affects *wh*-phrases that project focus alternatives, not traces of *wh*-movement, (16a).

(16) *Only the Rooth-Hamblin alternatives method is subject to intervention*
      a. Covert movement   b. Rooth-Hamblin alternatives

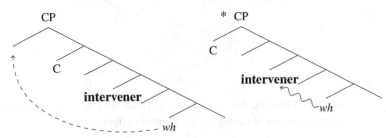

Beck's (2006) schema for intervention effects is summarized in (17). Given this schema, we expect to find intervention effects in Superiority-violating English questions when an intervener is introduced between the in-situ *wh*-word and C. We expect not to find intervention effects in Superiority-obeying English questions, since all *wh*-phrases in such questions move to C by LF. These structures are illustrated in (18a–b). We additionally expect to find intervention effects in all German questions, which have LFs as shown in (18b). These predictions are borne out by the findings of Beck (2006) and Pesetsky (2000).[8]

(17) *Intervention schema with in-situ* wh-*phrases (Beck 2006:5; adapted)*
      LF: *[C ... [**intervener** [... *wh*]]]

(18) *The interaction of superiority and interveners at LF (cf. (12))*
      a. English Superiority-obeying questions: No intervention effects
          [$_{CP}$ *wh*$_1$ *wh*$_2$ [C [$_{TP}$ ... **intervener** ... t_1 ... t_2]]]

      b. English Superiority-violating questions, all German questions: Intervention effects
          *[$_{CP}$ *wh*$_2$ [C [$_{TP}$ ... **intervener** ... *wh*$_1$ ... t_2]]]

5.3 Beck's (2006) Theory of Intervention Effects

In this section, I present Beck's (2006) formal theory of intervention effects. I take this proposal to be the most influential in the current literature on intervention, although it has also been criticized by various authors. In my own recent work, I have proposed an alternative theory of intervention, also relying on the principle that instances of *wh*-in-situ interpreted through focus alternatives are subject to intervention while instances interpreted through covert movement are immune from such effects (Kotek 2017b). Although the reasons for intervention are different, the basic ideas underlying the syntactic and semantic assumptions made here are similar to those made by Beck; therefore, I opt to present Beck's theory as it is more familiar.

An informal description of an intervention effect was given above: a linguistic structure is ungrammatical if a focus-sensitive operator (an **intervener**) occurs between *wh*-in-situ and the interrogative complementizer at LF.

(19) *Intervention schema with in-situ* wh-*phrases (Beck 2006:5; adapted)*
     LF: *[C … [**intervener** [… *wh*]

Beck (2006:sec. 3.2) proposes a formal semantic mechanism to predict this observed behavior. The proposal borrows from Kratzer (1991), Rooth (1992), and Wold (1996). Within this mechanism, each logical form α has an ordinary semantic value $[\![\alpha]\!]^g$ and a focus-semantic value $[\![\alpha]\!]^{g,h}$. The usual assignment function is g, and h is used for interpretation of "distinguished variables." In the syntactic structure for (20a), the squiggle operator $\sim$ is added, and *ALT* represents a set of alternatives provided by the context.[9]

(20) *A simple sentence with focus*
     a. **Only** Mary left.
     b. [[only *ALT*] [$\sim$*ALT* [Mary$_{F1}$ left]]]

A two-place semantics for *only* is given in (21). Here, *only* takes two arguments: the first is the set of alternatives *ALT*, and the second is the prejacent (i.e., the remainder of the sentence, including the $\sim$ operator).[10]

(21) *A two-place semantics for* only
     $[\![only]\!](\alpha)(\beta)(w) = 1$ iff for all p such that $p(w) = 1$ and $p \in \alpha, p = \beta$

The alternatives in *ALT* are computed from the focus-semantic value of the prejacent by replacing the F-marked constituent with other elements provided by the context. For (20a), the alternatives might contain propositions such as {*Mary* left, *Sue* left, *Bill* left, … }. The sentence is then true if the only true alternative is the one represented by the ordinary semantic value of the prejacent—that is, if it is true that Mary left and no one else left.

In (22), Beck defines the way that *ALT* comes to have the alternatives it does: the ordinary value of [$\sim$*ALT* Y] is undefined unless *ALT* only contains propositions that are possible alternatives to the prejacent. The focus-semantic value of the whole is reset to its ordinary value.

(22) *The meaning of a focused sentence (Beck 2006:15, (24); adapted)*
a. $[\![{\sim}ALT\ Y]\!]^g =$
$$\begin{cases} [\![Y]\!]^g \text{ if } g(ALT) \subseteq \{ [\![Y]\!]^{g,h'} : h' \in H \text{ and } h' \text{ is total} \} \\ \text{undefined otherwise} \end{cases}$$
b. $[\![{\sim}ALT\ Y]\!]^{g,h} = [\![{\sim}ALT\ Y]\!]^g$

Each focused constituent carries an index. The focus-semantic value of that constituent is set to be whatever the distinguished variable assignment function h assigns for that index. Otherwise, it is set to be the same as the ordinary semantics of the unfocused constituent, (23).

(23) *The semantics of a focused constituent*
$$[\![XP_{F1}]\!]^{g,h} = \begin{cases} h(1) \text{ if } 1 \in \text{Dom}(h) \\ [\![XP_{F1}]\!]^g \text{ otherwise} \end{cases}$$

The derivation of *Only Mary left*, (20a), is given in (24).

(24) *The derivation of (20a)*
a. $[\![\text{Mary}_{F1}\ \text{left}]\!]^g = \lambda w\ .\ \text{Mary left in } w$
b. $[\![\text{Mary}_{F1}\ \text{left}]\!]^{g,h} = \lambda w\ .\ h(1) \text{ left in } w$
c. $[\![{\sim}ALT\ [\text{Mary}_{F1}\ \text{left}]]\!]^g =$
$$\begin{cases} \lambda w\ .\ \text{Mary left in } w \\ \quad \text{if } g(ALT) \subseteq \{ \lambda w\ .\ h'(1) \text{ left in } w : h' \in H \text{ and } h' \text{ is total} \} \\ \text{undefined otherwise} \end{cases}$$
d. $[\![[\text{only } ALT]\ [{\sim}ALT\ [\text{Mary}_{F1}\ \text{left}]]]\!]^g =$
$$\begin{cases} [\![\text{only}]\!]\,(g(ALT))(\lambda w\ .\ \text{Mary left in } w) \\ \quad \text{if } g(ALT) \subseteq \{ \lambda w\ .\ h'(1) \text{ left in } w : h' \in H \text{ and } h' \text{ is total} \} \\ \text{undefined otherwise} \end{cases}$$
$$= \begin{cases} (1 \text{ iff for all } p \text{ such that } p(w) = 1 \text{ and } p \in ALT, p = \text{Mary left in } w) \\ \quad \text{if } g(ALT) \subseteq \{ \lambda w\ .\ h'(1) \text{ left in } w : h' \in H \text{ and } h' \text{ is total} \} \\ \text{undefined otherwise} \end{cases}$$
$$= \begin{cases} (1 \text{ iff for all } p \text{ such that } p(w) = 1 \text{ and } p \in ALT, p = \text{Mary left in } w) \\ \quad \text{if } g(ALT) \subseteq \{ \lambda w\ .\ x \text{ left in } w : x \in D \} \\ \text{undefined otherwise} \end{cases}$$

Next, we can turn to the derivation of a question. Beck (2006) assumes that *wh*-phrases have a focus-semantic value, but no ordinary semantic value (see (7) in section 3.2).

(25) *The semantics of* who
   Ordinary value: $[\![who_1]\!]^g$ = undefined

   Alternative value: $[\![who_1]\!]^{g,h} = \begin{cases} h(1) \text{ if } 1 \in \text{Dom}(h) \\ \text{undefined otherwise} \end{cases}$

Beck also assumes the following interpretability principle ((10) in chapter 3, repeated here).

(26) *Principle of Interpretability (Beck 2006:16; adapted)*
   An LF must have an ordinary semantic value.

Since a *wh*-phrase has a focus-semantic value but no ordinary value, a sentence cannot contain a *wh*-phrase unless it also contains an interrogative operator, which discards the (undefined) ordinary semantic value generated by the *wh*-word and uses just the focus-semantic value. (Note that in the terminology of my proposal from chapter 3, Q would be replaced with ALTSHIFT.)

(27) *The question operator and its meaning*
   a. $[\![Q_i \ Y]\!]^{g,h} = [\![Q_i \ Y]\!]^g$
   b. $[\![Q_i \ Y]\!]^g = \lambda p \ . \ \exists x \ [p = [\![Y]\!]^{g,h[x/i]}]$

Intervention effects occur if a focus-sensitive operator—associated with a $\sim$ operator—is encountered before the question operator, as in the LF in (28).[11]

(28) *LF of a question with an intervention effect*
   a. Only Mary$_{F1}$ saw *who*?
   b. [$_{CP}$ Q$_i$ [$_{IP3}$ [only *ALT*] [$_{IP2}$ $\sim$*ALT* [$_{IP1}$ Mary$_j$ saw *who$_i$*]]]]

In this structure, the $\sim$ operator is the first operator c-commanding the *wh*-phrase, and therefore it will operate on the focus instead of the question operator. The $\sim$ operator refers to the ordinary semantic value of its sister, in addition to the focus-semantic value. As a result, the ordinary semantic value at the IP$_2$ level will be undefined, because it contains a *wh*-phrase that, by definition, does not have an ordinary semantic value. At this point, the focus-semantic value of IP$_2$ is set to its ordinary semantic value, which again is undefined. Once this step takes place, there is no way for the derivation to recover. Even if a question operator is introduced later (e.g., above IP$_3$ in (28b)), discarding the undefined ordinary semantic value that has been inherited by IP$_3$ will not fix the problem, because the focus-semantic value that it will operate on is also undefined. The result is an uninterpretable structure, which leads to ungrammaticality, which we in turn diagnose as an intervention effect.

In more general terms, this system dictates that the first focus-sensitive operator c-commanding a *wh*-phrase must be a question operator, ALTSHIFT, in the system proposed here. All other focus-sensitive operators in natural language operate on the ordinary semantic value, as well as on the focus-semantic value of their sister,[12] and as a result will lead to an uninterpretable structure if they apply to a *wh*-phrase, which does not have an ordinary semantic value.

5.4   On the Surviving Single-Pair Reading of "Intervened" Questions

Before I conclude this chapter, an important note on the nature of the intervention effect is in order. As I mentioned in section 5.1, the intervention effects observed by Pesetsky (2000) were diagnosed by the unavailability of a pair-list reading of the question. The single-pair reading, on the other hand, remained available to at least some speakers who were consulted. This state of affairs will also hold for the new data I will present in chapters 6–7. Although this fact has been known for quite a while, it has never received much attention in the literature. However, I believe that it is important to keep this fact in mind when investigating intervention effects.

In what follows, I briefly explore the nature of the surviving single-pair reading of questions with intervention effects. I propose that the surviving single-pair reading in "intervened" questions is *not* a true single-pair reading and also not a functional reading; instead, it is a kind of echo question reading.

As noted above, it has been suggested that at least some speakers perceive a surviving single-pair reading in intervened questions. This has been reported, for example, for questions like (29b). Pesetsky (2000:60) remarks about such examples that "[f]or many speakers, at least as a first reaction, such examples are completely unacceptable. For other speakers (and perhaps for all speakers when the possibility is pointed out to them), the examples are acceptable so long as they receive a 'single-pair' rather than a pair-list reading."

(29) *Intervention effects affect Superiority-violating questions (adapted from Pesetsky 2000:60)*
   a.   *Which* student did**n't** ___ read *which* book?
   b. *[PL] *Which* book did**n't** *which* student read ___?

Pesetsky (2000:112n85) remarks that it was Sigrid Beck (pers. comm.) who first brought this fact to his attention, in the context of German, although Beck (1996a:3n2) does not mention improvement with a single-pair reading. Instead, she marks intervened questions with <u>??</u> and writes, "The '<u>??</u>' means that the data are incomprehensible (uninterpretable) rather than simply ungrammatical. I would accordingly ask native speakers to try and interpret the sentences, not simply judge whether they 'sound bad.'"

Here, it is important to note some characteristics of this surviving single-pair reading. As it is difficult to pinpoint the precise nature of this reading, I begin by describing what it is *not*. First, this reading is not the "true" single-pair reading in the sense observed by Wiltschko (1997), discussed in section 3.8 above. Moreover, it does not appear to be an "accidental" single-pair reading—that is, a situation in which it is possible to have several pairs in the answer set but it just happens to be the case that the answer applies to just one pair.

Instead, I suggest that this surviving reading of the question may be a kind of echo question reading. That is, the single-pair reading that remains available is one that requires strong contextual support, often including a sentence that already contains the illicit intervener, where the speaker simply failed to understand part of the information carried by that sentence. Below is an attempt to illustrate such a context:

(30) *Surviving single-pair reading in intervened question*
Mary: I heard a rumor that Chomsky hasn't ever read Rizzi's *Relativized Minimality*.
Jane: I'm sorry, what's that? *Which* book has**n't** *which* linguist read?

That is, the *wh*-phrases are used here as a kind of definite description, roughly standing in for "the thing you said (that I didn't understand)." If so, this explains why this surviving reading is not sensitive to intervention effects: the *wh*-words, representing definite descriptions, are not interpreted using focus alternatives, as in-situ *wh*-words in questions are.

An alternative is that this reading may be derived through a choice function mechanism, like the one that is independently necessary in order to model functional answers to questions, where a function can be defined to identify the relationship between the members of the pair in the answer (e.g., Chierchia 1993; cf. Dayal 2016; Reinhart 1997, 1998); see (31). If this proposal is on the right track, to preserve the insights into intervention that we have collected so far, it would be necessary that while this mechanism can be used to derive a single-pair reading of the question, it should not be able to derive pair-list readings.[13]

(31) *A functional reading of a question*
Q: *Who* does every boy love?
A: His mother.

Here, I will not attempt to provide a more comprehensive analysis of this reading. My main goal is to describe it well enough that it can be avoided as a potential confound when eliciting judgments with regard to intervention effects. In general, below and in consultation sessions, I do that by presenting examples containing potential intervention configurations in contexts that support the pair-list interpretation of the question, to avoid potential contamination from this surviving reading.

6 Intervention Correlates with Movement Possibilities for *Wh*-in-Situ

In this chapter, I more closely investigate of the distribution of intervention effects in English multiple *wh*-questions. Recall that Pesetsky (2000) observes a correlation between superiority and intervention effects in English questions, as in (1) and (2).[1]

(1) *Intervention effects correlate with superiority (adapted from Pesetsky 2000:60)*
    a.   *Which* student did**n't** ___ read *which* book?
    b. *PL *Which* book did**n't** *which* student read ___?

(2) a.   *Which* book did **no one** give ___ to *which* student?
    b. *PL *Which* student did **no one** give *which* book to ___?

To explain this correlation between superiority and intervention effects, Pesetsky argues that Superiority-obeying and Superiority-violating questions are derived from different LF structures—a proposal I have adopted in this book.

(3) *LFs of Superiority-obeying and Superiority-violating questions*
    a. $[_{CP}$ *wh*$_1$ *wh*$_2$ $[C$ $[_{TP}$ ... t_1 ... $t_2]]]$ (Superiority-obeying)

    b. $[_{CP}$ *wh*$_2$ $[C$ $[_{TP}$ ... *wh*$_1$ ... $t_2]]]$ (Superiority-violating)

We assume that *wh*-in-situ in Superiority-obeying questions is able to covertly move to C at LF, above any interveners in the structure. On the other hand, *wh*-in-situ in Superiority-violating questions remains in situ at LF, hence is subject to intervention effects if an intervener is introduced above the surface position of the *wh*. This explains the data in (1)–(2) and other examples presented in chapter 5. The general intervention schema is given in (4).[2]

(4) *The intervention configuration (Beck 2006:5; adapted)*
    a. LF: * $[_{CP}$ C ... $[$**intervener** $[$ ... *wh* ... $]]]$
    b. LF: $[_{CP}$ C ... $[$*wh* $[$**intervener** $[$ ... *t* ... $]]]]$

Below, I introduce new data to show that the presence of intervention effects in an English question does not correlate with superiority. Instead, intervention correlates with movement possibilities for the (phonologically) in-situ *wh*-phrase and for the intervener at LF.

This will serve to strengthen the motivation for the syntactic assumptions I have made throughout this book: the availability of covert movement of *wh*-in-situ varies according to the superiority status of the question, such that it is generally available in Superiority-obeying questions and absent in Superiority-violating ones. However, this basic state of affairs can be manipulated: we can find means of restricting covert movement in Superiority-obeying questions, or of moving *wh*-in-situ by means of noninterrogative movement in Superiority-violating questions. Moreover, when the intervener is moved out of the way, we again lack otherwise predicted intervention effects in Superiority-violating questions. In other words, it is the particular LF configuration of the question that matters, not its pronounced form.

6.1 Intervention in Superiority-Obeying Questions

Following the proposal sketched above, in-situ *wh*-phrases in Superiority-obeying questions are able to evade intervention through covert movement above the intervener at LF. This leads to a prediction that I will test in this section: if movement is blocked, intervention effects should reemerge.

I introduce three ways of blocking movement, using negative polarity items, focus association, and binding. (A fourth way of restricting movement using syntactic islands is the main focus of chapter 7.) The logic of the argument is as follows: (a) find an element that must take scope at a certain known position at LF; (b) construct a *wh*-phrase containing this element, hence marking the highest possible scope of *wh*-movement; (c) since covert *wh*-movement is now restricted, predict intervention effects to be found if an intervener is introduced above this highest landing site of *wh*-movement.[3]

6.1.1 Restricted Movement and Intervention: NPIs
I begin by using negative polarity items (NPIs) to restrict covert *wh*-movement. As is well-known, NPIs are licensed in nonveridical or downward-entailing environments (Giannakidou 1997; Ladusaw 1980; and much subsequent work).[4] Example (5) illustrates this with negation as the licensor. Notice that the multiple *wh*-question itself is not a sufficient licensor in the absence of negation.

(5) *NPIs are licensed in downward-entailing environments*
    a. Mary *(**didn't**) read <u>any</u> books.
    b. *Which* girl {✓ **didn't** give, *gave} *which* boy <u>any</u> flowers?

If an NPI occurs inside a *wh*-phrase, this *wh*-phrase will not be able to move out of the scope of the NPI's licensor. Here, I use negation; hence, the *wh*-phrase must remain below negation at LF. Recall, moreover, that negation acts as an intervener in English *wh*-questions (see (1)). Hence, this configuration should display an intervention effect: the (phonologically) in-situ *wh*-phrase may be able to undergo covert movement, but the target position of movement is necessarily below the intervener, leading to the illicit intervention configuration in (4a).[5]

Examples (6)–(7) instantiate this configuration. Example (6) provides a baseline to show that an NPI must be licensed by a c-commanding negation. Example (7a) provides a second baseline, a multiple *wh*-question with a (phonologically) in-situ *wh*-phrase that contains a non-NPI, *some*. This question is grammatical despite the presence of sentential negation, because the *wh*-phrase is able to move above the intervener at LF, undoing the intervention configuration. Example (7b) shows that intervention effects reemerge in this Superiority-obeying question when an NPI occurs inside a (phonologically) in-situ *wh*-phrase, because the *wh*-phrase is now unable to move above the intervener, leading to the illicit intervention configuration.

(6) *An NPI is licensed in a question when negation is present*
    Which girl {$\checkmark$ **didn't** read, *read} [a book about any president]?

(7) *An NPI restricts covert movement of* wh-*in-situ, causing intervention*
    a.   *Which* girl **didn't** read [*which* book about a/some president]?
    b. *[PL] *Which* girl **didn't** read [*which* book about any president]?

We thus observe an intervention effect in a Superiority-obeying question, when covert movement of the (phonologically) in-situ *wh*-phrase is restricted to a position necessarily lower than an intervener in the structure.

6.1.2   Restricted Movement and Intervention: Focus Association

The next argument comes from the nature of association-with-focus constructions (e.g., Rooth 1985, 1992). The interpretation of focus-sensitive operators such as *only* depends on the presence of an F-marked constituent within the scope of the operator. F-marked constituents that occur outside the scope of the operator do not contribute to the evaluation of that operator. This is explained by means of the Principle of Lexical Association.

(8) *Principle of Lexical Association (PLA) (Tancredi 1990:30)*[6]
    An operator like *only* must be associated with a lexical constituent in its c-command domain.

Evidence motivating this structural restriction on association with focus is shown in (9). The topicalization example in (9a) is ungrammatical under the intended interpretation, but the corresponding example in (9b) with in-situ focus is grammatical (intended associates of *only* are underlined).

(9) *F-marked constituents may not move out of the scope of* only
    a. * Mary$_F$, John **only** likes ___.
        Intended: 'As for Mary, John only likes her$_F$ (and no one else).'
    b. John **only** likes Mary$_F$.

Given the PLA, if F-marking is placed inside a *wh*-phrase, this *wh*-phrase will not be able to move out of the scope of the associating operator. In (10), the associating operator is *only*. Hence, to satisfy the PLA, the *wh*-phrase must remain within the scope of *only* at LF. However, recall from chapter 5 that *only* acts as an intervener in English questions. Hence, we predict an intervention effect in such a configuration.[7] Example (10a) provides a baseline, Superiority-obeying multiple *wh*-question that is able to have a pair-list answer. Example (10b) shows that intervention effects reemerge when F-marking is introduced inside the (phonologically) in-situ *wh*-phrase in this question, as predicted.

(10) *The PLA restricts covert movement of* wh-*in-situ, causing intervention*
    a. Baseline: I can tell you *which* student read *which* book.
    b. Context: The students in the class were supposed to read one book *and* one article about syntax. However, everyone got confused and read one book *or* one article. I've been reading everyone's squibs. I've finished all the ones about books, so:
        *PL I can tell you *which* student **only** read [*which* book$_F$ (about syntax)].   (based on Erlewine 2014:139)[8]

We thus again observe an intervention effect in a Superiority-obeying question, when covert movement of the (phonologically) in-situ *wh*-phrase is restricted to a position necessarily lower than an intervener in the structure. Moreover, when *only* associates with focus at a distance, in a way that does not block covert *wh*-movement, no intervention is observed.[9]

(11) *No intervention with long-distance association with focus*
    I can **only** tell you *which* student read *which* book$_F$.

Here, the availability of a pair-list reading is expected, as covert movement of the *wh*-phrase at LF will target a position that is still in the scope of *only*, but is above the position at which the interrogative complementizer occurs, thus not interfering with the interpretation of the question. Indeed, in the configuration in (11), the pair-list reading is available.

6.1.3 Restricted Movement and Intervention: Binding

Finally, I use Conditions A and B of binding theory to restrict the possible covert movement of a (phonologically) in-situ *wh*-phrase in a multiple *wh*-question. As in the cases we saw above, when movement is restricted, intervention effects reemerge above the landing site of movement in Superiority-obeying questions.

As a first step, I provide definitions of Conditions A and B and of the binding domain.

(12) *Condition A*
An anaphor must have a binder in its binding domain.

(13) *Condition B*
A pronoun must be free in its binding domain.

(14) *Definition: Binding domain*
The binding domain of a DP α is
a. if α is the subject of a tensed TP, the smallest TP containing α;
b. otherwise, the smallest TP containing α and a DP c-commanding α.

Lebeaux (2009) shows that Condition A applies at LF, whereas Conditions B and C apply at every stage of the derivation (including LF). Hence, we can use these binding conditions to restrict covert *wh*-movement in a multiple *wh*-question. In particular, if a *wh*-phrase contains a bindee, we expect that it cannot take scope above its binder at LF. Consequently, if an intervener is placed above this position, we expect to find an intervention effect.

The examples in (15) provide one relevant test case. Example (15a) provides a baseline for a Superiority-obeying multiple *wh*-question with an intervener, **no boy**. As with other such examples (cf. (1)–(2)), the pair-list reading of the question is available despite the presence of the intervener—that is, we do not observe an intervention effect. Following the explanation given in chapter 5, this is because the (phonologically) in-situ *wh*-phrase in this Superiority-obeying question is able to undergo covert movement to a position above the intervener at LF, avoiding the illicit intervention configuration.

Examples (15b–c) contain an anaphor and a bound pronoun, respectively, occurring inside the (phonologically) in-situ *wh*-phrase in the questions. The binder of this pronoun is the DP *no boy*, which also serves as an intervener. These examples are judged by native speakers as degraded.

(15) *Conditions A and B block covert movement, causing intervention*
  a.   *Which* girl gave **no boy** [*which* picture of Kennedy]?
  b. *PL *Which* girl gave **no boy** [*which* picture of himself]?
  c. *PL *Which* girl gave **no boy** [*which* picture of his best friend]?

The nature of the degraded status of (15b–c) differs across speakers. For some, the pair-list readings of the questions disappear—due to an intervention effect. However, at least some speakers prefer an interpretation of these questions that appeals to a functional reading.[10] For those speakers, examples (15a–b) may not be a useful test case; hence, I provide an additional set of examples below to further illustrate this point.

Examples (16a–b) vary minimally in the phrase that serves as the binder of a reflexive pronoun hosted by the (phonologically) in-situ *wh*-phrase in the question (for convenience, I underline the binder in the examples). In (16a), the binder is *daughter*, and the pair-list reading is available. This is because there are possible landing sites for movement (above *only Obama* but below *which daughter*) that would undo the intervention configuration and at the same time preserve the binding relation. On the other hand, in (16b) the binder is *(only) Obama*, and the pair-list reading is unavailable. This is because there is no landing site for movement that is both above the intervener and below the binder. Hence, an intervention effect is observed.[11]

(16) *No intervention effect if the intervention configuration can be undone*
       Context: Barack Obama has two daughters, Sasha and Malia.
       a.   *Which* <u>daughter</u> showed **only Obama** [*which* picture of herself]?
       b. *[PL] *Which* daughter showed **only <u>Obama</u>** [*which* picture of himself]?

Example (17), which has the same Condition A requirement but lacks an intervener, serves as a control. This example shows that it is possible for *himself* to be licensed by an element in object position, hence that the problem in (16b) relates to the presence of *only*.

(17) *Condition A can be satisfied from object position*
       Which daughter/girl showed <u>Obama/some man</u> *which* picture of himself?

These examples serve to show the importance of the intervention configuration and the LF position of (phonologically) in-situ *wh*-phrases. If movement can undo the intervention configuration, the pair-list reading of the question is available. Only if movement is forced to target a position below the intervener (or is generally unavailable) do we observe an intervention effect.

To summarize, we have seen three different ways of restricting covert *wh*-movement in a Superiority-obeying multiple *wh*-question: using NPI licensing, constraints on focus association, and constraints on binding. When covert *wh*-movement is restricted so that it cannot target a position above an intervener at LF, intervention effects are observed.

6.2 Missing Intervention Effects in Superiority-Violating Questions

In this section, I turn to the second half of Pesetsky's (2000) correlation: that Superiority-violating questions are subject to intervention effects. Following the analysis in chapter 5, this is because the (phonologically) in-situ *wh*-phrase in a Superiority-violating question is interpreted in situ at LF and cannot covertly move above any interveners in the structure. Below, I show that intervention can be avoided in Superiority-violating questions in at least three different cases: if (a) the intervener can scope out of the question, (b) the intervener can reconstruct below the in-situ *wh*-phrase, or (c) the in-situ *wh*-phrase can be given exceptionally wide scope by means of noninterrogative movement.

6.2.1 No Intervention If Intervener Scopes out of Question

I begin by showing that intervention effects in Superiority-violating questions can be avoided if the intervener can take scope outside of (and above) the question. This observation has in fact already been reported by Pesetsky (2000) for English, following parallel observation by Beck (1996a) for German. Schematically, the LF implicated in this situation is given in (18).

(18) *No intervention when the intervener scopes out of the question*

LF: intervener [$_{CP}$ wh_2 C ... **intervener** ... wh_1 ... t_2]

In this configuration, the intervener no longer separates the in-situ *wh*-phrase from the interrogative complementizer. Therefore, the illicit intervention configuration in (19a) is avoided, even though covert movement of the (phonologically) in-situ *wh*-phrase as in (19b) (repeated from (4)) is not possible.

(19) *The intervention configuration (Beck 2006:5; adapted)*

  a. * [$_{CP}$ C ... [**intervener** [... *wh* ...]]]

  b.   [$_{CP}$ C ... [*wh* [**intervener** [... *t* ...]]]]

The ability to move out of the question via QR is a property of universal quantifiers.[12] Consider first the Superiority-obeying question in (20), which has two possible readings. The first reading, (20a), is a list of triples, derived by assigning *everyone* wide scope over the question. In this case, people, newspapers, and books all vary at the same time. The second reading, (20b), is a list of pairs, derived by assigning *everyone* narrow scope in its pronounced position. Here, only books and newspapers vary. Pesetsky (2000) notes that the Superiority-violating variant of the question in (21) only has one reading, described in (20a)—the list-of-triples reading.

(20) *Everyone scopes out of Superiority-violating question to avoid intervention*
     Which newspaper did **everyone** write to ___ about *which* book?
     a. Wide scope answering pattern ($\forall$ > *newspaper-book pairs*)
        Bill wrote to the <u>New York Times</u> about book X,
        Mary wrote to the <u>Boston Globe</u> about book Y, and
        Tom wrote to the <u>Maquoketa Sentinel</u> about book Z.
     b. Narrow scope answering pattern (*newspaper-book pairs* > $\forall$)
        Everyone wrote to the <u>New York Times</u> about book X,
        everyone wrote to the <u>Boston Globe</u> about book Y, and
        everyone wrote to the <u>Maquoketa Sentinel</u> about book Z.

(21) *Which* book did **everyone** write to *which* newspaper about ___?
     Has answer pattern a, but not b.

We see, then, that the list-of-pairs reading is lost in (21). This is precisely
the reading that would require the illicit intervention configuration in (19a)—
where *everyone* takes narrow scope at LF, c-commanding the in-situ *wh*-phrase
which newspaper and separating it from the complementizer. The absence of
this reading in (21) is due to an intervention effect. On the other hand, in the
list-of-triples reading, the intervener no longer separates *wh*-in-situ from C;
hence, this reading is not blocked.

Pesetsky additionally shows that floating the quantifier (here: *each*) fixes its
scope in its pronounced position. This prevents the quantifier from moving out
of the way of the in-situ *wh*. As a result, the intervention configuration in (19a)
cannot be avoided, and the result is an intervention effect.

(22) *Floated quantifier blocks wide scope of* each, *leading to intervention*
     *PL Tell me *which* book the kids will **each** try to persuade *which* adult to
     read ___ .

This same effect has been shown to hold in German, regardless of superiority, as we would expect. Here, as in other cases of intervention effects in
German questions, intervention is avoided through overt scrambling of the *wh*-
phrase above the intervener. As a consequence, example (23a) can have only a
list-of-triples reading, where 'every' takes wide scope over the question, (24a).
Example (23b), on the other hand, can have both a wide scope list-of-triples
reading, (24a), and a narrow scope list-of-pairs reading, (24b).

(23) *Intervention above* wh-*in-situ, rescued by covert movement of 'every'*
     (Dayal 2016:246)
     a. *Wen* hat **jeder Junge** $\boxed{wann}$ beobachtet?
        who has every boy   when   observed
     b. *Wen* hat $\boxed{wann}$ **jeder Junge** beobachtet?
        who has when   every boy   observed

(24) *Only the wide scope reading is attested for (23a); both are available for (23b) (Dayal 2016:246)*
   a. 'For every boy, who did he observe when?'   (wide scope)
   b. 'Who is such that every boy observed him when?'   (narrow scope)

6.2.2 No Intervention If Intervener Reconstructs below *Wh*-Phrase

A second way to create a Superiority-violating structure that does not exhibit intervention effects is to reconstruct the intervener below the in-situ *wh*-phrase in the structure. This is illustrated schematically in (25). This structure again eliminates the intervention configuration in (19a) without allowing the in-situ *wh*-phrase to undergo covert movement.

(25) *No intervention when intervener reconstructs below in-situ* wh-*phrase*
   LF: [$_{CP}$ *wh*$_2$ C ... **intervener** ... *wh*$_1$ ... t_2 intervener]

To illustrate this configuration, I begin with the baseline example in (26), in which *all* is pronounced in an unraised position. This question has the reading that we are after: it is interpreted as a request for topic-professor pairs, such that the professor thought that all of the students enjoyed the topic—that is, a list-of-pairs reading.[13]

(26) *Baseline: Superiority-violating question with raising predicate and low* all
   Context: The first-year students took several classes this past semester, taught by different professors. Each professor thought that the students particularly enjoyed one topic that she taught. Tell me,

   Which topic did it seem to *which* professor that **all** of the students enjoyed ___?

Example (27) provides a second baseline, showing that a raised universal quantifier is generally able to reconstruct to its base position and take narrow scope in our test environment.

(27) *Baseline:* All *can reconstruct to its base position; inverse scope is possible*
   [All of the students]$_1$ seemed to some professor t_1 to have enjoyed learning about binding.   ($\forall > \exists, \exists > \forall$)

Example (28) provides the crucial test case. When read with the same context as in (26), supporting the list-of-pairs reading with narrow scope for the quantifier, the question is judged grammatical, despite the (surface) intervening quantifier.

(28) *Superiority-violating question with raised* all *can have a reconstructed reading*

Context: The first-year students took several classes this past semester, taught by different professors. Each professor thought that the students particularly enjoyed one topic that she taught. Tell me,

Which topic did **all** of the students seem to *which* professor to have enjoyed ___?

That is, we have successfully avoided intervention, despite appearing to have an illicit intervention configuration on the surface. However, at LF, the intervener is given narrow scope, below the in-situ *wh*, as is required to derive the list-of-pairs reading. That is, intervention is avoided by undoing the intervention configuration by means of reconstructing of the intervener to a position below *wh*-in-situ.

Notice that when the quantifier is floated, preventing it from reconstructing to its base position, the question is judged as degraded: the list-of-pairs reading becomes unavailable, and the list-of-triples reading causes an intervention effect.

(29) *Intervention effects reemerge with floated* all

*^{PL} *Which* topic did the students **all** seem to *which* professor to have enjoyed ___?

The question again becomes grammatical if the quantifier is floated in a lower position, below *wh*-in-situ. The narrow scope reading for *all* now becomes not only possible, but necessary.

(30) *Intervention effects disappear if* all *is floated below* wh

Which topic did the students seem to *which* professor to have **all** enjoyed ___?

6.2.3 No Intervention If *Wh* Scopes above Intervener

Although *wh*-in-situ in Superiority-violating questions cannot undergo covert *wh*-movement—given the assumptions about the syntax of these questions motivated in chapters 2–3 and to preserve the current explanation for the intervention data in chapters 5–6—we predict that intervention can be avoided if *wh* can be assigned wide scope above an intervener through another type of movement, which I will simply call noninterrogative movement. Here, I show that this is the case with right-node raising (RNR) constructions.[14]

It is well-known that RNR constructions allow exceptional extraction of *wh*-elements across certain islands (e.g., Bachrach and Katzir 2009). Example

(31a) illustrates a canonical relative clause island, which is ungrammatical. This example dramatically improves when it occurs as part of an RNR construction, (31b).[15]

(31) *RNR allows exceptional extraction of* wh-*items out of islands (Bachrach and Katzir 2009:283)*
   a. * *Which* book did John meet the man who wrote *t*?
   b. *Which* book did [John meet the man who wrote ___], and [Mary meet the woman who published ___] *t*?

It is also possible to extract only part of a right node, leaving overt material on the right. The conjuncts in (32) contain relative clause islands, making it unlikely that the *wh*-phrase was extracted before RNR applied to the remnant. Instead, it appears that the availability of RNR facilitates the exceptional *wh*-movement.

(32) *Movement can target just part of the* wh-*phrase (Bachrach and Katzir 2009:289)*
   Which animal$_1$ did John say that Mary knew [a man who wrote ___], and [a woman who published ___] an encyclopedia article about *t*$_1$?

Given this state of affairs, we predict that a multiple *wh*-question with RNR should allow the in-situ *wh*-phrase to take exceptionally wide scope, allowing it to evade intervention effects despite being in a Superiority-violating structure. This is indeed the case, as (33)–(34) illustrate.

(33) *No intervention in a Superiority-violating question with RNR*
   a. *[PL] *Which* book did **only Mary** allow *which* student to read ___ ?
   b. *Which* book did [**only Mary** allow ___], and [**only Sue** require ___], *which* student to read *t*?

(34) a. *[PL] *Which* topic did she **never** claim (that) *which* student would talk about ___ ?
   b. *Which* topic did [Mary **never** claim ___], and [Sue **never** promise ___], (that) *which* student would talk about *t*?

Here, (33a) and (34a) are classic intervention effect examples modeled after Pesetsky's (2000) examples in (1) and (2). Examples (33b) and (34b) add an RNR configuration. The resulting structures are no longer subject to intervention, because now the (phonologically) in-situ *wh* is able to take scope above the intervener at LF.

6.3   Intervention Is an LF Phenomenon

The data presented in sections 6.1–6.2 have consequences for the correct characterization of the environments that lead to intervention effects, and hence for the types of theories that might be able to correctly describe the phenomenon.[16] The data clearly show that intervention is the product of the LF configuration in (35).

(35)   *The intervention configuration (Beck 2006:5; adapted)*
          LF: *[$_{CP}$ C … [**intervener** [… *wh* …]]]

The grammar provides several different ways of avoiding or undoing this intervention configuration. Intervention effects are observed when there is no way of avoiding this configuration. Intervention thus reflects the available LF positions for the in-situ *wh*-phrase and the intervener.

(36)   *The intervention correlation*
          Intervention correlates with movement possibilities for the in-situ *wh*-phrase and the intervener at LF.

The grammar provides several strategies for avoiding intervention effects, all involving some form of movement of either the intervener or the in-situ *wh* (or both), undoing the intervention configuration.

(37)   *Strategies for avoiding the intervention configuration (35)*
          a. LF: [$_{CP}$ *wh* C … [**intervener** [… ___]   (*wh*-movement)
          b. LF: [$_{CP}$ C … *wh* [**intervener** [… ___]]]   (scrambling)
          c. LF: intervener [$_{CP}$ C … [**intervener** [… *wh*]]]   (QR)
          d. LF: [$_{CP}$ C … [**intervener** [… *wh* … intervener]]] (reconstruction)

The crucial conclusion is that we require an interrogative system that allows a syntax in which *wh*-phrases may either (covertly) move or remain in situ at LF and be interpreted without movement. Intervention effects are tied to movement, both overt and covert. When movement is available, intervention is avoided. When movement is unavailable, intervention emerges.

Although Pesetsky's (2000) claimed correlation between superiority and intervention is ultimately incorrect, his analysis of English multiple *wh*-questions nonetheless stands. That is, covert *wh*-movement is generally available in Superiority-obeying questions, unless it is blocked by independent factors; and covert *wh*-movement is not available in Superiority-violating questions, although other types of movement may still apply to the in-situ *wh*-phrase to give it wider scope at LF than its pronounced position.

These findings limit the types of theories that can explain intervention effects in English, and more generally crosslinguistically. For one, theories that rely solely on prosody—such as the one proposed by Tomioka (2007b) for Japanese—will have difficulty explaining the effects discovered here, as prosody does not reflect covert movement or in-situ interpretation. Intervention also cannot be given a purely syntactic account that directly ties it to the derivational probing mechanism for *wh*-phrases. Although derivations of Superiority-violating and -obeying questions may differ, intervention is possible in both types of questions, regardless of their superiority status.

Instead, theories of intervention must make reference to the LF representation of the question. In particular, the intervention configuration (35) shows that *wh*-phrases are sensitive to the presence of a c-commanding intervener when they are interpreted by means of a nonmovement mechanism. Theories such as Beck's (2006) and the version reformulated by Cable (2010) propose that this nonmovement mechanism is the projection of focus alternatives between the *wh*'s base position and C (e.g., Hamblin 1973; Rooth 1985, 1992), and that intervention is caused because this projection of alternatives is disrupted by the intervener, which blocks them from reaching C.[17] Other possible accounts of intervention that rely on a choice function theory of *wh*-in-situ (e.g., Reinhart 1998), instead of on focus alternatives, have to my knowledge not been explored in the literature; I leave these as a possibility for future work.

Finally, these findings concerning intervention effects have implications for the nature of grammar more generally. We learn that there must be at least two distinct ways of interpreting *wh*-elements: movement and an alternative, in-situ mechanism. Furthermore, we learn that grammar is equipped with several different ways of avoiding intervention configurations and that these movement mechanisms—(phrasal) *wh*-movement, QR, scrambling, and reconstruction—are employed quite frequently and may apply to different elements in the structure. Other movement operations may also apply to *wh*-phrases to move them out of the way: RNR, extraposition, subject raising, topicalization, and focus movement, among others. In fact, we have seen that significant effort and careful manipulation are necessary in order to prevent the grammar from finding a way to avoid the intervention configuration, leading to the quite complex structures that this chapter was concerned with. Only when all the possible intervention-avoiding strategies are unavailable do we detect an intervention effect.

III COVERT *WH*-SCRAMBLING

7 Covert *Wh*-Movement as Covert Scrambling

This chapter investigates the nature of covert movement in English multiple *wh*-questions.[1] In previous chapters, I adopted without argument the common assumption that covert *wh*-movement is a successive-cyclic operation targeting the interrogative CP layer, parallel to its overt counterpart.

(1) *The formation of a multiple* wh-*question*
   a. *Which student* read *which book*?
   b. LF: [$_{CP}$ *which student which book* C$_{+wh}$ [$_{TP}$ ___ read ___]]

Given this assumption, we would further assume that covert *wh*-movement is triggered by the same mechanism that triggers overt movement in English. This has been most explicitly spelled out by Pesetsky (2000) and Richards (1997): the *wh*-probe on C probes the structure more than once, until all phrases with *wh*-features have been found and agreed with. *Wh*-movement can be triggered immediately following an Agree operation. The following step-by-step derivation is assumed for (1a).[2]

(2) *The Agree/Attract model of covert* wh-*movement*
   a. *Step 1:* The interrogative probe on C probes its c-command domain. The base-generated higher *wh*, *which student*, is agreed with.

   [$_{CP}$ C$_{+wh}$ [$_{TP}$ *which student* read *which book*]]

   b. *Step 2: Which student* is attracted to the interrogative Spec,CP.

   [$_{CP}$ *which student* C$_{+wh}$ [$_{TP}$ ___ read *which book*]]

   c. *Step 3:* The probe again probes its c-command domain. The base-generated lower *wh*, *which book*, is agreed with.

   [$_{CP}$ *which student* C$_{+wh}$ [$_{TP}$ ___ read *which book*]]

d. *Step 4: Which book* is attracted to Spec,CP.

[$_{CP}$ *which student* *which book* C$_{+wh}$ [$_{TP}$ ___ read ___]]

In this chapter, I argue for a different view of covert *wh*-movement. I show that covert *wh*-movement can target positions other than interrogative C, and I argue that this movement is best viewed as a covert form of scrambling, triggered for the interpretational needs of the *wh*-phrase itself and not by an Attract operation triggered following Agree between the interrogative probe on C and the *wh*.

The evidence comes from (a) Superiority-obeying multiple *wh*-questions in which a (phonologically) in-situ *wh*-phrase occurs inside a syntactic island and (b) their behavior with regard to intervention effects. Intervention effects can be used to diagnose whether a *wh*-phrase is interpreted in situ in a structure or by means of covert movement: we observe an intervention effect when *wh* is LF-in-situ, but not when *wh* moves over an intervener. I show that intervention happens when an intervener occurs *above* an island but not *inside* it, a pattern consistent with covert movement that takes place inside the island to positions other than interrogative C, but which cannot escape the island. In chapter 8, I provide additional evidence—from online sentence processing—in favor of the view of covert *wh*-movement as covert scrambling.

7.1   Intervention Effects in Multiple *Wh*-Questions with Islands

Intervention effects can be used as a diagnostic for whether or not covert *wh*-movement has taken place in the derivation of a question: the presence of an intervention effect shows that a (phonologically) in-situ *wh*-phrase must be interpreted below an intervener at LF, whereas the lack of an intervention effect shows that the *wh*-phrase must have moved above the intervener by LF.[3]

The crucial data in this chapter come from the interaction of intervention effects with English multiple *wh*-questions in which the (phonologically) in-situ *wh*-phrase occurs inside a syntactic island. I take as my starting point the fact that multiple *wh*-questions with islands can have pair-list readings, as illustrated in (3). This is contrary to Dayal's (2002) claim that such questions do not have pair-list readings.[4]

(3) *A multiple* wh-*question with an island can also have a pair-list reading (Cheng and Demirdache 2010:466; context attributed to Chris Tancredi)*
    Context: Each of two philosophers will be offended if we invite one of two linguists. What I want to know is:

    Which philosopher will be offended if we invite *which linguist*?

a.   Pair-list
      Quine will be offended if we invite Chomsky, and Lewis will be
      offended if we invite Kayne.
b.   Single-pair (infelicitous due to context)
      #/*Quine will be offended if we invite Chomsky.

This is important since it is specifically the pair-list reading of a multiple
wh-question that is sensitive to intervention effects. With a single exception,
I have found that native speakers of English find the target sentence in (3a)
grammatical and felicitous in the context.

With this baseline established, I now turn to an investigation of the presence and extent of covert *wh*-movement in English multiple *wh*-questions
with islands. As shown in previous chapters, Superiority-obeying multiple *wh*-
questions in English are generally immune from intervention effects. Focusing
on questions with islands, I will ask two related questions about covert *wh*-
movement. First, if covert *wh*-movement happens, must it target interrogative
C? This is standardly assumed in theories of interrogative semantics: For questions to be interpretable, the mechanism that interprets them by means of
movement requires all *wh*-phrases to occupy positions local to interrogative C
(Karttunen 1977 and much subsequent work). Alternatively, *wh* may be interpreted in situ without movement (Hamblin 1973 and much subsequent work).
This all-or-nothing stance is often implicitly adopted in theories of interrogative syntax, including those that have been proposed for English multiple
wh-questions. A third option, compatible with at least some in-situ approaches
to *wh*-in-situ, is to allow *wh* to be interpreted in positions that are neither
interrogative C nor fully in situ. This will be the view endorsed in this chapter.

Second, is covert *wh*-movement sensitive to syntactic islands? If movement
is able to target positions other than interrogative C—as I will argue—one
way to show this is to restrict its possible landing sites. Syntactic islands are
known to block overt movement out of them (Ross 1967), and they have been
argued to affect at least some instances of covert movement (e.g., Huang
1982b). If covert movement in English differs from overt movement only in
the choice of which copy of the movement chain is pronounced (as in, e.g.,
Bobaljik 1995; Chomsky 1995, 2000; Pesetsky 2000), it should be similarly
sensitive to islands.

With this background in mind, let us turn to the data. To foreshadow, I will
show that the following generalization holds:

(4) *Generalization: The interaction of intervention effects and islands*
    Intervention occurs when an intervener is placed *above* an island contain-
    ing a *wh*, but not when an intervener is placed *inside* the island.

First, let us reexamine (3), repeated here as the slightly modified (5).[5] As suggested above, this question has two felicitous readings: single-pair and pair-list. Since in this section we are only interested in the presence or absence of the pair-list reading of a given question, I restrict my attention to this reading alone. All the examples below have felicitous single-pair readings.[6]

(5) *Lower* wh *inside adjunct island: Pair-list reading is available*
Context: The linguists at the conference are very picky about attending the conference dinner. However, each of them adores one philosopher and will certainly attend the dinner if that philosopher is invited. What I want to know is:

Q: *Which* linguist will come [if we invite *which* philosopher]?
A: Chomsky will come if we invite Quine,
Kayne will come if we invite Lewis,
Bresnan will come if we invite Arendt, …

Similarly, when the in-situ *wh*-phrase is inside a complex NP (CNP) island, the resulting question can again have a pair-list reading.

(6) *Lower* wh *inside CNP island: Pair-list reading is available*
Context: The linguists at the conference are very suspicious of rumors. However, each of them believed one of the rumors going around that we invited a particular famous philosopher to the conference party. What I want to know is:

Q: *Which* linguist believed the rumor [that we invited *which* philosopher]?
A: Chomsky believed the rumor that we invited Quine,
Kayne believed the rumor that we invited Lewis,
Bresnan believed the rumor that we invited Arendt, …

Examples (5) and (6) thus provide baselines for the crucial test cases. Next, we introduce interveners into these questions, (7)–(8). We find that an intervention effect, diagnosed by the loss of the pair-list reading, occurs when an intervener (here: *only* or negation, in boldface) occurs above the island, but not when it is inside the island.[7]

(7) *Adjunct island: Intervention above but not inside island*
a. Context: The linguists at the conference don't really want to attend the conference dinner. However, each of them adores one philosopher and has said that they will come just in case that philosopher is invited. What I want to know is:

Q: *Which* linguist will **only** come [if we invite *which* philosopher]?
A: *PL Chomsky will only come if we invite Quine,
      Kayne will only come if we invite Lewis,
      Bresnan will only come if we invite Arendt, ...

  b. Context: The linguists at the conference are looking forward to the conference dinner. However, each of them dislikes all but one philosopher and will attend the dinner just in case that philosopher alone is invited. What I want to know is:

Q: *Which* linguist will come [if we **only** invite *which* philosopher]?
A: Chomsky will come if we only invite Quine,
     Kayne will come if we only invite Lewis,
     Bresnan will come if we only invite Arendt, ...

(8) *CNP island: Intervention above but not inside island*
  a. Context: The linguists at the conference are very gullible and believe lots of rumors. However, each of them is suspicious of one rumor about a philosopher that we supposedly invited to the conference party. What I want to know is:

Q: *Which* linguist **didn't** believe [the rumor [that we invited *which* philosopher]]?
A: *PL Chomsky didn't believe the rumor that we invited Quine,
      Kayne didn't believe the rumor that we invited Lewis,
      Bresnan didn't believe the rumor that we invited Arendt, ...

  b. Context: The linguists at the conference are very suspicious of rumors. However, each of them believed the rumor that we failed to invite one philosopher to the conference party. What I want to know is:

Q: *Which* linguist believed [the rumor [that we **didn't** invite *which* philosopher]]?
A: Chomsky believed the rumor that we didn't invite Quine,
     Kayne believed the rumor that we didn't invite Lewis,
     Bresnan believed the rumor that we didn't invite Arendt, ...

Some speakers report similar contrasts in questions with an in-situ *wh*-phrase inside the complement clause of a nonbridge verb, such as *dream* or *shout*. Such verbs have been argued to be islands for extraction (e.g., Erteschik-Shir 1973; Zwicky 1971), and we therefore predict that interveners that occur above the complements of such verbs but not ones that occur inside them should cause an intervention effect. This prediction is indeed borne out, as illustrated in (9a–b).

(9) *Nonbridge verbs: Intervention above but not inside island*[8]

    a. *[PL] *Which* protester **didn't** shout [that we invited *which* politician]?

    b.   *Which* protester shouted [that we **didn't** invite *which* politician]?

Furthermore, configurations with three *wh*-phrases similar to those studied by Cheng and Demirdache (2010), where two *wh*-phrases are inside an island and one is outside, again exhibit intervention effects; the effects are diagnosed here by the loss of the list-of-triples reading, when an intervener occurs above the island, (10a), but not when it is inside it, (10b). This is consistent with the behavior of multiple *wh*-questions that we have seen in (7)–(9).

(10) *Questions with* wh-*phrases: Intervention above but not inside the island*

    a. Q: *Which* linguist **didn't** believe the rumor [that *which* student invited *which* philosopher]?

       A: *[PL] Chomsky didn't believe the rumor that Sue invited Quine,
          Kayne didn't believe the rumor that Jane invited Lewis,
          Bresnan didn't believe the rumor that Anya invited Arendt, ...

    b. Q: *Which* linguist believed the rumor [that *which* student **didn't** invite *which* philosopher]?

       A: Chomsky believed the rumor that Sue didn't invite Quine,
          Kayne believed the rumor that Jane didn't invite Lewis,
          Bresnan believed the rumor that Anya didn't invite Arendt, ...

If two *wh*-phrases occur outside the island and only one *wh*-phrase is inside it, we predict a pair-list reading with the answer for the third *wh*-phrase held constant. This prediction is borne out, as illustrated by the possible answer in (11a), where only the two higher *wh*-phrases vary and the third *wh*-phrase is held constant, as opposed to the unavailable answer in (11b), where all three *wh*-phrases vary simultaneously.[9]

(11) *Questions with three* wh-*phrases: Pair-list reading for* wh-*phrases above the island*

    Which linguist **didn't** tell *which* philosopher about the rumor [that *which* student had won a dissertation prize]?

    a. Possible answer: List of pairs (varying only the higher pair of *wh*-phrases)

       Chomsky didn't tell Quine about the rumor that Sue had won ... ,
       Kayne didn't tell Lewis about the rumor that Sue had won ... ,
       Bresnan didn't tell Arendt about the rumor that Sue had won ... , ...

b. Impossible answer: List of triples (varying all *wh*-phrases at once)
Chomsky didn't tell Quine about the rumor that Sue had won … ,
Kayne didn't tell Lewis about the rumor that Jane had won … ,
Bresnan didn't tell Arendt about the rumor that Anya had won … , …

I note that German questions in configurations such as (7)–(8)—where the intervener occurs *inside* the island together with the *wh*-phrase—are ungrammatical. This is in line with previous evidence (see, e.g., Beck 1996, 2006) that the only way to escape intervention effects in German is to overtly scramble the in-situ *wh*-phrase above the intervener.

(12) *An intervener* inside *an island causes an intervention effect in German (Martin Hackl, pers. comm.)*

Welcher Philosoph   wird sich ärgern   wenn {✓ wir/***niemand**}
which   philosopher will self be.upset if   we   no.one
welchen Linguisten einladen/einlädt?
which   linguist   invite/invites

'Which philosopher will be offended if we/no one invite(s) which linguist?'

Finally, following the logic of chapter 6, if the in-situ *wh*-phrase can be given exceptionally wide scope, so that it occupies a position above the intervener at LF, we expect the question to become grammatical again. Here, I use attachment height of relative clauses. In particular, we expect high attachment of a relative clause containing an in-situ *wh* in examples like (8a–b) to assign the *wh* wider scope than when it is attached low. The relevant examples are given in (13). Example (13a), repeated from (8a), provides a baseline without extraposition, where the pair-list reading is blocked because of an intervention effect.[10] When the noun-complement clause is extraposed and attached above the temporal adjunct *yesterday*, giving the clause exceptionally wide scope above the intervener, the pair-list reading becomes available, (13b).[11]

(13) *High attachment allows exceptionally wide scope for in-situ* wh-*phrase*

a. *[PL] *Which* linguist **didn't** believe the rumor that we invited *which* philosopher?

b.   ? *Which* linguist **didn't** believe the rumor *yesterday* [that we invited *which* philosopher]?

To summarize, the structural description of the configuration yielding intervention effects can be stated as in (14), repeated from (4).

(14) *Generalization: The interaction of intervention effects and islands*
Intervention occurs when an intervener is placed *above* an island containing a *wh*, but not when an intervener is placed *inside* the island.

7.2   Covert Movement and the Nature of Syntactic Derivations

I began section 7.1 by asking two related questions. First, if covert *wh*-movement happens, must it target interrogative C? Second, is covert *wh*-movement sensitive to syntactic islands? In this section, I argue that the intervention pattern in (14) shows that covert movement must take place in the English questions discussed, that this movement is sensitive to syntactic islands, and that it must be able to target positions other than interrogative C.

As discussed at the beginning of this chapter, current theories of interrogative syntax/semantics assume that a *wh*-phrase must either covertly move to interrogative C or else be interpreted in situ at LF.[12] For example, following Pesetsky (2000) and others, we may assume that Superiority-obeying questions with interveners such as (15a) have derivations such as (15b). Here, the (phonologically) in-situ *wh*-phrase *which philosopher* covertly moves to C at LF, correctly predicting the lack of an intervention effect in that question.

(15) *Covert movement available: No intervention in Superiority-obeying question*
   a. *Which* linguist **didn't** ___ invite *which* philosopher?
   b. LF: [$_{CP}$ *which* linguist *which* philosopher [C [$_{TP}$ t_1 **didn't** invite t_2]]]

Next, consider (16a–c), summarizing the pattern discovered in section 7.1. If we assume that covert movement is insensitive to islands, movement of *which philosopher* to C—along the lines of the derivation sketched in (15b)—should be possible for all of (16a–c). This clearly cannot derive the correct judgment pattern, and in particular the ungrammaticality of (16c). Hence, we conclude that covert movement is sensitive to syntactic islands.

(16) *Questions with islands are grammatical, if the intervener is inside the island*
   a.   *Which linguist* believed the rumor [$_{Island}$ that we invited *which philosopher*]?
   b.   *Which linguist* believed the rumor [$_{Island}$ that we **didn't** invite *which philosopher*]?
   c.   *[PL] *Which linguist* **didn't** believe the rumor [$_{Island}$ that we invited *which philosopher*]?

This conclusion has consequences for our understanding of the nature of islands. First, the data in this chapter are unexplained if islands are a PF phenomenon, as often assumed for example in the literature on the amelioration of island effects through ellipsis (see, among many others, Merchant 2001; Ross 1969). Under such an approach, islands should not restrict covert movement, and we would hence expect no intervention effects in any of the questions in (16a–c), contrary to fact. Moreover, a theory in which islands can be covertly pied-piped to C, as has been proposed for Japanese (Nishigauchi 1990; Richards 2000), incorrectly predicts no intervention effects for interveners occurring above the island. Under such a theory, the entire island in (16c) would undergo massive pied-piping to the matrix interrogative Spec,CP, resulting in a structure in which *wh* is not c-commanded by the intervener and hence no intervention effect would be expected.[13]

Alternatively, we might imagine that in-situ *wh*-phrases never undergo covert movement—that is, an approach in which *which philosopher* in (16) is interpreted in situ at LF. This type of derivation would correctly predict that (16a) is grammatical and that (16c) is ungrammatical, since it contains an in-situ *wh*-phrase c-commanded by an intervener. However, this type of derivation would incorrectly predict that (16b) should also be ungrammatical, because it too would have an in-situ *wh*-phrase c-commanded by an intervener. Hence, a derivation without any covert *wh*-movement is untenable.

A derivation that predicts the full pattern in (16) is one involving a movement step to a position above the intervener and possibly as high as the edge of the island, followed by in-situ interpretation of the *wh* between the landing site of movement and C. Here, I refer to this movement step as *partial movement*. Two possible characterizations of partial movement are described in (17).

(17) *Two ways to characterize partial movement*
　　　a. "Move as much as possible"
　　　　Move as close to interrogative C as possible in the derivation.
　　　　In the absence of islands, move all the way to C. In the presence of an island, move to the edge of the island.
　　　b. "Move just as much as necessary"
　　　　Move only as far as necessary to render a structure interpretable.
　　　　All things being equal, remain in situ. In the presence of an intervener, move above it but no further.

Both characterizations of partial movement are able to derive the pattern of judgments in (16a–c), but they have different consequences. If movement targets a position as close to C as possible, the presence of an intervener is irrelevant as a trigger for movement. If an island is lacking, we predict movement to always target interrogative C. If an island is present, movement would always target its edge. We hence predict the derivation in (18a) for the question in (16a), which lacks an island. We predict the derivation in (18b) for the question in (16b), which has an intervener inside an island. And we predict ungrammaticality in the case of (16c), since an intervener occurs above the island, but movement can only target the edge of the island—nothing further.

(18) *Derivations under the "Move as much as possible" view*
    a. No island: Move to Spec,CP

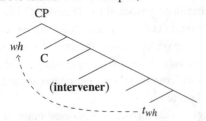

    b. Island: Move to edge of island

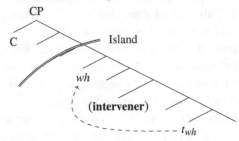

Alternatively, if covert movement takes place just when necessary and targets the first position that would yield an interpretable structure, interveners act as triggers for movement. In the absence of an intervener, all things being equal, we expect no movement to take place. If an intervener is present, movement targets a position immediately above the intervener, unless this movement is blocked by an island barrier. Hence, we predict a derivation without any movement for the question in (16a), which lacks an intervener, (19a). We predict a derivation for the question in (16b) with *wh* moving just above the intervener inside the island, (19b). And we predict ungrammaticality in the case of (16c), since an intervener occurs above the island, but movement cannot escape the island.

(19) *Derivations under the "Move just as much as necessary" view*
    a. No intervener: No movement

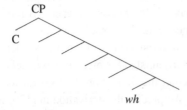

b. Intervener: Move above intervener

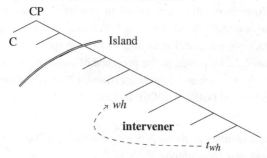

These two possible characterizations of partial movement follow naturally from two different models of structure building in syntax: a bottom-up model would naturally predict movement as in the "Move as much as possible" view, while a left-to-right, top-down model would predict movement as in the "Move just as much as necessary" view.

7.2.1 English as Covert Romanian

Consider first a bottom-up model of syntax. In such a model, *wh*-phrases carrying interrogative features enter into the derivation in earlier cycles (phases) than the C that they eventually agree with.[14] *Wh*-phrases are then "carried along" into higher phases using edge features (e.g., Chomsky 2001, 2008) or a similar mechanism, or through "greedy" movement (Chomsky 1995). In a question without islands, movement is thus predicted to terminate in interrogative Spec,CP, where *wh* and C can enter into a local relationship.

This view of covert *wh*-movement is standardly assumed in work on English questions—for example by Pesetsky (2000) and Richards (1997), who propose to view English as a covert version of a multiple *wh*-fronting language, such as Bulgarian or Romanian. Bulgarian and Romanian require all *wh*-phrases in a question to overtly front to the specifiers of interrogative C. English question LFs are argued to have a similar structure, but there is a pronunciation rule that dictates that only one *wh*-phrase is pronounced in its moved position, all other *wh*-phrases being pronounced in their base-generated positions, as discussed in more detail in section 2.2.1.

If a barrier to movement such as an island is present, we may assume that it will restrict movement, so that the *wh*-phrase will move to the edge of the island but will be unable to proceed any further. From its landing site, *wh* will be interpreted using an in-situ mode of composition such as alternatives computation or choice functions. This will give rise to a structure such as (18b) and will correctly predict the observed generalization regarding intervention effects in English multiple *wh*-questions, (14).

As noted by Cheng and Demirdache (2010), citing Ratiu (2005, 2007), a derivation of this form is overtly exemplified in multiple *wh*-questions in Romanian. Romanian is a multiple *wh*-fronting language, normally requiring all *wh*-phrases in a multiple *wh*-question to overtly front to specifiers of interrogative C (see section 4.2). However, in the presence of an island we observe a different behavior: *wh* cannot move outside an island, (20a), and it also cannot stay in its base-generated position, (20b). Instead, *it* moves to the edge of the island, (20c).

(20) *Overt multiple* wh-*fronting in Romanian questions (Ratiu 2005, 2007; as reported in Cheng and Demirdache 2010:474)*

a. *Wh* cannot move out of the island

$*[_{CP}$ *Cine$_i$ ce$_k$* $[_{IP}$ *t$_i$* o   cunoaşte pe   studenta
    who   what   CL.3.FSG know   PREP student

$[_{Island}$ *căreia*   i   s-a   dedicat   *t$_k$* ieri]]]?
    which.DAT CL.DAT EXPL-AUX dedicated   yesterday

b. *Wh* cannot stay in situ

$*[_{CP}$ *Cine$_i$* $[_{IP}$ *t$_i$* o   cunoaşte pe   studenta
    who   CL.3.FSG know   PREP student

$[_{Island}$ *căreia*   i   s-a   dedicat   *ce$_k$* ieri]]]?
    which.DAT CL.DAT EXPL-AUX dedicated what yesterday

c. *Wh* moves to the edge of the island[15]

$[_{CP}$ *Cine$_i$* $[_{IP}$ *t$_i$* o   cunoaşte pe   studenta
    who   CL.3.FSG know   PREP student

$[_{Island}$ *căreia*   *ce$_k$* i   s-a   dedicat   *t$_k$* ieri]]]?
    which.DAT what CL.DAT EXPL-AUX dedicated   yesterday
'*Who* knows the student to whom *what* was dedicated yesterday?'

Cheng and Demirdache (2010) motivate a partial movement derivation for English questions with islands, building on this parallel with the overt behavior of Romanian and on a consideration of the readings of English questions with three *wh*-phrases where some *wh*-phrases are "trapped" inside an island. The proposal in (18) is thus equivalent to Cheng and Demirdache's proposal. See Cheng and Demirdache 2010 for details.[16]

This model of structure building is naturally consistent with a "Move as much as possible" approach: in most cases, we will end up with a derivation in which covert movement targets interrogative Spec,CP, as in the traditional theory. However, within this model movement must be caused by the needs of the *wh* itself and not by the needs of C: if C required all *wh*-phrases to reach its edge, be it for syntactic or for semantic reasons, we would be unable to correctly predict any partial movement and hence would be unable to model the pattern of intervention effects presented in section 7.1.

However, once a syntax and a semantics are put in place that allow *wh*-phrases to be interpreted without requiring movement to interrogative C, the mechanisms of edge features and greedy movement become conceptually difficult to justify. Edge features may fail to attract a *wh* across an island but not lead to a crash in the derivation (Preminger 2011). Similarly, the greedy movement mechanism pushes a *wh*-phrase as far as it can, but the derivation does not crash if the *wh* does not reach its destination. But why would we assume the existence of these mechanisms in the first place, if we independently must assume a syntax/semantics that is able to interpret *wh*-phrases partially or completely in situ, in noninterrogative positions?

A more parsimonious syntax would not assume such syntactically driven mechanisms as a general rule. Instead, it would model covert *wh*-movement as being triggered only when necessary for the interpretational needs of the question: here, *wh* cannot be interpreted if it is c-commanded by an intervener and hence the only convergent LF for such a structure must involve movement of the *wh* above the intervener. All things being equal, for economy reasons such movement would be predicted to be as short as possible, targeting a position immediately above the intervener. However, this is not straightforwardly accommodated in a bottom-up model of syntax, involving probes and goals, edge features, and greedy movement, without encountering a lookahead problem: how can we know what the lowest position is at which the *wh* is interpretable before we know what the path between *wh* and C looks like—and specifically, where interveners occur, if any?

As an alternative, we may be able to predict that movement will target the lowest possible position in a bottom-up model through a theory of economy that utilizes transderivational competition (e.g., Reinhart 2006).[17] However, this movement is naturally predicted in a top-down model of syntax that does not require transderivational competition, as I will illustrate next.

7.2.2 English as Covert German

Consider next a left-to-right, top-down model of syntax, often used to describe the processing of natural language (e.g., Phillips 1996). Under such a model, the parsing of a question is straightforward in English: the presence of an interrogative C heading a question is made explicit by the overt fronting of a *wh*-phrase to Spec,CP and T-to-C movement. It is now possible to keep track of any interveners and islands occurring in this question. If a second *wh*-phrase is encountered—marking the fact that we are constructing a multiple *wh*-question—it is immediately clear that this *wh*-phrase cannot occupy a position below an intervener, because it would not be interpretable in such a position. The lowest target position of covert movement is also immediately clear: it is the position immediately above the intervener.[18] If the *wh* is trapped inside an island, the extent of movement will be limited by its presence.

For illustration purposes, it may be beneficial to think of the covert movement envisioned by this kind of approach as movement to the right, as in the (simplified) sketch in (21).[19]

(21) *Covert* wh-*movement viewed as movement to the right*

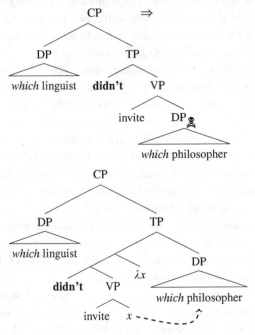

The (phonologically) in-situ *wh*-phrase *which philosopher* cannot be integrated into the structure in situ, as this would lead to an intervention effect because of the c-commanding sentential negation. As soon as this *wh*-phrase is encountered, the structure must undergo a *reanalysis* step, resulting in the integration of the *wh* in a position above the intervener. This reanalysis step is parallel to the reanalysis required in garden path sentences.

(22) *A garden path sentence*
    I convinced her children are noisy.

Here, the structure undergoes reanalysis from an initial assumption by the parser that a DP *her children* should be constructed to a structure in which *her* alone acts as the first internal argument of *convince*, and *children are noisy* acts as the second argument.[20]

This model of structure building is thus naturally consistent with the "Move just as much as necessary" approach, where movement happens only when it is necessary for interpretability. Therefore, no movement happens if no intervener is present in a question, and movement would target a position immediately above an intervener if one is present, to avoid an intervention effect. However, movement cannot escape an island; hence, interveners occurring outside the island lead to ungrammaticality.

This state of affairs is parallel to cases of overt scrambling observed in German multiple *wh*-questions. As we have seen, in-situ *wh*-phrases in German scramble above any interveners in the structure in order to avoid ungrammaticality: although in-situ *wh*-phrases can normally be interpreted in their base positions, (23a), they cannot be c-commanded by an intervener and instead must scramble above it, (23b).

(23) *German: Intervention above* wh-*in-situ is avoided by scrambling (Beck 1996a:6)*

    a.   * *Wer* hat **niemanden** $\boxed{wo}$ angetroffen?
             who has no.one   where met

    b.   *Wer* hat $\boxed{wo}$ **niemanden** ___ angetroffen?
             who has where no.one   met
             'Who didn't meet anybody where?'

We can capitalize on this parallel by proposing that covert *wh*-movement in English is a more restricted, local operation than the unbounded dependency we normally conceive of for overt *wh*-movement. Specifically, it may be fruitful to think of covert *wh*-movement as a form of *covert scrambling*. I discuss this option in the next section.

7.3 Evidence for Covert *Wh*-Scrambling

In this section, I further explore the idea that the covert partial movement step in Superiority-obeying English questions should be thought of as *covert scrambling* of the in-situ *wh*. If this idea is correct, the movement of the in-situ *wh* is not traditional *wh*-movement. Instead, it should be characterized as an instantiation of a more general QR operation that applies to other nominals as well. Proposals that QR is in fact covert scrambling—not just in the case of *wh*-movement but more generally whenever quantifiers participate in covert scope-taking operations—have been made for English in the previous literature (Akahane 2007; Beck 1996b; Diesing 1992; Johnson 2000b; Johnson and Tomioka 1997; Miyagawa 2011; Takano 1998[21]).[22]

For Johnson (2000b) and Johnson and Tomioka (1997), the analysis of QR as covert scrambling explains scope relations in quantified sentences, and in particular quantifiers' interpretation with respect to sentential negation. For

Diesing (1992), covert scrambling affects English bare plurals, which must occur higher than their base position, in order to receive a generic interpretation (cf. Kratzer 1995). Thus, bare plurals can facilitate ACD, since they are in fact not in situ but have undergone a short movement step. This is in contrast to the definite DP, which does not make as good a host for ACD.[23]

(24) *Bare plurals facilitate ACD (Diesing 1992:94)*
    Oscar usually reads books that Olga does.
    cf. Oscar read the book that Olga did.

I adopt the standard assumption that QR targets the nearest node of propositional type in the structure, namely, the nearest vP (e.g., Heim and Kratzer 1998). Hence, I assume that the scrambled object adjoins to vP above the original position of the external argument (Bruening 2001; Diesing 1992; Fox 2000; Johnson 2000b).[24] This is also the position typically targeted by short scrambling in languages such as Dutch and German.

Examples (25a–b) show overt short scrambling in German. As German is head-final, no DP can follow the verb. Unscrambled pronouns, following negation, must be interpreted as stressed (contrastively focused) to be licit. Full DPs may be scrambled above negation or may remain below negation.

(25) *Optional overt short scrambling in German (Richards 2004:3)*
    a. Peter hat (es/das Buch) nicht (das Buch/*es) gelesen (*es/*das Buch).
       Peter has (it/the book) not   (the book/*it) read   (*it/*the book)
       'Peter didn't read (it/the book).'
    b. ... dass Peter (das Buch/es) nicht (das Buch/*es) las   (*das Buch/*es).
       ... that Peter (the book/it) not   (the book/*it) read (*the book/*it)
       ' ... that Peter didn't read (it/the book).'

Hallman (1997) shows that although full DPs in German can optionally remain in situ, *wh*-phrases always obligatorily undergo a short scrambling step. The data are given in (26). We see that a full DP (*das Buch, die Maria*) can occur on either side of the adverbial *gestern*, but a *wh*-phrase can only appear above the adverbial.[25]

(26) *Obligatory overt short* wh-*scrambling in German (Hallman 1997:45)*
    a. *Wer* hat denn (das Buch) gestern   (das Buch) gelesen?
       who has DENN (the book) yesterday (the book) read
       'Who read the book yesterday?'
    b. *Wer* hat denn (*was*) gestern   (**was*) gelesen?[26]
       who has DENN (what) yesterday (what) read
       'Who read what yesterday?'

    c. *Wer* hat denn (die Maria) gestern   (die Maria) angerufen?
       who has DENN (the Maria) yesterday (the Maria) called
       'Who called Maria yesterday?'
    d. *Wer* hat denn (*wen*)   gestern   (*wen) angerufen?
       who has DENN (whom) yesterday (whom) called
       'Who called whom yesterday?'

Moreover, this short scrambling step in (26) does not result in freezing of the in-situ *wh*. In fact, a longer scrambling step can be observed in questions with interveners, as illustrated in (23).

Given these similarities between the behavior of German and that of English, I propose that covert *wh*-movement in English precisely parallels its German counterpart: obligatory short movement to the edge of the nearest vP, with a longer movement step to a position above interveners taking place when necessary for interpretability. The single difference between the two languages lies in the fact that movement is covert in English, but overt in German.

Finally, I note that the proposal that covert *wh*-movement in Superiority-obeying English questions should be modeled as covert scrambling makes an interesting prediction with regard to intervention effects. As we have seen in this chapter, we observe an intervention effect when a *wh*-word occurs inside an island and an intervener occurs above it, in a different clause. Given the proposal here, however, we should find difficulty whenever an intervener occurs in a higher clause than the *wh*-phrase, regardless of islandhood, since QR/scrambling is often clause-bound.

(27) *Predicted intervention schema: Intervener in higher clause than* wh
    $[_{CP}\ wh_1\ [_{C}\ [_{TP}\ \ldots\ \textbf{intervener}\ \ldots\ [_{CP}\ C\ [_{TP}\ \ldots\ wh_2\ [_{vP}\ \ldots\ t_2\ \ldots\ ]]]]]]$

We have already seen evidence, in (9), that this behavior extends to embeddings with nonbridge verbs. This prediction appears to be borne out, although the judgments are not uniform across all my consultants. If my proposal is on the right track, the variability in judgments should correlate with the extent to which QR is clause-bound for different speakers.

(28) *Finite embeddings as islands for extraction*
    a. ?? *Which* linguist **didn't** believe/claim/say [$_{CP}$ that we invited *which* philosopher]?
    b. *Which* linguist believed/claimed/said [$_{CP}$ that we **didn't** invite *which* philosopher]?

7.4 Some Consequences

Modeling covert *wh*-movement as covert scrambling has several advantages
for the theory of grammar. From a theoretical standpoint, we are able to provide a more parsimonious theory of movement, where covert *wh*-movement,
QR, and scrambling are modeled as one and the same operation. This is conceptually superior to a theory that posits three different types of movement
operations, each with its own properties, but all potentially covert and therefore
perhaps not easily acquired.[27]

The QR-as-covert-scrambling proposal thus allows a clear division of labor
between syntax and semantics. If scope is determined by QR, and QR is the
covert counterpart of scrambling, languages differ along a single parameter:
whether they have overt scrambling (German) or covert scrambling (QR in
English). As a consequence, crosslinguistic variation is restricted to different
parameter settings in overt syntax, while the semantic component can be kept
uniform across all language types, presumably a desirable result in itself (see
also discussion in Lechner 2013).

This proposal is more generally advantageous from the point of view of
learnability and language acquisition: one puzzle regarding the behavior of
multiple *wh*-questions and intervention effects is how they come to be acquired
by children. The positive evidence for these phenomena is in general quite
impoverished: the patterns we have seen are complex, involving at least two
wh-phrases and an additional intervener, and they are rare. How, then, do native
speakers converge on their adult grammars? This is puzzling under previous
theories of multiple *wh*-questions, which propose quite different LF structures
for English and German, despite their similar surface appearances.

Here, a natural answer to the question can be provided. The grammars of
English and German are the same with respect to the syntax/semantics of
questions and intervention effects, with the exception that scrambling is overt
in German but covert in English. QR, modeled in terms of scrambling, not
only affects in-situ *wh*-phrases in multiple *wh*-questions, but also is ubiquitous
and affects all quantifiers in the language. Therefore, children need not decide
whether there is covert *wh*-movement in their target language and what syntactic position this movement targets. Instead, they simply determine whether
or not the language has overt scrambling—a question for which there is ample
evidence in the input. If a language does not exhibit overt scrambling, then it
must have covert scrambling. A language with overt scrambling will exhibit
rigid scope, while a language without overt scrambling will allow for a covert
variant of this operation, resulting in possible scope ambiguities.

Finally, the view of *wh*-movement and QR as covert scrambling can be accommodated in a single-output model of the grammar (Bobaljik 1995; Fox and Nissenbaum 1999; Groat and O'Neil 1996; Pesetsky 2000), in which overt and covert movement operations are not distinguished by relative timing; instead, they are the same operation in the narrow syntax, and are then distinguished by whether the higher or lower copy of the movement chain is pronounced. Hence, we do not require the familiar Y-model of grammar, under which "covert" operations are operations that occur after the "split" in the grammar that takes a single input and leads to separate phonological (PF) and semantic (LF) representations.

This state of affairs thus leads to the conclusion that overt *wh*-movement and covert *wh*-movement are qualitatively different from one another. While overt *wh*-movement always targets one and the same position—in English and German, the specifier of interrogative C—and must take place without exception, covert movement can target different positions in the structure and may not occur at all in some cases. Given an appropriate semantics that allows for in-situ interpretation of *wh*-phrases, the purpose of this obligatory overt step of movement to Spec,CP cannot be the semantic interpretation of the question, since we already have a mechanism that can interpret questions without movement. An alternative motivation for this movement will have to be assumed—often, this involves EPP features. See Pesetsky 2000 for a detailed version of this syntactic (EPP-based) view and Richards 2010, 2016 for a prosody-based account.

If proposals such as Johnson and Tomioka's (1997) are on the right track, QR in English should also be recast as covert scrambling. If so, English has exactly one covert scope-taking operation—scrambling—parallel to its overt counterpart in German. English, then, is not a covert version of Romanian, as often assumed in the literature (e.g., Richards 1997); instead, it is a covert version of German.[28] In the next chapter, I present experimental evidence in support of this conclusion, along with a revised denotation for *wh*-expressions as quantifiers that captures the scrambling-as-QR idea.

8 Processing Evidence for Covert Scrambling

In this chapter, I provide novel experimental evidence that supports the view of covert *wh*-movement as covert scrambling.[1] I begin by contrasting the predictions made by a theory in which *wh*-phrases undergo covert *wh*-movement at LF with one where they remain in situ. As ample offline evidence has shown, we expect to find evidence for covert movement of the in-situ *wh*-phrase in Superiority-obeying English questions, but not in Superiority-violating questions.

Once I establish the methodology and basic processing signature of movement, I then use the intervention effect diagnostic to test the nature of this movement more closely. In particular, as spelled out in section 7.2, if the covert *wh*-scrambling proposal is on the right track, we expect the size of movement to correlate with the presence and height of interveners: a higher intervener should require a longer movement step than a lower intervener in the structure. I show that this prediction is indeed borne out.

I conclude this chapter by briefly entertaining the source of short *wh*-scrambling: by combining the Hamblin set approach to *wh*-expressions with Karttunen-based approaches that view *wh*-expressions as quantifiers, we may be able to combine the results developed throughout this book into a single coherent proposal. The denotations of *wh*-expressions that I eventually propose, then, consist of *a set of alternative quantificational interpretations* (i.e., of alternative $\langle et, t \rangle$ denotations).

8.1 Three Approaches to Covert Movement

As we have seen throughout this book, the literature on the syntax semantics of *wh*-questions provides two conceptual approaches to the interpretation of in-situ *wh*-phrases: covert movement and in-situ composition. Under the covert movement approach, all *wh*-phrases must be structurally adjacent to the head that interprets them in the CP periphery. The in-situ approach invokes a mechanism that interprets *wh*-phrases without any movement. I have argued in this book for a combined approach, where covert *wh*-movement is modeled as short scrambling, with in-situ composition affecting the interpretation of everything between the landing site of scrambling and C. Here, I will briefly sketch LFs based on these three approaches to movement and spell out predictions for sentence processing, which will be the main focus in this chapter.

The predicted LF under the traditional covert movement approach, where all *wh*-phrases must occur in the CP periphery by LF, is given in (1) (=(1) of chapter 7).[2]

(1) *A covert movement approach to question formation*
    a. *Which* student read *which* book?
    b. LF: [CP *which* student *which* book C [TP ___ read ___]]

This view of covert movement predicts pervasive covert movement in multiple *wh*-questions, parallel to the overtly observed behavior of multiple *wh*-fronting languages such as Bulgarian (e.g., Richards 1997) (see section 7.2.1). Moreover, movement is always triggered for one and the same reason—the semantic needs of the *wh*-phrases themselves—and it always targets the same syntactic position at LF: C. This approach makes the prediction in (2).

(2) *A prediction of the "traditional" covert movement approach*
    All *wh*-phrases in a question must (overtly or covertly) move to C for interpretation.

Against this backdrop stands the traditional in-situ approach to *wh*-in-situ, according to which the meaning of a question can be calculated through a mechanism that passes the meanings of *wh*-words up the structure until they reach C, where they can be interpreted (Hamblin 1973; Rooth 1985, 1992). No movement needs to be assumed for the interpretation of *wh*-phrases in the structure.

(3) *An in-situ approach to question formation*
    [CP *which* student [C [TP ___ read *which* book]]]

This approach to questions makes no particular predictions about the position of *wh*-phrases at LF. Following standard assumptions in the theoretical literature that the simplest syntactic structure for a sentence is always preferred to a less simple one (see Chomsky 1995, 2000; Collins 2001; Epstein 1992; Fox 2000; Kitahara 1997; Reinhart 2006), it is predicted that *wh*-phrases occupy the position at which they were merged into the syntactic structure, unless another syntactic process triggers their movement.

(4) *A prediction of the in-situ approach*
    Wh-phrases can be interpreted in situ and do not require any movement.

Evidence from previous chapters has led me to argue for a combined account of *wh*-in-situ in English questions. We have seen that *wh*-phrases covertly move in Superiority-obeying questions, but that movement need not target interrogative C. I have argued that movement should be modeled as covert scrambling: *wh*-in-situ undergoes a short covert movement step when it is merged into the structure, and additional movement is motivated if it is necessary for interpreting the *wh*-phrase—for example, in order to avoid an intervention effect.

(5) *A covert scrambling approach to question formation*
    [CP *which* student [C [TP ... *which* book [vP ___ read ___]]]]

This is a logical consequence of a liberal interpretation of Hamblin 1973: *wh*-phrases may be able to undergo a *partial* movement step to positions other than interrogative C, and then be interpreted through the projection of Rooth-Hamblin alternatives between this landing site and C. Such movement will not be triggered for the reasons proposed in Karttunen 1977, as this would necessitate movement to C, but other factors may drive covert movement at LF.

(6) *A prediction of the scrambling approach*
    Wh-phrases may undergo a short movement step, and will only move further if there are external reasons requiring this movement.

8.2   Experimental Background

In section 8.3, I present a series of experiments supporting the view that instances of English *wh*-in-situ undergo a short covert scrambling step and can be interpreted without any further movement between their landing site and C. In this section, I introduce the experimental methodology. Specifically, I present background on ACD, which will be central to the experiments, the Hackl, Koster-Hale, and Varvoutis (2012) paradigm, and a general discussion of how syntax and online processing interact.

8.2.1   Antecedent-Contained Deletion
ACD is a phenomenon found in certain VP-ellipsis contexts. For VP-ellipsis to be licensed, a pronounced antecedent VP must exist that is identical to the missing VP.[3] This is straightforward in examples like (7), where the only

pronounced VP in the sentence—*read a book*—can serve as an antecedent for the missing VP. In ACD cases like (8), however, the missing VP appears to be properly contained inside the only possible antecedent VP in the sentence. Matching the missing VP with the [antecedent VP] should be impossible since the missing VP is properly contained inside its antecedent and so cannot be identical to it.

(7) *VP-ellipsis and its resolution*
    a. Sue [read a book] and Mary did ⟨missing VP⟩, too.
    b. Sue read a book and Mary did ⟨read a book⟩, too.

(8) *ACD and the containment problem*
    a. Sue [read every book that Mary did ⟨missing VP⟩].
    b. Sue read every book that Mary did ⟨??⟩.

To solve the containment problem in (9a), the standard analysis of ACD assumes that the object is covertly moved out of TP$_1$ to a syntactic position in the higher TP$_2$, yielding the LF in (9b). The resulting VP, containing only the verb and the trace of covert movement, can then be used as an antecedent for the missing VP (see Fox 2003; Larson and May 1990; May 1985; Sag 1976; Williams 1974, 1977).

(9) *Resolution of ACD using covert movement*
    a. [$_{TP_1}$ Sue [read [every book that Mary did ⟨missing VP⟩]]]
    b. [$_{TP_2}$ [every book that Mary did read t] [$_{TP_1}$ Sue [read t]]]

For additional details on the interaction of ACD with multiple *wh*-questions, see the appendix to chapter 2.

8.2.2 Self-Paced Reading and the Hackl, Koster-Hale, and Varvoutis (2012) Paradigm

In this section, I present the methodology that is used in the experiments in section 8.3. These experiments use the paradigm developed by Hackl, Koster-Hale, and Varvoutis (HKV) for studying the real-time processing of sentences where covert movement has been argued to occur, concentrating on the universal quantifier *every*.

This paradigm takes advantage of the inherently linear organization of real-time sentence processing: the human parser integrates material that occurs earlier in a sentence before it encounters material that occurs later. The paradigm relies on two underlying assumptions about the economy of structure building: (a) the linguistic parser always builds the simplest syntactic structure consistent with the linguistic input, and (b) structures without covert movement are simpler than structures with covert movement.

Given these assumptions, we expect the parser not to postulate covert movement in the parse of a sentence until the point at which it determines that such movement is necessary. From that point on, one might expect to find online consequences (detectable as a delay in Reading Times, RTs) of the *reanalysis* of the structure to a less preferred parse.

HKV (2012) compare the processing of sentences that contain nonquantificational objects (*the*, (10a–c)) to sentences with quantificational objects (*every*, (10d–f)). This factor is crossed with three different gap sizes inside an attached relative clause: (a) *no ellipsis* using a lexical <u>verb</u>; (b) *small ellipsis* marked by <u>did</u>, where the antecedent of the ACD is the embedded VP$_2$ headed by *treat*; and (c) *large ellipsis* marked by <u>was</u>, where the antecedent of the ACD is the matrix VP$_1$ headed by *reluctant*.

(10) *The HKV (2012) paradigm*

The doctor was [$_{VP_1}$ reluctant to [$_{VP_2}$ treat …

   a. **the** patient that the recently hired nurse <u>*admitted*</u>   *(no ellipsis)*
   b. **the** patient that the recently hired nurse <u>*did*</u>   *(small ellipsis)*
   c. **the** patient that the recently hired nurse <u>was</u>   *(large ellipsis)*
   d. **every** patient that the recently hired nurse <u>*admitted*</u>   *(no ellipsis)*
   e. **every** patient that the recently hired nurse <u>*did*</u>   *(small ellipsis)*
   f. **every** patient that the recently hired nurse <u>was</u>   *(large ellipsis)*

                          …after looking over the test results.

Under a standard analysis, ACD resolution involves at least three steps: (i) creating a structure in which antecedent containment is undone, (ii) identifying an appropriate antecedent for the ellipsis, and (iii) filling the antecedent into the gap and computing the resulting meaning. Steps (ii) and (iii) are required in all cases of VP-ellipsis. Step (i)—reanalysis of the structure to undo antecedent containment—is only required in the case of ACD. HKV (2012) generate specific predictions for language processing in real time based on these properties and the assumptions that (a) step (i) of ACD resolution requires covert movement, and (b) quantificational objects (but not nonquantificational objects) require covert movement (in particular, QR) for their interpretation, and that this movement targets the lowest position in the structure where the object can be interpreted (see Fox 1995, 2000; Heim and Kratzer 1998; May 1985).

In the *definite* conditions in (10a–c), no covert movement is predicted to take place when the definite article is processed. The parser will only assume covert movement if and when it determines that the sentence contains an instance of ACD. This will happen after encountering the auxiliaries *did* and *was* in (10b–c), which, together with the immediately following word, signal the presence of an ACD site and thus trigger reanalysis in order to resolve ACD. This reanalysis should incur a processing cost detectable as a slowdown in RTs following the ellipsis site, compared to the baseline with *no ellipsis* (10a). Furthermore, the difference in the locality of covert movement and, concomitantly, the size of the antecedent VP should also be reflected in RTs: the covert movement in (10c) must target a nonlocal position, above the matrix VP_1 headed by *reluctant*, in order to make the matrix VP available for ACD resolution, while the covert movement in (10b) targets a closer position above the embedded VP_2 headed by *treat*. On the assumptions that nonlocal movement and the retrieval of a larger antecedent VP are more costly than local movement and the retrieval of a smaller antecedent VP, and that the nonlocal VP instantiates a more complex meaning than the local VP, (10c) is expected to produce longer RTs than (10b). These predictions are summarized in (11). Here and in (12) triggers for movement are boxed.

(11) *Predictions for the* definite *conditions*
     a. The doctor was reluctant to treat **the** patient that the nurse *admitted*.
       ⇒ Lexical verb condition: No movement is assumed at all.
     b. The doctor was reluctant to treat **the** patient that the nurse $\boxed{did.}$
       ⇒ Movement is assumed after *did* is encountered.   (late trigger)
       Movement targets a position above *treat*.   (short movement)
     c. The doctor was reluctant to treat **the** patient that the nurse $\boxed{was.}$
       ⇒ Movement is assumed after *was* is encountered.   (late trigger)
       Movement targets a position above *reluctant*.   (long movement)

For the *quantificational* conditions, different predictions are made. In all of (10d–f), the parser must assume covert movement as soon as it encounters the quantificational object headed by *every*. Furthermore, the movement is expected to be *local* and to target a position just above the embedded VP_2 headed by *treat*: this is the first position where quantifiers in object position can be integrated into the structure without causing a type mismatch. Importantly, this position is high enough to preemptively undo antecedent containment in the case of *small ellipsis* (10e) but not in the case of *large ellipsis* (10f): the movement triggered by *every* targets the same position that would be independently targeted for the resolution of the *small ellipsis*. Because this movement has already happened earlier in the parse, step (i) of ACD resolution can be avoided, and only steps (ii)–(iii) must apply when the ellipsis marker *did* is encountered. This means that at the point of identifying the ACD site, no reanalysis is predicted for this sentence. Hence, ACD resolution is expected to be easier in (10e) than in (10b) since part of the work necessary to resolve ACD has already happened prior to encountering the ACD marker _did_ with _every_, but all three steps of ACD resolution must happen when _did_ is encountered with _the_. In other words, we expect a _facilitation effect_ of ACD resolution, detectable as relatively fast RTs, in the _every-did_ condition.

In the case of the _large ellipsis_ in (10f), by contrast, the covert movement step that is assumed following the processing of _every_ is not sufficient to furnish a suitable antecedent VP: following this local movement, the missing VP is still contained inside its antecedent. Hence, when the auxiliary _was_ is reached, the parser must again reanalyze the structure, covertly moving the object a second time, from its position above the embedded VP to a position higher than the matrix VP. This means that no facilitation of ACD resolution is expected in (10f) even though the host DP is quantificational in nature.

These predictions are summarized in (12).

(12) _Predictions for the_ every _conditions_

   a. The doctor was reluctant to treat ⟨every⟩ patient that the nurse _admitted._

   ⇒ Movement is assumed after **every** is encountered.   (early trigger)
   Movement targets a position above _treat._   (short movement)

   b. The doctor was reluctant to treat ⟨every⟩ patient that the nurse _did._

   ⇒ Movement is assumed after **every** is encountered.   (early trigger)
   Movement targets a position above _treat._   (short movement)

   c. The doctor was reluctant to treat ⟨every⟩ patient that the nurse ⟨was.⟩

   ⇒ Movement is assumed after **every** is encountered.   (early trigger)
   Movement targets a position above _treat._   (short movement)
   ⇒ **Additional** movement is assumed after _was_ is encountered.

   (late trigger)
   Movement targets a position above _reluctant._   (long movement)

HKV (2012) used sentences in a paradigm like (10) in a self-paced reading study (Just, Carpenter, and Wooley 1982): participants read sentences that appeared on the screen one word at a time using a moving-window display. Residual Reading Times (RRTs) were analyzed for each word in the sentence. Note that RRTs measure whether a given word in a given trial in the experiment was read at the average speed for all words of the same length throughout the experiment for each participant (represented by RRT = 0 in figure 8.1), faster than expected (negative RRT values), or slower than expected (positive RRT values).[4]

Figure 8.1 shows RRTs two words after the ellipsis site. These results indicate that the predictions described above are borne out. When the object is

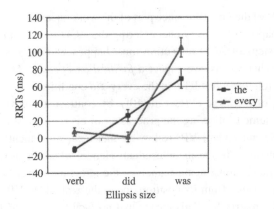

Figure 8.1
Results of Hackl, Koster-Hale, and Varvoutis 2012. Mean Residual Reading Times two words after the embedded verb.

definite, ACD resolution is associated with longer RRTs than in the baseline condition, *no ellipsis (verb)*. The increase in RRTs is linear across the three gap size levels (*the-verb* vs. *the-did* vs. *the-was*). When the object is *quantificational*, however, an interaction pattern emerges. No increase is observed between the *every-verb* condition and the *every-did* condition (*small ellipsis*), while a large increase is observed between the *every-did* condition and the *every-was* condition (*large ellipsis*).

This is unexpected if the two factors (quantificational vs. nonquantificational object and ACD size) are not linked in some form, but it is the expected result under the assumptions that (a) covert movement is required to accommodate both a quantificational object and an ACD site, as the first step in resolving ACD, and that (b) quantifiers undergo a short QR step sufficient to facilitate ACD resolution with *did*, but insufficient in the case of *was*.[5]

8.2.3 How Syntax and Online Processing Interact
At this point, let us step back and look in more detail at the assumptions that self-paced reading paradigms rely on. This discussion will serve as the basis for the experiments presented in section 8.3.

8.2.3.1 Structure Building and Processing
First, let us consider how online sentence processing corresponds to structure building in syntax. The predictions laid out above assume that linguistic structure can be built in real time from left-to-right. This is enforced

rather straightforwardly by the self-paced reading paradigm: participants encounter material on the left before they reach material on the right; hence, processing of linguistic material proceeds similarly from left-to-right (Phillips 1996).

Next, consider when the parser begins to build a parse for the material it encounters. A consensus in the literature is that the parser does not wait until a full sentence has been uttered in order to begin imposing a structure on it. Instead, structure is built "online," in tandem with reading or hearing the sentence. The literature offers two approaches to this process: *serial processing*, where the parser pursues just one parse of a sentence at a time (e.g., Ford, Bresnan, and Kaplan 1982; Frazier and Rayner 1982; Pritchett 1992), and *parallel processing*, where the parser pursues multiple analyses at once (e.g., MacDonald, Perlmutter, and Seidenberg 1994; Tanenhaus and Trueswell 1995). A third, intermediate way of viewing processing is to assume a *serial parser*, which assumes one particular parse of the sentence at a time, but evaluates multiple potential parses at each step of the derivation before converging on a single one. Here, I will be using rhetoric that assumes a serial parse, but the conclusions I draw are compatible with parallel models as well. The important assumption—a standard and well-motivated one—is that the parse is built simultaneously with reading or hearing the sentence, not after it has been completed.

Although processing happens from left to right and is very fast, it may not be instantaneous or strictly incremental in the sense that each new word is fully processed and integrated before the next word is processed. In fact, effects in the self-paced reading paradigm often show up not on the word expected to trigger an effect, but downstream from that word. The more costly the expected computation, the longer it takes for the effect to show up. For this reason, it is advisable to employ precautionary measures that make it possible to isolate the hypothesized effects of specific triggers in a sentence. First, possible triggers for slowdown—for example, suspected triggers of covert movement—are separated from one another by additional lexical material. In the HKV (2012) paradigm in (10), two factors are varied: the quantifier heading the relative clause (*the* vs. *every*) and the ellipsis marker at the right edge of that clause (*verb* vs. *did* vs. *was*). These two factors are separated by six words, to ensure that effects from the earlier trigger do not interfere with those form the later trigger.[6] Second, a "continuation" is used following the second trigger, to allow for a spillover region where effects of this trigger might show up, if they are not instantaneous. These can sometimes make for a long

and perhaps cumbersome sentence, but this complication is an inherent component of all Self-paced reading experiments, and experimenters work to ensure
that while long, the sentences are as easy to process as possible.

8.2.3.2   Covert Movement and Self-Paced Reading

With this in mind, consider how movement is integrated into an online parse
of a sentence. Overt movements (to the left) constitute *filler-gap dependencies,* which have a well-known processing signature: the parser encounters a
linguistic element in a position other than its θ-position; this element must
be stored in memory until its gap position is found, so that it can be integrated into the structure there. There is a rich literature surrounding the
mechanisms that are implicated in processing such filler-gap dependencies.
For example, it is known that the difficulty of processing these dependencies increases with distance (Gibson 1998), interference effects (Van Dyke
and McElree 2006; Gordon, Hendrick, and Johnson 2004), and processing
load imposed by other referential entities along the filler-gap path (Warren and
Gibson 2002).

Much less is known about the effects of covert movement operations on
real-time sentence processing. To begin with, I need to make explicit two
assumptions that will play a role in the reasoning below. First, I assume,
following Frazier and Fodor 1978 and much subsequent work, that processing is not just incremental from left to right but also biased toward simplicity
along the lines of the Minimal Attachment Principle, (13) (see also, e.g., Bever
1970; Frazier 1982; Phillips 2003). Second, I assume that, all else being equal,
a parse without covert movement is simpler than a parse with covert movement, and that a parse with local (short) covert movement is simpler than a
parse with nonlocal (long) covert movement (e.g., Anderson 2004; Fox 1995,
2000; Frazier 1999; Tunstall 1998).

(13) *Minimal Attachment Principle*
     Attach each new item into the current phrase marker, postulating only as
     many syntactic phrase nodes as the grammar requires.

Given these assumptions, we expect the parser not to postulate covert movement in the parse of a sentence until the point at which it determines that such
movement is necessary. Therefore, we expect the parser to assume no covert
movement upon encountering a definite object DP, since definite descriptions
are able to semantically merge with a verb in situ. This step in the parse is
illustrated in (14).[7]

(14) *Integrating a definite object into the parse in online processing*

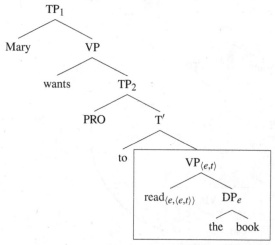

Conversely, we expect movement to be assumed as soon as a quantificational object is encountered. Following the principles laid out above, we expect this movement to be as short as possible, to avoid assuming more structure than necessary. This step in the parse is illustrated in (15). The quantificational object cannot be integrated into the structure as the sister of the verb, because of a type mismatch. Instead, it is integrated into the first position at which it is interpretable—here, immediately above TP_2.[8] As in chapter 7, I illustrate QR as movement to the right in these trees, although nothing hinges on this assumption.

(15) *Integrating a quantificational object into the parse in online processing*

a.

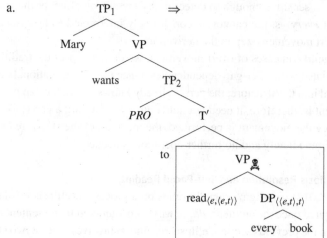

b.

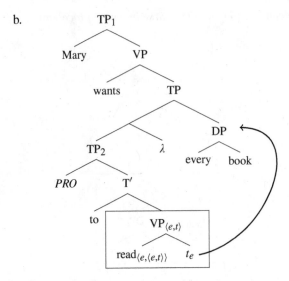

Since going from the original parse in (15a) to the alternative one in (15b) amounts to a *reanalysis* triggered by the quantificational DP *every book*, one might expect to find online consequences of this move to a less preferred parse. Alternatively, a slowdown might be attributed simply to the presence of the quantifier in the structure: since quantifiers are less frequent in text and speech than definite articles, a slowdown in RTs might reflect low-level surprisal due to lexical infrequency. Moreover, it is worth pointing out that observing no slowdown after a quantificational object does not mean that reanalysis as described in (15) did not take place. It could simply be that this sort of reanalysis is performed by the parser with sufficient automaticity that self-paced reading is not sensitive enough to detect it. As a result, an effect or the lack of an effect of *every* vs. *the* cannot be conclusively interpreted to be associated with a covert movement step in the derivation.

Finally, unlike in cases of overt movement, we do not expect the traditional costs associated with filler-gap dependencies. Once the quantificational object is integrated into the structure, the parser already knows where the gap position of movement is; therefore, it need not hold onto the filler until a gap is located. That is, once the movement is performed, the meaning of the structure can be computed immediately and no further operation is needed.

8.2.3.3 Ellipsis Resolution and Self-Paced Reading

The HKV (2012) paradigm crucially relies on a process of ellipsis resolution that is triggered once the auxiliary *did* or *was* is encountered in the sentence. As discussed in the previous section, ellipsis resolution involves at least two steps:

(i) identifying an appropriate antecedent for the ellipsis, and (ii) filling the antecedent into the gap and computing the resulting meaning of the sentence. In the case of ACD, an additional step is necessary: an appropriate antecedent must first be constructed, before steps (i) and (ii) can proceed. In the HKV (2012) paradigm, this involves covert movement of the object to a position above the verb heading the antecedent VP.

The movement step involved in this process may proceed in more than one way. The parser may always assume movement above the most local VP, as a first step. It then attempts to use this VP as an antecedent. If the resulting meaning is convergent, the parse may continue. Otherwise, the parser must assume additional movement, and it will attempt to use the next higher VP as the antecedent for ellipsis. Thus, in the case of *small ellipsis*, the first assumption about movement is sufficient, but in the case of *large ellipsis*, a second movement step must be assumed in order to form an appropriate antecedent for the ellipsis. Alternatively, we can assume that the parser is able to immediately target the correct antecedent in both the *small* and *large ellipsis* conditions. In this case too, the large ellipsis has a richer content than the small ellipsis, and therefore integrating the former into the structure and computing the resulting meaning of the sentence may be more costly.[9]

Under either formulation, we might expect to find slower RTs with larger ellipsis than with smaller ellipsis. As we will see, such an effect is indeed present in all of the experiments reported here. Thus, a main effect of ellipsis size alone will not be taken as an indication of movement. Instead, the crucial question will be whether an earlier trigger for movement facilitates ACD resolution downstream—the RT signature of facilitation being an interaction. This is expected under a movement analysis of ACD, but is unexpected if ACD resolution does not involve movement.

8.2.3.4   The Timing of Effects in Self-Paced Reading Paradigms

Finally, we can now ask when we might expect to detect an effect of covert movement in a self-paced reading paradigm. One obvious prediction is that we should not detect an effect *before* a trigger is encountered. However, it is common to find an effect not *on* the trigger word itself, but in the spillover region *following* that word (e.g., Clifton, Frazier, and Deevy 1999; Kazanina and Phillips 2000; Polinsky et al. 2012; Polinsky and Potsdam 2014; Wagers and Phillips 2009; Xiang et al. 2011). The more costly the computation associated with the trigger, the further downstream an effect may occur.

In the case of the HKV (2012) paradigm, the crucial region of interest starts with the later trigger for movement: the auxiliary verbs *did* and *was*, which signal the presence of antecedent containment in the structure. More accurately, the earliest point at which the parser has conclusive evidence for the presence of an ACD site is arguably the word following the auxiliary verb and not the auxiliary itself: at this point in the sentence, readers encounter a conjunction or disjunction that can only be attached at the clausal level, indicating that the previous clause contained ellipsis. For ease of exposition, however, I will assume in what follows that the trigger is the auxiliary verb itself and start counting words in the spillover region from there on.

The question, then, is when we should expect to detect effects of covert movement, as revealed by ease of processing an ACD site. As shown above, the HKV (2012) effects appear not on the auxiliary verb itself, but two words after the verb/auxiliary. We will see that all five experiments presented in this chapter also exhibit an effect in this same region: effects consistently show up two and three words after the auxiliary verb.

In this context, it is again important to recall an inherent limitation of the self-paced reading paradigm: it does not allow us to predict the precise location of an effect a priori, as long as the effect happens inside the spillover region. To interpret the effects of experiments based on the HKV (2012) paradigm as stemming from covert movement triggered by the need to resolve ACD, the effects must happen only after the parser encounters the triggers *did/was*, and they must happen within a region that is uniform across all conditions so that nothing else in that region could have generated them. The materials below were constructed to ensure this. Moreover, important strategies for confirming the validity of results of self-paced reading experiments are replication and consistency: crucial effects reported in the experiments below survive replication and show up in the same region across all experiments.

8.3   Experimental Evidence for Covert Scrambling

With this background established, in this section I present experimental evidence that supports the covert scrambling view of covert *wh*-movement. All of the experiments rely on the HKV (2012) paradigm, building on multiple *wh*-questions that host an ACD site, like (16).

(16) *ACD hosted by in-situ* wh-*phrase*
　　　Mary asked *which soloist* [$_{VP_1}$ wanted to [$_{VP_2}$ play *which concerto* that
　　　the brilliant protégé did Δ]].   (ambiguous)
　　　Δ = VP$_2$ "play *t*"   (*small ellipsis*)
　　　Δ = VP$_1$ "wanted to play *t*"   (*large ellipsis*)

Recall the predictions from section 8.1, summarized here for convenience:

(17) *Predictions for online sentence processing*
   a. If covert movement targets interrogative C, then all *wh*-phrases move *nonlocally* to C. As a result, we predict that both *small ellipsis* (targeting VP_2) and *large ellipsis* (targeting VP_1) should be relatively easy to process, because antecedent containment will have been undone by covert *wh*-movement before the parser reaches the gap site. When the parser encounters the gap site, all it needs to do is find an antecedent for the missing VP and nothing more.
   b. If *wh*-phrases are interpreted in situ, the parser will only reanalyze the structure and covertly move the *wh*-object to undo antecedent containment once an ellipsis site is reached, in order to construct an appropriate antecedent for the ellipsis. Hence, a high processing cost should be associated with resolution of the ACD site in both the *small* and *large ellipsis* cases (with a potentially larger cost for large ellipsis).
   c. If *wh*-phrases covertly scramble a short distance, using a movement step akin to QR, we expect the movement to target a position above VP_2 but below VP_1. As a result, we predict that *small ellipsis* (targeting VP_2) should be relatively easy to process, but *large ellipsis* (targeting VP_1) should incur a high processing cost.

The following three experiments were designed to test these predictions.

8.3.1   Experiment 1: *Every* vs. *Which*

Experiment 1 compares ACD facilitation effects in multiple *wh*-questions to ACD facilitation with quantifiers. Since HKV (2012) looked at QR with *every*, this experiment will provide a baseline: we compare the behavior of *every* to that of *wh*-in-situ and ask whether the effects are stronger (favoring the "traditional" covert movement view), weaker (favoring an in-situ view), or parallel (favoring a covert scrambling view). I elaborate on these predictions below.

8.3.1.1   Design and Materials

Experiment 1 presented participants with (embedded) *wh*-questions headed by a subject *wh*-phrase. Two factors were crossed: (a) *determiner*: whether the embedded question contained the quantificational determiner *every*, yielding a simplex *wh*-question, or a second *wh*-phrase, yielding a multiple *wh*-question; and (b) *ellipsis size*: whether the sentence contained a *small ellipsis* marked by <u>did</u>, where the antecedent of the ACD site is the embedded VP_2, or a *large ellipsis* marked by <u>was</u>, where the antecedent of the ACD site is the matrix VP_1.[10] A sample item is given in (18).[11]

(18) *Sample target item in Experiment 1*
   The conductor asked *which soloist* was [$_{VP_1}$ willing to [$_{VP_2}$ play ...
   a. **every** concerto that the brilliant protégé *did*   *(small ellipsis)*
   b. **which** concerto that the brilliant protégé *did*   *(small ellipsis)*
   c. **every** concerto that the brilliant protégé *was*   *(large ellipsis)*
   d. **which** concerto that the brilliant protégé *was*   *(large ellipsis)*
                                   ... and restructured the rehearsal accordingly.

There were 28 sentence templates modeled similarly to the sample paradigm in (18). Each sentence in a template employed either *every* or *which* as the determiner of the object DP. This DP hosted a relative clause with an ACD site marked with an auxiliary verb. The auxiliary *did* marked a *small ellipsis* corresponding to the embedded predicate, VP_2, and the auxiliary *was* marked a *large ellipsis* corresponding to the matrix predicate, VP_1. After the ellipsis site, the sentences had continuations beginning with a clausal conjunction or disjunction, which varied in length but were at least five words long, providing a spillover region for detecting possible processing difficulties associated with ACD resolution. See the appendix for a full list of the materials for all the experiments presented in this chapter.

Because the experiments were conducted online, it was not possible to control the participants' screen size. Consequently, to ensure that the region of interest was read without interruptions that might artificially affect the data, all the sentences were presented on two lines; the line break in target sentences was always placed immediately after the verbal complex (i.e., the first line of the sentence was the first line in (18), and the second line contained the text in lines a–d and the continuation following these lines).[12]

The 28 target items were counterbalanced across four lists using a Latin square design and were combined with 48 filler sentences of various types, resulting in a total of 76 sentences. Nontarget items included sentences that were similar to the target items in structure, in length, and in containing quantifiers. Of the 48 filler sentences, 18 resembled the target sentences in all respects but contained a lexical verb instead of ellipsis (*did*, *was*). Additionally, these filler sentences contained line breaks in different positions, making it impossible for participants to anticipate where a line break might occur, or whether or not there would be ellipsis in the sentence.[13] The remaining 30 filler sentences were taken from an unrelated study.

Each experimental item was followed by a *yes/no* comprehension question. The questions asked about different aspects of the sentences, including asking about material inside the relative clause and about the predicates used in the sentences, to ensure that participants were processing all parts of each sentence at a deep level. The correct answer to half of the questions was *yes* and to the other half was *no*.

8.3.1.2   Methods

Experiment 1 used the moving-window self-paced reading methodology and was hosted on Ibex Farm.[14] Participants were presented with sentences that appeared on the screen one word at a time in a moving-window display. After the final word of each sentence, the comprehension question appeared. Participants responded by pressing "1" for *yes* or "2" for *no*. No feedback was given about whether the answer to the question was correct or incorrect.

Before beginning the experiment, participants were given detailed instructions about the experiment and then read and accepted a consent statement. Participants were instructed to read the sentences at a natural rate to ensure understanding. They were also instructed to answer the comprehension questions as accurately as possible. There were three practice items before the experiment began. The experiment took approximately 30 minutes to complete.

Participants were recruited through Amazon Mechanical Turk and were paid $1.50 for their participation. Participants were asked about their native language but were told that payment was not contingent on their response. To further ensure that only native speakers of English participated in the experiments, IP addresses of participants were restricted to the United States, using Amazon Mechanical Turk's user interface. Only Turk Workers with an overall approval rate of over 95% of all their submissions were allowed to participate.

8.3.1.3   Predictions

The *every* conditions are expected to replicate the results reported by HKV (2012). That is, we expect to find a main effect of *ellipsis size*, such that *small ellipsis* is easier to process than *large ellipsis*: since *every* triggers covert movement to a position above the embedded VP$_2$ (headed by *play* in (18)) as soon as the quantifier is encountered, we expect antecedent containment to be preemptively undone in the case of *small ellipsis* (18a), leading to facilitation of ACD resolution. However, since this movement does not target a position high enough to undo antecedent containment in the case of *large ellipsis* (18c), we expect ACD resolution to be more difficult in this case: once the auxiliary <u>was</u> is reached, the parser must perform a second reanalysis, covertly moving *every* from its position above the embedded VP$_2$, where QR placed it, to a position above the higher VP$_1$ (headed by *willing* in (18)), in order to allow for ACD resolution. These two conditions thus provide a baseline contrast against which to compare the *which* conditions in (18b,d).

For the *which* conditions, the three approaches to in-situ *wh*-phrases make different predictions. Under the "traditional" covert movement approach, all *wh*-phrases must move *nonlocally* to C for interpretation. Both *small* and *large ellipsis* are predicted to be relatively easy to process because antecedent containment is undone by covert *wh*-movement before the parser reaches the ellipsis site. We thus expect an interaction, such that the *which-did* and *which-was* conditions pattern with *every-did* and exhibit facilitation effects, whereas we predict participants to exhibit increased difficulty with ACD resolution in the *every-was* condition.

Under the in-situ approach, the in-situ *wh*-phrase can be interpreted without any movement. Hence, only upon reaching the ellipsis site will the need for reanalysis be apparent. Thus, processing costs for ACD resolution are predicted to reflect both covert movement of the *wh*-object to a position above the missing VP and the retrieval of the appropriate antecedent for the elided VP; hence, they should be relatively higher for both the *small* and *large ellipsis* conditions. We thus expect to find a main effect of the object type, such that the *which* conditions are more difficult to process than the *every* conditions. This main effect may be accompanied by an interaction, such that the two *which* conditions pattern with *every-was* and are more difficult to process than *every-did*, or they may be even more difficult than the *every-was* condition.

Finally, under the covert scrambling approach, *wh*-in-situ undergoes a short scrambling step akin to QR. Hence, we predict that results for the *which* conditions in the experiments should be similar to the results for the *every* conditions. That is, we expect to find a main effect of *ellipsis size* such that the *did* conditions are easier to process than the *was* conditions, but no effect of determiner.

8.3.1.4 Results

Sixty-one native speakers of English participated in this study. The following exclusion criteria were used to filter the results of this experiment and all subsequent ones: participants who held the spacebar continuously pressed instead of reading the sentences one word at a time as instructed, participants who participated in the study more than once, participants who submitted the entire survey in less than 10 minutes, participants with an average reaction time of over 700 ms,[15] and participants with low accuracy rates in response to comprehension questions ($<$ 75% on filler trials and $<$ 75% on target trials) were excluded from the study. Twenty participants in Experiment 1 were excluded from the analysis for these reasons.[16] In addition, two target sentences were excluded from the analysis because of low accuracy ($<$ 60% across participants).

Questions across the full experiment (targets and fillers) were answered correctly 87.5% of the time across participants; questions for target items were answered correctly on 83.3% of trials. The data were trimmed as follows: RTs from the first and last words of all items, RTs faster than 90 ms or slower than 2,000 ms, and any RTs that were more than 2 standard deviations faster or slower than the average RTs for each subject (calculated per condition) were excluded from the analysis. Overall, less than 1% of the data was lost due to these criteria.[17] Figure 8.2 shows the mean Residual Reading Times (RRTs)[18] for the two regions of interest for the four target conditions. (For more detailed graphs that include error bars, visit http://hkotek.com/composing-questions.)

A linear mixed-effects model was fit to the data using *R* and the *R* package *lme4* (Bates and Sarkar 2007). The model predicted RRTs from the two factors of interest: *determiner* (*every* vs. *which*) and *ellipsis size* (*small ellipsis* marked by *did* vs. *large ellipsis* marked by *was*).[19] The model contained random intercepts and slopes for both predictors for subjects and items (Baayen 2004; Barr et al. 2013).

The results show a main effect of *determiner* at the slot at which the determiner appeared in the sentence (log likelihood tests comparing a model with and without the effect of *determiner*, $p < .05$). This result is driven by the fact that RTs in the *which* condition were slower than RTs in the *every* condition, across both ellipsis conditions.[20]

The results additionally show a main effect of *ellipsis size* two words and three words after the auxiliary verb (log likelihood tests, p's $< .05$). This result

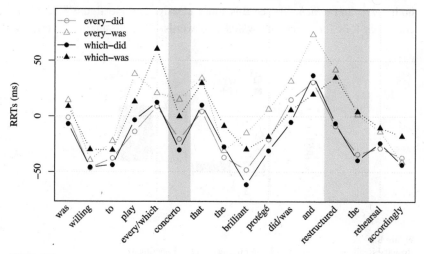

Figure 8.2
Residual Reading Times for target items in Experiment 1

Table 8.1
Results of Experiment 1

Predictor	Coefficient	Standard error	t value
Intercept	−31.591	18.851	−1.676
Determiner	3.586	16.018	0.224
Ellipsis size	39.8416	15.651	2.546
Determiner × Ellipsis size	2.665	20.628	0.129

is driven by the fact that the resolution of *small ellipsis* is faster than the resolution of *large ellipsis* for both *every* and *which*. The results of the model for the third word after the auxiliary verb are summarized in table 8.1.[21]

8.3.1.5 Discussion

There are two effects of interest in Experiment 1. First, the main effect of *determiner* in the first region of interest may be attributed to the fact that a multiple *wh*-question is more complex than a simplex *wh*-question, or to the fact that simplex *wh*-questions occur more frequently than multiple *wh*-questions. Regardless of the cause of this effect, it shows that the participants were processing the sentences at least at a depth sufficient for detecting the difference in determiner.

Second, we observe a main effect of *ellipsis size* in the second region of interest, following the auxiliary verb, such that sentences with a *small ellipsis* are read faster than sentences with a *large ellipsis*. This is the case for both *every* and *which*. To see this more clearly, observe figure 8.3, which compares RTs for *every* and *which* two words after the auxiliary verb. As

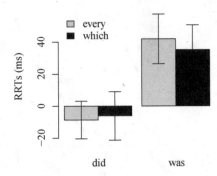

Figure 8.3
Residual Reading Times two words after the auxiliary in Experiment 1

the figure shows, the *ellipsis size* manipulation affects the two determiners equally.

This is the result predicted by the covert scrambling view of covert movement: covert *wh*-movement is a short movement that facilitates *small ellipsis*, but is insufficient to preemptively undo antecedent containment in the case of *large ellipsis*.

8.3.2 Experiment 2: *The* vs. *Every* and *The* vs. *Which*

Experiments 2a–b provide an important baseline to strengthen the results of Experiment 1. In particular, this experiment compares the behavior of the non-quantificational determiner *the* with that of *every* and of *which*, to eliminate two possible concerns regarding Experiment 1: (a) that the paradigm it uses is not sensitive enough to detect ACD resolution facilitation effects, because of the added complexity of the embedded questions in the paradigm as compared to the original HKV (2012) paradigm; and (b) that participants are not processing the sentences at a deep level.

8.3.2.1 Design

To allow for a direct comparison with Experiment 1, Experiment 2 uses the same materials and methods as Experiment 1, with minor changes to accommodate its experimental manipulation. *Determiner* was treated as a between-subjects factor: Experiment 2a compares *every* and *the*, and Experiment 2b compares *which* and *the*. The missing comparison, *which* and *every*, was the focus of Experiment 1.

(19) *Sample target item in Experiment 2a*
  The conductor asked *which soloist* was [$_{VP_1}$ willing to [$_{VP_2}$ play …
  a. **every/the** concerto that the brilliant protégé *did*   (*small ellipsis*)
  b. **every/the** concerto that the brilliant protégé *was*   (*large ellipsis*)
            … and restructured the rehearsal accordingly.

(20) *Sample target item in Experiment 2b*
  The conductor asked *which soloist* was [$_{VP_1}$ willing to [$_{VP_2}$ play …
  a. **which/the** concerto that the brilliant protégé *did*   (*small ellipsis*)
  b. **which/the** concerto that the brilliant protégé *was*   (*large ellipsis*)
            … and restructured the rehearsal accordingly.

The same 48 filler items from Experiment 1 were used. The comprehension questions to some items were minimally changed to accommodate the change of determiners in the sentences.

8.3.2.2 Predictions

We expect Experiment 2a to replicate HKV's (2012) results. In particular, we expect to see an effect of *ellipsis size*, such that *small ellipsis* is easier to process than *large ellipsis* for both *the* and *every*. In addition, we expect to find a difference in the processing of ACD in sentences with a relative clause headed by *every* and sentences with a relative clause headed by *the*, such that the processing of ACD in sentences with *every* is easier than processing of ACD in sentences with *the*. This is because we assume QR of *every* but no movement of *the* in the target sentences.

Furthermore, we expect to find the same behavior pattern with *which* in Experiment 2b: if *which*, like *every*, undergoes a short movement step targeting a position above the lower VP$_2$, we expect to find that *which*, like *every*, facilitates the resolution of *small* ellipsis with *did*, but not of *large* ellipsis with *was*, for the same reasons as described above for *every*. We expect *the* not to facilitate ACD resolution of any size; hence, we predict sentences with *the* to be more difficult to process than sentences with *which*.

8.3.2.3 Results

One hundred sixty-five native speakers of English participated in this study: 84 participated in Experiment 2a and 81 participated in Experiment 2b. Of these, 21 participants were excluded from the analysis of Experiment 2a and 24 participants were excluded from the analysis of Experiment 2b, using the same exclusion criteria specified in Experiment 1. Three target sentences and one filler sentence were excluded from the analysis of Experiment 2a and three target sentences and two filler sentences were excluded from the analysis of Experiment 2b because of low accuracy (< 60% across all participants).

Questions across the full experiment (targets and fillers) were answered correctly 86.7% of the time in Experiment 2a and 85.8% of the time in Experiment 2b; questions for target items were answered correctly on 84.7% of trials in Experiment 2a and on 83.8% of trials in Experiment 2b. The data were trimmed using the same criteria described for Experiment 1. Overall, less than 1% of the data was excluded from the analysis. Figure 8.4 shows the mean RRTs for the region of interest for the four target conditions in Experiment 2a, comparing the processing of sentences with *the* and *every*.

A linear mixed-effects model with random intercepts and slopes for *ellipsis size* for subjects and items was fit to the data.[22] The model predicted RRTs from the two factors of interest: *determiner* (*every* vs. *the*) and *ellipsis size* (*small ellipsis* marked by *did* vs. *large ellipsis* marked by *was*). The results show a main effect of *ellipsis size* two and three words after the auxiliary verb

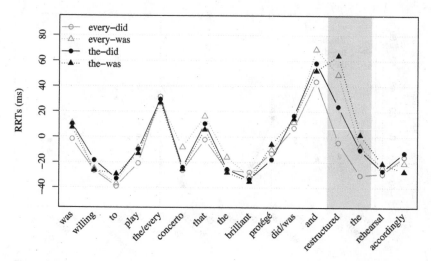

Figure 8.4
Residual Reading Times for target items in Experiment 2a

Table 8.2
Results of Experiment 2a

Predictor	Coefficient	Standard error	*t* value
Intercept	3.304	20.959	0.158
Determiner	21.780	16.517	1.319
Ellipsis size	39.008	19.510	1.999
Determiner × Ellipsis size	12.207	23.441	0.521

and a main effect of *determiner* two words after the auxiliary verb (log likelihood tests, *p*'s < .05). These results are driven by the fact that the resolution of
small ellipsis is faster than the resolution of *large ellipsis* for both determiners,
and furthermore that the resolution of ACD in the *every* conditions is faster
than in the *the* conditions. The results of the model for the second word after
the auxiliary verb are summarized in table 8.2.

Next, we examine the results of Experiment 2b, comparing the determiners
the and *which*. Figure 8.5 shows the mean RRTs for the regions of interest for
the four target conditions.

A linear mixed-effects model with random intercepts and slopes for *ellipsis
size* for subjects and items was fit to the data. The model predicted RRTs from
the two factors of interest: *determiner* (*which* vs. *the*) and *ellipsis size* (*small*

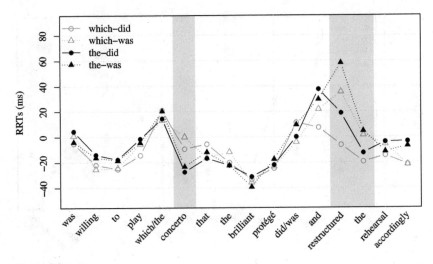

Figure 8.5
Residual Reading Times for target items in Experiment 2b

Table 8.3
Results of Experiment 2b

Predictor	Coefficient	Standard error	*t* value
Intercept	16.572	15.716	1.054
Determiner	22.748	14.213	1.600
Ellipsis size	42.714	15.949	2.678
Determiner × *Ellipsis size*	5.117	20.483	0.250

ellipsis vs. *large ellipsis*). The results show a main effect of *ellipsis size* two and three words after the auxiliary verb and a main effect of *determiner* two words after the auxiliary verb (log likelihood tests, *p*'s < .05). These results are driven by the fact that the resolution of *small ellipsis* is faster than the resolution of *large ellipsis* for both determiners, and furthermore that the resolution of ACD in the *which* conditions is faster than in the *the* conditions. The results of the model for the second word after the auxiliary verb are summarized in table 8.3.

8.3.2.4 Discussion

The results of Experiments 2a–b confirm that the HKV (2012) paradigm extends to the context of an embedded question. In particular, we find—in addition to the main effect of *ellipsis size*—a main effect of *determiner*, such that sentences with *every* are processed faster than sentences with *the*, and

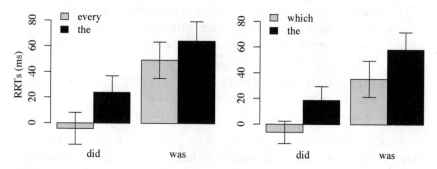

Figure 8.6
Residual Reading Times two words after the auxiliary in Experiments 2a (left) and 2b (right)

sentences with *which* are similarly processed faster than sentences with *the*. That is, *every* and *which* pattern together and facilitate ACD resolution more than parallel sentences with *the*. To see this more clearly, consider figure 8.6, which compares the RTs of *the*, *every*, and *which* two words after the auxiliary verb site.

For the results of Experiment 2a, I adopt HKV's (2012) explanation and assume that these results are the way they are because the parser must assume covert movement with *every* as soon as it encounters the quantifier, but assumes no such covert movement with *the*.[23] As a result, covert movement is always assumed to take place at the point of ACD resolution in the case of *the* but not in the case of *every*: when a *small ellipsis* is encountered, the parser need not assume any additional covert movement, since sufficient movement has taken place earlier in the parse. To explain the fact that non-local ACD resolution is less difficult with *every* than with *the*, I hypothesize that the second QR step to a position above the matrix VP_1 is easier in the case of *every*, perhaps because the object must move a shorter distance than in the case of *the*.

The results of Experiment 2b again show that *which* patterns with *every*. These results can be understood if we assume that the in-situ *wh*-phrases in the target items of Experiment 2b undergo a covert movement step similar in extent to that of *every*; that is, movement appears to target the lower VP_2, and not the higher VP_1 or interrogative C.

8.3.3   Experiment 3: *Every* vs. *Which* with Interveners

Experiment 3 tests a further prediction of the covert *wh*-scrambling proposal. Recall that we predicted a short covert scrambling step of a (phonologically) in-situ *wh*-phrase similar to the overt scrambling step observed in German, as in (21a–b), repeated from (26a–b) of chapter 7.

(21) *Obligatory overt short* wh-*scrambling in German (Hallman 1997:45)*

    a. *Wer* hat denn (das Buch) gestern   (das Buch) gelesen?

       who has DENN (the book) yesterday (the book) read

       'Who read the book yesterday?'

    b. *Wer* hat denn *(was)* gestern   (**was*) gelesen?

       who has DENN (what) yesterday (what) read

       'Who read what yesterday?'

We also predict that the presence of an intervener in the question can drive additional movement beyond this initial target position of movement. Again, following the overt behavior exhibited by German questions as in (22), repeated from (23) of chapter 7, we expect covert scrambling to target the first position above the intervener where the *wh* can be integrated into the structure. I assume that this is the first node with (extensional) propositional type in the structure.

(22) *German: Intervention above* wh-*in-situ is avoided by scrambling (Beck 1996a:6)*

    a. * *Wer* hat **niemanden** $\boxed{wo}$ angetroffen?

       who has no.one   where met

    b. *Wer* hat $\boxed{wo}$ **niemanden** ___ angetroffen?

       who has where no.one   met

       'Who didn't meet anybody where?'

This prediction will be the focus of Experiments 3a–b, and we will see that it is indeed borne out.

8.3.3.1 Design

Experiment 3 is an extension of Experiment 1, where an intervener—specifically, the focus-sensitive adverb *also*[24]—is added to the questions.[25] Three factors are crossed: (a) *determiner* (*every* vs. *which* as the head of the object relative clause hosting the ACD site); (b) *ellipsis size* (*small ellipsis* marked by *did* vs. *large ellipsis* marked by *was*); and (c) *position of also* (low *also* occurring above the embedded VP_2 vs. high *also* occurring above the matrix VP_1). To simplify the design and the analysis of the results, Experiment 3 is divided into two subexperiments, each using just one determiner, *every* or *which*. Sample items for Experiments 3a–b are given in (23)–(24).

(23) *Sample target item in Experiment 3a* (every)[26]

    The conductor asked *which soloist* was ...

    a. [$_{VP_1}$ **also** willing to [$_{VP_2}$ play every concerto that the brilliant protégé
       <u>did</u>   *(small ellipsis)*

    b. [$_{VP_1}$ willing to [$_{VP_2}$ **also** play every concerto that the brilliant protégé
       <u>did</u>   *(small ellipsis)*

    c. [$_{VP_1}$ **also** willing to [$_{VP_2}$ play every concerto that the brilliant protégé
       <u>was</u>   *(large ellipsis)*

    d. [$_{VP_1}$ willing to [$_{VP_2}$ **also** play every concerto that the brilliant protégé
       <u>was</u>   *(large ellipsis)*

               ... and restructured the rehearsal accordingly.

(24) *Sample target item in Experiment 3b (*which*)*

    The conductor asked *which soloist* was ...

    a. [$_{VP_1}$ **also** willing to [$_{VP_2}$ play which concerto that the brilliant protégé
       <u>did</u>   *(small ellipsis)*

    b. [$_{VP_1}$ willing to [$_{VP_2}$ **also** play which concerto that the brilliant protégé
       <u>did</u>   *(small ellipsis)*

    c. [$_{VP_1}$ **also** willing to [$_{VP_2}$ play which concerto that the brilliant protégé
       <u>was</u>   *(large ellipsis)*

    d. [$_{VP_1}$ willing to [$_{VP_2}$ **also** play which concerto that the brilliant protégé
       <u>was</u>   *(large ellipsis)*

               ... and restructured the rehearsal accordingly.

Experiment 3 contained the same 48 filler items from Experiment 1. The target items from Experiment 1 were minimally changed to add the intervener *also* in the appropriate places. No changes were made to the comprehension questions.

8.3.3.2 Predictions

We expect interveners to interact with *wh*-phrases and force covert scrambling of the in-situ *wh*-phrase to a position above the intervener. Following our assumptions about the parser, we expect it to posit the shortest movement step possible. Hence, in the *low also* condition we expect *wh*-scrambling to target a position above *also* but below VP_1, while in the *high also* condition we expect long-distance movement above *also* and thus above VP_1.

Crucially for this experiment, we do not expect interveners to interact with *every*, since the literature provides no evidence that conventional quantifiers interact with focus interveners. Hence, we expect *every* to undergo a small QR step and not move any further unless and until the need for long-distance movement becomes apparent, once the parser reaches an ACD site marked by <u>was</u>.

As a consequence, we expect Experiment 3a to replicate the results of Experiment 1, since interveners should not affect the parsing of sentences with *every*. That is, we expect to find a main effect of *ellipsis size* and, crucially, no effect of *also*. Different predictions are made in the case of Experiment 3b. Here, we expect the position of *also* to affect the extent of covert *wh*-movement in the question, regardless of the size of ACD.

In the *low also* conditions (24b,d), we expect the results to resemble those of Experiment 1 and of Experiment 3a. The position of *also* above the embedded VP_2 will force scrambling to a position above *also* in the embedded VP_2 but below the matrix VP_1. This position is high enough to preemptively undo antecedent containment in the case of *small ellipsis*, (24b) but not in the case of *large ellipsis*, (24d). Consequently, we expect ACD resolution to be facilitated in the case of *small ellipsis* but not in the case of *large ellipsis*.

In the *high also* conditions (24a,c), the position of *also* is above the matrix VP_1. As always, the parser must assume covert movement as soon as it encounters *which*. Unlike in the case of *low also*, here the movement must be nonlocal and target a position above the matrix VP_1. This position is high enough to preemptively undo antecedent containment in the case of both *small ellipsis*, (24a) and *large ellipsis*, (24c). As a result, when the parser reaches the gap site, no reanalysis is necessary in order to construct an appropriate antecedent for the ellipsis. We thus expect ACD resolution to be facilitated in both the *small* and *large ellipsis* conditions.

8.3.3.3 Results

Two hundred forty-three native speakers of English participated in this study: 123 participated in Experiment 3a and 120 participated in Experiment 3b. These numbers represent the aggregate results of performing each experiment twice: the original experiment and a replication undertaken to ensure that the results reported here are robust. Of these, 27 participants were excluded from the analysis of Experiment 3a and 25 participants were excluded from the analysis of Experiment 3b, using the same exclusion criteria specified for Experiment 1. Two target sentences and three filler sentences were excluded from the analysis of both experiments because of low accuracy ($< 60\%$ across all participants).

Questions across the full experiment (targets and fillers) were answered correctly 84.9% of the time across participants in Experiment 3a and 86% of the time across participants in Experiment 3b; questions for target items were answered correctly on 82.42% of trials in Experiment 3a and on 82.47% of trials in Experiment 3b. The data were trimmed as described for Experiment 1 above. Overall, less than 1% of the data was excluded. Below, I present

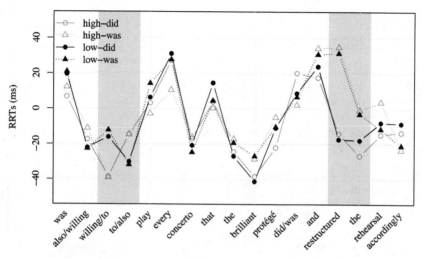

Figure 8.7
Residual Reading Times for target items in Experiment 3a

first the results of Experiment 3a and then those of Experiment 3b. Figure 8.7 shows the mean RRTs for the region of interest for the four target conditions in Experiment 3a.

A linear mixed-effects model with random intercepts and slopes for the effect of *ellipsis size* and the effect of *also* (for subjects only) was fit to the data[27]. The model predicted RRTs from the two factors of interest: *position of also* (*low*, above the embedded verb, vs. *high*, above the matrix verb) and *ellipsis size* (*small* vs. *large*). The results show a main effect of *also* at the third and fourth words in the region of interest (where *also* occurs in the sentence). The results additionally show a main effect of *ellipsis size* two and three words after the auxiliary verb (log likelihood tests, p's $< .05$). These results are driven by the fact that the resolution of *small ellipsis* is faster than that of *large ellipsis* for both *also* conditions. The results of the model for the third word after the auxiliary verb are summarized in table 8.4.

Next, we examine the results of Experiment 3b. Recall that in this experiment, the determiner heading the object relative clause in all four target conditions was *which*. Figure 8.8 shows the mean RRTs for the region of interest for the four target conditions.

A linear mixed-effects model with random slopes and intercepts for subjects and items was fit to the data. The model predicted RRTs from the two factors of interest: *position of also* (*low* vs. *high*) and *ellipsis size* (*small* vs. *large*). The results show a main effect of *also* at the third and fourth words in the

Table 8.4
Results of Experiment 3a

Predictor	Coefficient	Standard error	*t* value
Intercept	−28.342	11.909	−2.380
Position of also	7.449	8.282	0.900
Ellipsis size	25.073	10.653	2.354
Position of also × *Ellipsis size*	−14.070	13.034	−1.079

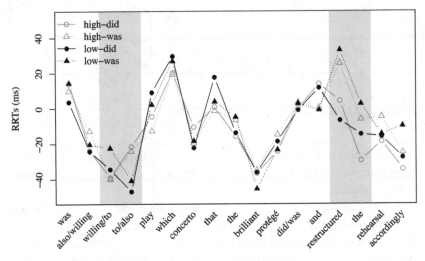

Figure 8.8
Residual Reading Times for target items in Experiment 3b

region of interest (where *also* occurs in the sentence). The results additionally show a main effect of *ellipsis size* two and three words after the auxiliary verb and a main effect of *also* three words after the auxiliary (log likelihood tests, *p*'s < .05).[28] The main effect of *ellipsis size* reflects the fact that the resolution of *small ellipsis* is faster than the resolution of *large ellipsis* for both *also* conditions, while the main effect of *also* arises because the processing of the *high also* conditions is overall faster than the processing of the *low also* conditions. The results of the model for the third word after the auxiliary verb are summarized in table 8.5.

Finally, an analysis was conducted pooling data from the *high also* condition across Experiments 3a–b. A linear mixed-effects model predicting RRTs from the two factors of interest, *determiner* (*every* vs. *which*) and *ellipsis size* (*small* vs. *large*) was fit to the data. The model included random slopes and intercepts

Table 8.5
Results of Experiment 1

Predictor	Coefficient	Standard error	*t* value
Intercept	−29.634	9.056	−3.272
Position of also	17.017	7.584	2.244
Ellipsis size	21.984	9.215	2.386
Position of also × *Ellipsis size*	−6.791	11.810	−0.575

Table 8.6
Results of comparison of the *high also* conditions in Experiments 3a–b

Predictor	Coefficient	Standard error	*t* value
Intercept	−25.08	14.32	−1.751
Determiner	34.87	11.12	1.810
Ellipsis size	52.06	19.27	4.680
Determiner × Ellipsis size	−30.06	15.20	−1.978

for the factors of interest. The results show a main effect of *ellipsis size* two and three words after the auxiliary site, such that *small ellipsis* was processed faster than *large ellipsis* (log likelihood tests, *p*'s < .05). In addition, the results show a *determiner × ellipsis size* interaction two words after the auxiliary verb, driven by the fact that the difference between the *every* conditions is greater than the difference between the *which* conditions across the two *ellipsis size* conditions. The results of the model for the second word after the auxiliary verb are summarized in table 8.6.[29]

8.3.3.4 Discussion

Several effects can be observed in both Experiment 3a and Experiment 3b. First, participants react similarly to reading the word *also* itself. We can take this to indicate that participants were paying attention to this experimental manipulation. Additionally, there is a main effect of *ellipsis size* in both experiments, occurring on the second and third words after the ellipsis site. This effect is more pronounced on the second word following the auxiliary verb (see figure 8.9). This is again consistent with the effects observed in Experiments 1 and 2a–b.

In both Experiment 3a and Experiment 3b, we observe the main effect of *ellipsis size* not only on the second word following the auxiliary verb but also on the third word. More importantly, we find that on this word, the presence and position of *also* affects the resolution of ACD differently in the

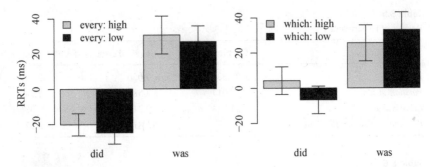

Figure 8.9
Residual Reading Times two words after the auxiliary in Experiments 3a (*every*, left) and 3b (*which*, right)

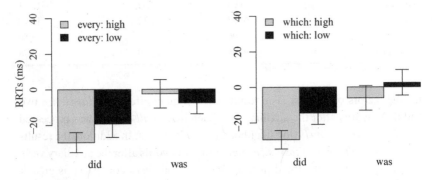

Figure 8.10
Residual Reading Times three words after the auxiliary in Experiments 3a (*every*, left) and 3b (*which*, right)

two experiments. Specifically, *also* does not have an effect in Experiment 3a (*every*), but in Experiment 3b (*which*), we find a main effect of *also* in addition to the main effect of *ellipsis size*. To see this more clearly, consider figure 8.10.

The main effect of *also* in Experiment 3b reflects a facilitation effect of non-local ACD resolution with *high also*, such that it is processed at a speed similar to that of the *local* ACD with *low also* (i.e., of the <u>*did*</u>–*low also* condition). This is consistent with the proposed covert scrambling analysis of English *wh*-in-situ: if interpretability requirements force long-distance covert scrambling, we expect ACD to be facilitated in the entire domain of movement. In Experiment 3b, *high also* forces scrambling above VP$_1$ and, as a result, antecedent containment is preemptively undone not only in the case of small ellipsis but also in the case of large ellipsis.

As discussed above, comparison of the *high also* conditions across the two experiments yields an interaction, attributable to the fact that the difference between the *small* and *large ellipsis* conditions with *every* is greater than the difference between the two conditions with *which*. Again, this is predicted if *high also* facilitates the resolution of ellipsis in both the *small* and *large ellipsis* conditions with *which*, but if *every* facilitates it only in the *small ellipsis* condition.

8.3.4 An Alternative Account

Before concluding this chapter, I would like to address an alternative interpretation of the experimental results presented above. This interpretation accepts the finding that *wh*-in-situ is in fact not interpreted in situ at LF, but it attempts to reconcile the data with the traditional covert movement view, under which covert *wh*-movement necessarily targets interrogative C.[30]

Let us return to the sample item (18) from Experiment 1, repeated here for convenience. Recall that this experiment compared the behavior of *every* with that of *which* with regard to facilitation of ACD resolution, and found that the two items facilitate ACD resolution to the same extent.

(25) *Sample target item in Experiment 1*
   The conductor asked *which soloist* was [$_{VP_1}$ willing to [$_{VP_2}$ play ...
   a. **every** concerto that the brilliant protégé *did*   *(small ellipsis)*
   b. **which** concerto that the brilliant protégé *did*   *(small ellipsis)*
   c. **every** concerto that the brilliant protégé *was*   *(large ellipsis)*
   d. **which** concerto that the brilliant protégé *was*   *(large ellipsis)*
   ... and restructured the rehearsal accordingly.

Our starting point here was the assumption that *every* undergoes a short QR movement step to a position above the lower VP$_2$—here, *play*—in order to resolve a type mismatch as soon as the parser encounters it. This assumption was based on the results reported by HKV (2012), surveyed in section 8.2.2. Specifically, HKV (2012) showed that such movement indeed takes place in their items. However, the items used in the present study differ from HKV's (2012) in that they are embedded inside a question.

Questions with quantifiers are ambiguous between two readings.

(26) *The two readings of a question with a quantifier*
   Which book did *every boy* read?
   a. Which book is such that all the boys read it?   *(which > ∀)*
   b. For each boy, which book did he read?   *(∀ > which)*

The reading in (26a) involves narrow scope for *every* with respect to *which* and is consistent with the assumption that *every* undergoes only a short movement step. On the other hand, the reading in (26b) involves wide scope for *every* with respect to *which* and would require *every* to take scope above the question. There are several theories of how this scope is obtained, but it is at least possible that it is obtained through long-distance covert movement of *every* (cf. Chierchia 1993; Krifka 2006; Nicolae 2013).

The HKV (2012) methodology does not allow us to test which interpretation the experimental participants accessed. As a result, we must entertain the idea that at least some speakers accessed this reading for some of the items. This is made more plausible by the fact that multiple *wh*-questions themselves admit a similar ambiguity, between a single-pair and a pair-list reading. At least the pair-list reading has been argued to require covert movement for its interpretation (see chapter 3); and this is perhaps true for the single-pair reading as well.

(27) *The two readings of a multiple* wh-*question*
      Which book did *which* student read?
      a. Which book and which student are such that the student read the book?
                                                                                      (single-pair)
      b. For each book, which student read it?   (pair-list)

If the items in the present experiments were read with a pair-list reading, we might expect *every* to undergo long-distance movement to a position above the question—hence above both the embedded VP_2 and the higher VP_1. Consequently, ACD should be preemptively undone in both the *small* and the *large ellipsis* conditions, and ACD resolution should be facilitated when the parser encounters both <u>did</u> and <u>was</u>. The fact that *every* patterns with *which*, then, teaches us not that *every* and *which* both underwent a short QR movement step just above VP_2, but that they both underwent long-distance movement, targeting a position higher than VP_1. The difference between the *small* and the *large ellipsis* could be attributed to the fact that the latter is richer and therefore may be more costly to integrate into the structure than a simpler antecedent, and not to any additional covert movement in the structure.

The results of Experiment 2 could be consistent with this view of interrogative syntax: we observe that sentences with *every* and *which* are both processed faster than corresponding sentences with *the*, and this could be explained either under a theory where both have undergone a short movement step (as I proposed above) or under the theory entertained here, that they both underwent a long-distance covert movement step.

However, this alternative proposal is inconsistent with the results of Experiment 3. If in-situ *wh*-phrases always covertly move to C, *also* should not be able to affect *which*, since sufficient movement to avoid an intervention effect would be performed regardless of the presence and position of *also*.

To maintain the idea that *wh*-movement always targets C in view of the results of Experiment 3, we could propose that *also* interacts with *every* so as to slow down the processing of the items in Experiment 3a. This could come about if *also* marks the possible scope of *every*: *low also* would force a short QR step, and *high also* would be compatible with a longer movement step. Crucially, we would have to assume that such a constraint does not affect the movement of *which*. However, if this were the case, we would expect an interaction in Experiment 3a, such that the *low also–was* condition suffers, as it would be the only condition in that experiment where movement of *every* is unable to preemptively undo antecedent containment. This is not the result observed in Experiment 3a: instead, we observe a main effect of *ellipsis size* but no interaction. This result was replicated twice, as described in section 8.3.3, to ensure its validity.[31]

To summarize, the idea that questions with *every* are assigned a pair-list reading, consistent with long-distance movement of the quantifier, may be true in some cases; but a proposal that attempts to explain the experimental data in this chapter solely on the basis of pair-list LFs in which *every* and *which* take nonlocal scope is not consistent with the results of Experiment 3. Consequently, I propose to adopt the *covert scrambling* approach to *wh*-in-situ, allowing *wh*-in-situ to be interpreted not only at C but also at other positions in the structure.

8.4   A Hamblin Semantics with Covert Scrambling

The experiments presented here lend further support to the idea that (phonologically) in-situ *wh*-phrases in Superiority-obeying English questions undergo a short covert scrambling step immediately upon being integrated into the structure, parallel to the overt scrambling step observed in German. Further movement can then be forced by interpretability considerations, such as the need to avoid intervention effects or to construct an appropriate antecedent for ellipsis.

Following Beck's (2006) influential proposal, *wh*-phrases are sensitive to intervention effects only if they are interpreted via focus-alternatives computation, not if they undergo (covert) movement to a position above the intervener, (28). The need to avoid intervention effects is thus the driving force behind the extended scrambling observed in Experiment 3: *wh* is unable to remain below the intervener and be interpreted using Rooth-Hamblin alternatives; instead, it can only project alternatives from a position above the intervener.

(28) *Only* wh*s interpreted via focus alternatives are subject to intervention*

    a. LF: [$_{CP}$ C ... *wh* **intervener** ... *t* ...]

    b. LF: *[$_{CP}$ C ... **intervener** ... *wh* ...]

Finally, I introduce one additional extension to the proposal: the notion that *wh*-phrases may not be simple Hamblin sets of individuals, as suggested above, but instead are *interrogative quantifiers* of some kind. Such proposals have been made for a variety of languages (see Karttunen 1977; Baker 1970; Dornisch 2000 for Polish; Huang 1995; Kim 1991 for Korean; Rullmann and Beck 1998). This proposal is suggestive, given the parallels between *every* and *which* observed in Experiments 1–2. However, such a proposal is not able to explain the interaction with intervention effects observed for *wh*-phrases in Experiment 3b, nor can it explain why *every* is not similarly sensitive to intervention effects, as observed in Experiment 3a and independently known in the literature.[32]

A way to integrate both sets of results from this book, then, would be to suggest that *wh*-expressions have as their interpretation *a set of alternative quantificational interpretations* (i.e., a set of alternative ⟨*et, t*⟩ denotations). This could be implemented by replacing, for example, the set of individuals {Abby, Betty, ... } as the denotation of *who* with the type-lifted denotation in (29) (Partee 1986; Partee and Rooth 1983; Rooth and Partee 1982).

(29) Wh-*expressions as sets of type-lifted individual alternatives*

    {λP . P(Abby), λP . P(Betty), ... }

An even more ambitious proposal would be to allow *wh*-expressions to denote sets of existential quantifiers, modeled after Karttunen-style denotations for *wh*-words.[33]

(30) Wh-*expressions as sets of existential alternatives*

    {λP . $\exists x$(P(x) & x = Abby), λP . $\exists x$(P(x) & x = Betty), ... }

This provides an automatic explanation for the short movement of object *wh*-expressions observed in chapters 7 and 8, although at this point this solution is merely a technical one, and one that will perhaps only be allowed if the simpler set-of-individuals interpretation is unavailable. I leave for future work a more detailed argument in favor of this more complex quantificational set denotation over the more traditional one, as a set of individuals, or alternatively a proposal that motivates short scrambling in English and German on different grounds, independent of quantification.[34]

8.5   Appendix: Materials for Experiments 1–3

Below is the full list of items used in Experiments 1–3. The same templates were used in all three experiments, with different choices of determiner and placement/position of *also* as described in the body of the chapter. Recall that in all experiments, the sentences were presented on two lines, with the line break always placed immediately following the verbal complex.

1. The orderly learned which doctor was (also) planning to (also) monitor *the/every/which* patient that the duty nurse *did/was* and immediately updated the charts.
2. The principal determined which instructor was (also) able to (also) teach *the/every/which* class that the substitute teacher *did/was* and accordingly finalized the schedule.
3. The conductor asked which soloist was (also) willing to (also) play *the/every/which* piece that the brilliant protégé *did/was* and restructured the rehearsal accordingly.
4. The coordinator learned which tutor was (also) scheduled to (also) teach *the/every/which* topic that the Physics professor *did/was* and assigned them to classrooms.
5. The prosecutor asked which witness was (also) told to (also) discredit *the/every/which* defendant that the corrupt detective *did/was* but only one witness revealed anything.
6. The teacher found out which student was (also) eager to (also) attend *the/every/which* trip that the class president *did/was* and organized the field trips accordingly.
7. The detective found out which guard was (also) willing to (also) hassle *the/every/which* prisoner that the sadistic warden *did/was* and included the names in his report.
8. The analyst predicted which investor was (also) prepared to (also) buy *the/every/which* stock that the hedge fund *did/was* and then sent a memo to the bank management.
9. The realtor asked which trainee was (also) able to (also) show *the/every/which* property that the experienced secretary *did/was* but nobody was available that weekend.
10. The carpenter asked which apprentice was (also) qualified to (also) use *the/every/which* technique that the licensed electrician *did/was* and then assigned personnel to projects.

11. The choreographer determined which dancer was (also) ready to (also) perform *the/every/which* dance routine that the Russian ballerina *did/was* and then started the dance recital.

12. The organizers found out which announcer was (also) willing to (also) cover *the/every/which* game that the notorious commentator *did/was* and then finalized the broadcasting schedule.

13. The librarian learned which teacher was (also) planning to (also) borrow *the/every/which* book that the visiting scholar *did/was* and accordingly shortened the loan periods.

14. The attorney clarified which witness was (also) supposed to (also) support *the/every/which* alibi that the undercover informant *did/was* and then gave his closing argument.

15. The dispatcher clarified which apprentice was (also) scheduled to (also) accompany *the/every/which* crew that the experienced engineer *did/was* and sent the crews on their way.

16. The programmer realized which update was (also) certain to (also) solve *the/every/which* problem that the old software *did/was* but surprisingly decided not to tell anyone.

17. The focus-group explained which discount was (also) likely to (also) attract *the/every/which* demographic that the Spring sale *did/was* and then several TV ads were launched.

18. The secretary found out which professor was (also) going to (also) question *the/every/which* student that the disciplinary committee *did/was* and then scheduled the hearings.

19. The general forgot which unit was (also) scheduled to (also) attack *the/every/which* target that the nuclear submarine *did/was* and sent a messenger to headquarters.

20. The biologist discovered which reptile was (also) likely to (also) have *the/every/which* gene that the Tyrannosaurus Rex *did/was* and proposed additional tests.

21. The admiral specified which ship was (also) ordered to (also) attack *the/every/which* position that the navy jet *did/was* and then the joint army-navy exercise began.

22. The engineer explained which apprentice was (also) asked to (also) service *the/every/which* engine that the sick crew member *did/was* and then called the train company.

23. The colonel explained which officer was (also) ordered to (also) interrogate *the/every/which* prisoner that the CIA agent *did/was* and then described what methods not to use.

24. The log showed which detective was (also) sent to (also) arrest *the/every/which* suspect that the FBI agent *did/was* and additionally where the arrest took place.

25. The detective discovered which mobster was (also) about to (also) blackmail *the/every/which* business that the street gang *did/was* and immediately informed his superiors.

26. The sheriff knew which marshal was (also) excited to (also) chase *the/every/which* fugitive that the state police *did/was* but doubted that the fugitives would be caught.

27. The scientist discovered which antibody was (also) likely to (also) attack *the/every/which* virus that the standard medication *did/was* but needed funding to complete her study.

28. The warden guessed which inmate was (also) trying to (also) smuggle *the/every/which* contraband that the corrupt guard *did/was* and therefore intensified the security screens.

9 Epilogue

Some open questions remain. An important question that I have mostly left aside in this book concerns the precise nature of intervention effects and of interveners. An explanandum that I take to be key to any theory of intervention effects is the fact that intervention affects just one of (at least) two modes of composition of *wh*-questions: it affects *wh*-phrases that are truly in situ at LF, and not ones that have been moved above the intervener. Moreover, I take the mode of in-situ composition that is affected by intervention to be Rooth-Hamblin alternatives. Throughout this book, I adopted Beck's (2006) proposal as the correct theory of intervention. I believe that the insight behind Beck's work is on the right track, but I also have some concerns about the implementation.[1] In ongoing work, I develop an alternative proposal that maintains the idea that in-situ *wh*-phrases are interpreted using focus alternatives and that this mode of composition is sensitive to intervention effects, but attributes intervention to a problem with the definition of Predicate Abstraction over alternatives in simple semantic models. I believe that important insights from this new mode of thinking about intervention will not alter the way the results in this book should be interpreted, but of course any revised theory of intervention may lead to a new and different interpretation of the data and conclusions I have presented here.[2]

Another open avenue of research concerns the crosslinguistic typology of questions. In chapter 4, I presented a sketch of the main ways in which interrogative syntax can vary crosslinguistically. A full description of every type of structure in every language is of course beyond the scope of this book, but the proposals offered here make predictions about the kinds of variation we expect to find. They also make predictions for the types of readings and the distribution of intervention effects crosslinguistically. In most cases, the data that would verify or falsify these predictions have not yet been collected. A third avenue for future work concerns variation in the availability of ALTSHIFT in syntax. I proposed that limiting its distribution in different languages—for example, to necessarily occur at FocP in Hungarian and to be available in DPs in Japanese—can help us understand some types of variation not only in questions but in other related constructions as well. More data need to be collected to inform other ways in which the distribution of ALTSHIFT may vary across languages.

Finally, several unifying themes emerge from this book, which I would like to highlight here.

The first recurring theme concerns economy. Movement is assumed only when necessary, and a shorter movement step is preferable to longer ones. In online processing, a more parsimonious parse is adopted until evidence is encountered forcing reanalysis to a more complex one. In chapter 7, I proposed that this property of grammar can be exploited for understanding the nature of derivations. The common bottom-up model may necessitate a form of trans-derivational economy and may still run into lookahead problems. A top-down, left-to-right model may instead yield predictions that are more in line with the data presented here. Such a model may also be more psychologically real, but would require many of the working assumptions adopted by linguists today to be revised or recast in other terms. I take this to be an important next step in the development of the theory of syntax and semantics, which I of course leave for future work.

A second recurring theme concerns the versatility of grammar. I argued throughout the book for an interrogative syntax/semantics that allows *wh*-phrases to occupy different positions at LF, beyond their base position and the interrogative CP layer. Concomitantly, I argued for a semantic framework that employs at least two ways of interpreting *wh*-phrases: movement and in-situ composition using Rooth-Hamblin alternatives. Looking beyond the data that were the focus of this book, it seems plausible that at least one and perhaps two more ways of interpreting *wh*-phrases should be allowed: choice functions are necessary for functional readings of questions (and perhaps other uses as well), and still another mechanism may be required for echo questions. An overarching result, then, is that grammar possesses multiple means of achieving the same ultimate goal of question formation. Likewise, we observed multiple ways of undoing an intervention configuration, including QR, reconstruction, *wh*-movement, RNR, extraposition, and scrambling.

These two results exist in a curious state of tension. On the one hand, the semantics allows for flexibility in several aspects of the derivation of a question. On the other hand, as we have seen, the syntax of multiple *wh*-questions is *not* flexible in several ways that the semantic proposal put forth here predicts that it could be.

(1) *Determinism in the derivation of multiple* wh-*questions*[3]

    a. The in-situ *wh*-phrase in a Superiority-obeying question always undergoes a short QR/scrambling step to the nearest vP node.

    b. The in-situ *wh*-phrase in a Superiority-obeying question can move higher if necessary—for example, to avoid an intervention effect or to construct an appropriate antecedent for ellipsis. This movement would again be to the nearest position that would render the sentence grammatical.

    c. The in-situ *wh*-phrase in a Superiority-violating question may not undergo interrogative movement under any circumstances, including to undo an intervention configuration or to construct an appropriate antecedent for ACD resolution.

Finally, even though the smallest movement possible in a question is no movement at all, this appears not to be an option in the derivation of either Superiority-obeying questions in English or multiple questions in German. In fact, Superiority-violating English questions with pair-list readings may be the sole exception to the rule that every *wh*-phrase in the structure must undergo at least some movement following its merger into the derivation. This aspect of interrogative syntax—the fact that in-situ *wh*-phrases in Superiority-violating questions do *not* appear to move, not even in order to host ACD (which is generally possible even for DPs that the parser normally assumes to be interpreted in situ; see chapter 8)—is particularly puzzling and, I suspect, holds the key to understanding the nature of covert *wh*-movement in general. I hope to return to this issue in future work.

Notes

Chapter 1

1. Other readings that have been discussed in the literature include the functional reading (e.g., Chierchia 1993; Engdahl 1986) and the mention-some reading (e.g., George 2011). These will not be the focus of this book; hence, I do not discuss them here.

Chapter 2

1. In this book, I will limit my attention to *wh*-questions with *wh*-arguments rather than *wh*-adjuncts.

2. In other words, the Hamblin/Karttunen denotation contains more information than a partition; hence, it is possible to go from the former to the latter but not the other way around.

3. Other theories argue that at least in some cases, it is not full *wh*-phrases but an operator that moves at LF (e.g., Aoun and Li 1993; Hagstrom 1998). Since the target position of movement and the reasons for this movement are the same as in the approach introduced here, I classify these theories as consistent with the covert movement approach. Nothing hinges on these details.

4. Alternative mechanisms for in-situ interpretation involve the use of choice functions (Reinhart 1997) or unselective binding (Nishigauchi 1986, 1990). Here, I do not discuss these mechanisms in detail. As will become clear in subsequent sections, there are theories of intervention effects that rely on the use of Alternative Semantics, but there is no theory I am familiar with that uses other in-situ modes of composition and is able to explain intervention effects. I will leave open the question of whether it is possible to relate intervention effects to a choice function analysis of *wh*-in-situ.

5. Here, I will not be presenting computations of Rooth-Hamblin alternatives beyond the toy example in (25). For the technical details of Rooth-Hamblin (focus) alternatives computation, see Hamblin 1973, Rooth 1985, 1992, and subsequent work.

6. The semantic denotations here must be interpreted intensionally. To simplify the presentation, world variables are not illustrated.

7. In fact, Aoun and Li (2003) show that superiority is relevant not only for movement structures but also for some nonmovement constructions involving resumption.

8. As Richards notes, a tucking-in derivation is "countercyclic" in that it does not extend the tree. This violates the Extension Condition (Chomsky 1993). See Richards 1997 for discussion of this issue.

9. See Büring 2003, Constant 2014, Jackendoff 1972, Roberts 1996, and citations therein for further discussion of contrastive topics and question-answer congruence. Further discussion of this issue is beyond the scope of this book.

10. Some English speakers I have consulted with observe an additional uniqueness presupposition on the lower *wh*-expression. This makes a pair-list interpretation of the question in the following example bad (Chris Tancredi, pers. comm.):

(i) *Context*: Mary and John have five children, Alice, Betty, Charles, David, and Ellen. They decided to take the children out to see a movie. Mary wanted to see a sci-fi movie, but John wanted to watch a romance drama instead. John and Mary decided to each go watch a different movie, and left it to the children to decide which parent to go with.

    #Which child went with which parent?

Here, exhaustivity with respect to *which child* makes it necessary for multiple children to be paired with each parent, but this is something that such speakers do not allow. Instead, for such speakers each value of the higher *wh*-expression must be paired with a different value from the lower one. This does not fall out either from the presuppositions described here or from the semantics I develop based on them. I leave the issue of this possible additional presupposition to future work.

11. Nissenbaum (2000) argues that in-situ *wh*-phrases in English multiple *wh*-questions undergo covert movement not only in Superiority-obeying questions but also in Superiority-violating ones, given the possible licensing of parasitic gaps in both types of questions. Here, on the basis of Pesetsky's (2000) ACD argument and the behavior of these questions with regard to intervention effects, I adopt the view that covert movement is available only in Superiority-obeying questions. I leave to future work the reconciliation of these facts with Nissenbaum's parasitic gap data.

12. See Pesetsky 2000:31–33 for a discussion and dismissal of several possible alternative explanations for the difference between (39) and (40).

13. This example is judged as slightly degraded because of the repetition of the predicate in the matrix and embedded clauses. The predicate must be downstressed in this situation. When this happens, it has been argued that the structure exhibits behavior and licensing conditions very similar to those of VP-ellipsis structures (of which ACD structures are a subtype); see, for example, Tancredi 1992.

14. These examples are naturally read with accent on *Mary* inside the relative clause. This seems necessary for them to be grammatical.

Chapter 3

1. In later chapters, I will modify and refine this assumption: I will argue that *wh*-in-situ in Superiority-obeying questions undergoes covert scrambling that may be shorter-distance and need not necessarily target C, although it may do so. I furthermore show that *wh*-in-situ may not undergo covert interrogative movement in Superiority-violating

questions, but it may be subject to other types of movement, such as extraposition, raising, or RNR. These details are irrelevant at this point. As I will show in chapter 4, the system I develop is able to yield the desired question semantics given a variety of assumptions about interrogative syntax.

2. I acknowledge that this assumption is carried over from the prior literature. I am not claiming here that every different answer pattern to a question must correspond to a difference in LF. In fact, my analysis aims to preserve the same LFs for both answer patterns, varying only in the presence or absence of an answer operator ALTSHIFT, in the left periphery of the question. This allows, then, for additional answer patterns, including partial answers, functional answers, and so on.

3. This is a simplification: the restriction to nonhumans is more nuanced. It's possible to answer a *what* question with *A person*, as in (i).

(i) Q: What should we have as our mascot?
   A: A person.

Indeed, this phrase can be included in the question itself.

(ii) Q: What should we have as our mascot, a person or a cat?

Consequently, the tendency toward not using *what* for people could simply be Gricean: *who* is used specifically to refer to humans; therefore, *who* must be used whenever the questioner expects a human answer. If there is no specific expectation, however, *what* may be used. *What* is then necessary whenever there is an expectation that the answer is non-human, but it will also be appropriate when the answer is potentially human, even if it is potentially the name of a specific person.

(iii) Q: What just came in the door, a robot or Bill?

I set this complication aside, as it will not be relevant to the discussion, and I continue to use the simplified denotation in the text.

4. Note that these definitions assume contextual domain restriction. For simplicity, in the derivations that follow I ignore this detail.

A complication that I will mostly ignore is the question of how Predicate Abstraction is defined. As discussed in Rooth 1985: 45–59 and Shan 2004, Predicate Abstraction is not well-defined in simple semantic models. Several solutions have been proposed for this problem (see, e.g., Charlow 2017; Ciardelli, Roelofsen, and Theiler 2017; Novel and Romero 2009). See also the discussion in Kotek 2017b for whether any of these solutions should be adopted. While this is an important point that may affect the subsequent analysis, it is the subject of ongoing research and as such I leave it open at this point. I simply assume that one way or another, any complete theory of focus will eventually have to develop some way of composing structures across λ-abstracted sets.

5. Although, as noted below, the denotation I propose for ALTSHIFT may be viewed as a generalized version of the denotation of *ka* as proposed by Shimoyama (2001) (see in particular the discussion in section 2.5, and footnote 36) or Beck and Kim's (2006) Q operator.

6. Logically, this operator could perhaps be thought of as the inverse of the $\sim$ operator, which similarly operates over focus-semantic values but generates ordinary semantic values without alternatives.

7. In (10) in chapter 2, I illustrated C as the operator responsible for interrogative semantics, in keeping with the more standard notation in the literature, but from now on I will use the operator ALTSHIFT for this purpose.

8. I adopt standard assumptions about the derivation of *wh*-questions: successive-cyclic *wh*-movement through phase edges, A-movement of the vP-internal subject to Spec,TP, T-to-C movement of the auxiliary verb, and so on. For simplicity, I do not illustrate these here.

9. For completeness, in (13) and all derivations below, I show not only the sets that we derive as the denotation of the question, but also their characteristic functions.

10. To simplify the notation, throughout I represent assignment-dependent elements in the denotation using unbound variables.

11. I take ANS to be an operator that occupies the left periphery of the clause and may be selected by certain question-embedding predicates such as *know* and *ask*.

12. Dayal does not use the term Max_{inf}, but the definition she provides is equivalent to Max_{inf}, as proposed in Fox and Hackl 2006 and subsequent work. See also von Fintel, Fox and Iatridou 2014.

13. Recall again that complex propositions such as "Abby read MD and JE" are not in this set because our question, *Which book did Abby read?*, contains singular agreement on the *which*-phrase.

14. It is worth noting at this point that a parallel derivation, involving movement of only the base-generated higher *wh*-phrase to C and leaving lower ones fully in situ, would similarly yield a single-pair reading of the Superiority-obeying question. Here, I showed the derivation of this reading from a syntax involving covert movement of *wh*-in-situ, following arguments in the literature that such movement does indeed take place. However, as we will see in chapter 4, such a derivation of a Superiority-obeying question may be appropriate for multiple *wh*-questions in other languages—for example, in German.

15. See alternative proposals in Dayal 1996, Fox 2012b, and Nicolae 2013.

16. Thanks to David Lahm and the Frankfurt semantics reading group for noticing a typo in (23) in an earlier version of this book.

17. Here, I use the notation $\lambda \alpha : \beta \, . \, \gamma$, following Heim and Kratzer (1998). β denotes a definedness condition on the applicability of the λ-expression to its argument α, and γ denotes the output of the function.

18. But see appendix 2 to this chapter for more discussion of the readings of Superiority-violating questions.

19. Recall that *wh*-movement is triggered immediately following an agreement operation. Hence, once DP_x has been agreed with and not moved (allowing DP_y to move over it to the outermost Spec,CP), it follows that DP_x can no longer undergo *wh*-movement, although other movement operations may still be available to it. We will see such movement operations in other languages (e.g. focus movement) in chapter 4 and in English (e.g., right-node raising) in chapter 6. Note additionally that in the LFs shown here, DP_x is not blocked from undergoing subject raising from vP to TP, as usual.

20. The discussion in this appendix is based in part on joint work with Michael Yoshitaka Erlewine.

21. I thank Michael Yoshitaka Erlewine for discussing this proposal this me. Erlewine attributes this idea to an anonymous *Journal of Semantics* reviewer of a manuscript of his.

22. Notice further that we might argue that *what* enters into an Agree relation with the complementizer, further supporting the fact that its behavior is distinct from that of focused nominals.

23. More specifically, a single-pair reading of the question may be predicted. The data in (37) and the proposed solution in (40) already show that a multiple *wh*-question denotation will not be available here, since ALTSHIFT cannot apply to a part of structure containing just the focused expression to yield a question. Recall that this step is necessary for the derivation of a multiple *wh*-question, where alternative-generating (*wh*-)expressions and ALTSHIFT operators are interleaved.

24. Two observations are in order here. First, Barss (2000) argues that D-linked Superiority-violating questions lack the pair-list answer and instead can only have a single-pair answer. However, I believe that both Superiority-obeying and Superiority-violating questions of the kinds I investigate here allow a pair-list reading.

Second, David Pesetsky (pers. comm.) offers the following context, with the judgment that a single-pair reading is available if the phonologists are for some reason more salient than the syntacticians. I agree with this judgment and believe that it points to the importance of the context in the examples given in this appendix. In particular, it is important that only one pair is logically possible in these contexts. It is not sufficient that the answer happens to be true of just one pair. Hence, I propose to distinguish "true" single-pair from "accidental" single-pair readings, the latter being a special case of a pair-list construal of the question.

(i) *Superiority-violating question with an apparent single-pair reading (English)*
    Context: To foster the atmosphere in our Linguistics unit, every day one syntactician and one phonologist go out to lunch together, at the department's expense. You know who all went out to lunch together this week, so tell me:
    a. *Which* syntactician ___ took *which* phonologist out to lunch today?
    b. *Which* phonologist did *which* syntactician take out ___ to lunch today?

25. Nissenbaum (2000) notices a similar finding in questions with an overtly moved *wh*-phrase and a lower quantifier, *each*. Example (i) can only have a pair-list reading, where *each* has apparently moved above the *wh* via QR.

(i) *Which* car did you persuade *each* senator to borrow ___ [after getting an opponent of *pg* to put a bomb in *pg*]?

Nissenbaum (2000) attributes the possibility of a pair-list interpretation to Fox's (2000) Scope Economy principle, arguing that covert movement of the quantifier above the *wh*-phrase is allowed because it creates a new scope relation that did not exist with the quantifier in situ. However, more needs to be said in order to predict that the pair-list reading is *forced* in this case. This could perhaps be related to the fact that distributive quantifiers such as *each* tend to take wide scope. A related question that I leave open at this point is whether Nissenbaum's finding extends to other quantifiers as well.

26. This logic crucially relies on a notion of cross-derivational economy that makes a Superiority-obeying question preferable to a Superiority-violating one. This may not be desirable from a computational standpoint; nonetheless, it yields the correct results here.

Chapter 4

1. This generalization has one interesting exception: the base-generated highest *wh*-phrase in the question must be pronounced first, but if there are two additional *wh*-phrases, they may occur in either order.

(i) Wh$_1$ wh$_2$ wh$_3$ *and* wh$_1$ wh$_3$ wh$_2$ *both possible*
    a.   *Koj* na *kogo kakvo* dade?
        who to whom what gave

        'Who gave what to whom?'
    b.   ? *Koj kakvo* na *kogo* dade?

Richards (1997) dubs this the Principle of Minimal Compliance. The precise characterization of this condition is not important here. Informally, Richards describes this as an "AC-tax": Attract Closest must be satisfied by *wh$_1$*, but once the "tax" has been paid, the relative ordering of *wh$_2$* and *wh$_3$* does not matter.

2. Some Austronesian languages have also been described as having (optional) multiple *wh*-fronting of the Bulgarian type. See Sabel 2003 for Malagasy facts regarding superiority that parallel the Bulgarian data, although data on the readings of the question are still needed.

3. A further complication is a point of variation relating to complex questions: Russian never shows superiority effects, Bulgarian always does, and Serbo-Croatian has been shown to exhibit them in *some* complex cases—in long-distance questions, embedded questions, and overt *li* questions (Bošković 2002). As this complication would take us too far afield, I will put it aside for present purposes.

4. An additional restriction on such questions is that they must operate on the same domain, so while questions like 'Who fought with whom?' are acceptable, minimally different questions like 'Who bought what?' are ungrammatical. See É. Kiss 2002:100 and Lipták 2000 for details.

5. Movement to the focus projection can be identified through the demotion of the verb marker (VM) in the sentence to a postverbal position. See É. Kiss 2002 for arguments that there is only one focus projection per clause.

6. If a sentence contains two 'only'-phrases, either one can move, resulting in unambiguous scope of the moved phrase above the in-situ one.

(i) *Only one* only-*phrase moves; unambiguous scope*
    a. Csak Mari kapott   csak két tárgy-ból   jelest.
        only Mary received only two subject-from A+

        only M > only two: 'It was only Mary who got an A+ only in two subjects.'
    b. Csak két tárgy-ból   kapott csak Mari jelest.
        only two subject-from received only Mary A+

        only two > only M: 'It was only two subjects in which only Mary got an A+.'

If a sentence contains a *wh*-phrase and two 'only'-phrases, the *wh*-phrase is fronted, but now the two 'only'-phrases have ambiguous scope with respect to one another. This suggests an interesting interaction between moved and (phonologically) in-situ focused phrases.

(ii) Wh-*phase moves; the two 'only'-phrases' relative scope is ambiguous*
   a. *Melyik* félé-ben kapott   csak három lány csak két tárgy-ból   jelest?
      which term-in received only three girl only two subject-from A+
      only three girls > only two subjects: 'In which term was it only three girls who
      received an A+ only in two subjects?'
      only two subjects > only three girls: 'In which term was it in only two subjects
      that only three girls received an A+?'
   b. *Melyik* félé-ben kapott   csak két tárgy-ból   csak három lány jelest?
      which term-in received only two subject-from only three   girl A+
      = (a), both readings

7. Recall that for English and German I propose that the lowest adjunction site for
ALTSHIFT is in the CP layer.

8. I thank Michael Yoshitaka Erlewine for a discussion of these and other focus-related
effects in Hungarian.

9. Other focus-sensitive operators, which I have proposed may be adjoined at this position when other focus-sensitive elements occur in the derivation, will lead to a crash
if combined with a *wh*-phrase. Only the ALTSHIFT operator can successfully handle a
wh-phrase, as the only element in grammar that takes only the focus-semantic value of
its sister. Other focus-sensitive operators require both the ordinary and focus-semantic
values of their sisters. See Beck 2006 for discussion.

10. In the absence of this operator, the question will not have an ordinary value. It will
hence be ruled out by Beck and Kim's (2006) Principle of Interpretability in (10) of
chapter 3: An LF must have an ordinary semantic interpretation.

11. I remain agnostic here about whether this CP projection is the same as the Hungarian
DistP. For parsimony, I would suggest that these are one and the same, but I leave the
details open at this point.

12. As far as I can see, in the case of Superiority-obeying questions, the highest projection targeted by *wh*-fronting could be either FocP or CP. In the case of
Superiority-violating questions, Attract Closest requires that the higher projection be
different in nature from the lower one: the higher projection, CP, hosts wh_2, while
the lower projection, FocP, hosts other *wh*-phrases, which have fronted by means of
noninterrogative movement.

13. Of course, the full data set to be described for each of these languages is more
diverse than I have shown here. Here, I have sketched some basic assumptions that can
model important points of variation in multiple *wh*-fronting languages. I leave a fuller
description of these languages for future work.

14. To be more precise, it is in fact the Q-particle *ká* that moves; alternatively, *ká*
marks the scope of the phrase that moves—namely, the entire island. Therefore, examples (ia–b) are grammatical, as long as the Q-particle occurs outside of the island. See
Sulemana 2017 for details.

(i) *No island sensitivity in Bùlì questions when the Q-particle is outside the island*
   a. Fí á-yáalí   ká [núrpók wāi   ālì dà $b^w\bar{a}$ lá:?]
      2SG IMPV-love Q woman REL.PRO C buy.PST what PRT
      'You love the woman who bought what?'

b. Azuma dà   ká [gbáŋ ālī b^wā:?]
   Azuma buy.PST Q   book CONJ what
   'Azuma bought a book and what?'

15. For simplicity, I illustrate all LFs as head-initial, but of course for a head-final language we would adapt the LF so that all phrases are right-branching instead.

16. Note further that adopting an LF in like (32), with an ALTSHIFT operator adjoined directly to the *wh*-DP, but without projecting an existential quantifier on top of the DP, will allow us to derive the pair-list readings of a question in the event that a second *wh*-phrase occurs in the structure.

17. A related but different phenomenon is the formation of 'how-many' questions, a form of a "separation" construction, where either the entire 'how-many' phrase moves, or only the *wh*-part. Where only the *wh*-part moves, the relation between the moved part and the part that remains in situ is said to be established through focus alternatives. See Mathieu 2002 for discussion.

(i) *'How-many' questions may involve a "separation" construction (Mathieu 2002:14)*
   a. [$_{CP}$ *Combien* de livres$_i$ as-tu   'lus t_i]?
      how.many of books have you read.AGR
   b. [$_{CP}$ *Combien$_i$* as-tu   lu   [t_i de livres]]?
      how.many have you read   of books
      'How many books have you read?'

18. The paper identifies the movement strategy as focus movement, although the translations provided use cleft constructions.

19. For this reason, Kobele and Torrence concentrate on nonsubjects, which allow comparison of the two strategies. Such restrictions on subject questions are, in fact, quite common crosslinguistically.

20. Adverbial *wh*-words such as 'why' and 'how' cannot be left in situ and instead must move, at least partially. This is to be contrasted with nominal adjuncts such as 'where', which can be left in situ. See Cole and Hermon 1998 for details.

21. This Edge Generalization is very important for related work reported in Kotek and Erlewine 2016 on the nature of intervention effects in pied-piping constituents in English. See that article for details.

22. QPs that do not move to the CP layer undergo existential closure at the TP layer and become *wh*-indefinites.

23. Similar heads would have to be added in order to deal with questions with three QPs, four QPs, and so on.

24. Cable (2010) in fact does not develop a semantics for pair-list readings of multiple *wh*-questions within his original theory.

Chapter 5

1. Not to be confused with a host of other effects that have been called "intervention" effects (most famously, defective intervention) but that are unrelated to the phenomenon at hand.

2. Although this pattern in *wh*-in-situ languages is not without exceptions. See, for example, Branan 2017b and Eilam 2008.

3. Pesetsky uses the notation $\overset{??}{=}$ to indicate this loss of the pair-list reading due to intervention effects. For transparency, I use the notation $*^{PL}$ instead.

4. Chris Tancredi (pers. comm.) notes that there may be a way to rescue Superiority-violating questions with interveners such as (8b). He observes that (8a) is acceptable in both contexts (i) and (ii), whereas (8b) is acceptable only in context (ii) and requires accent on the two occurrences of *which* and nothing else. The crucial property of this context is that the intervener is explicitly mentioned in the context.

(i) Three girls were standing near the dance floor where three boys were gathered. Mary and Sue got the two groups together and made introductions.

(ii) Three girls were standing near the dance floor where three boys were gathered. Mary and Sue got the two groups together and made introductions. In most cases, a girl got introduced multiple times to the same boy, once by Mary and once by Sue. However, for each boy there was one girl—a different one for each—that only Mary introduced to him.

The pair-list reading may not go away altogether, then. It disappears in some contexts but not in others. As a first approximation, we may speculate that we observe an intervention effect if the intervener does not qualify as Given in the context. We might additionally speculate that focus on *which* (or possibly on *which girl*) is also a requirement. Under the current analysis, this would give an alternative reason for movement in the structure and so would be predicted to be sufficient to generate the interpretation in question. I leave this issue open at the moment.

5. Büring (1996) argues that sentential negation is not a focus-sensitive operator, possibly raising a problem for the theory proposed by Beck (2006). He argues that apparent focus-sensitive effects of the interpretation of negation in declaratives can be reduced to the idea that sentences with different prosody are congruent to different questions under discussion. (A similar argument is made in Beaver and Clark 2008:chap. 3.) I note, however, that these arguments are based solely on the contribution of negation in declaratives. A full investigation of the potential effects of focus on negation in interrogatives is outside the scope of this book. Here, I simply follow Beck (2006) and Pesetsky (2000), who show that sentential negation in English patterns with the other items as an intervener.

Note, however, a possible concern stemming from the contrast between *didn't* and *shouldn't* (and *couldn't*) in (i). I leave this as a curious but potentially important point, which I have no explanation for at the moment.

(i) *Not all questions are similarly affected by the presence of negation*
    a.   *Which* student did**n't** ___ read *which* book?
    b.   * *Which* book did**n't** *which* student read ___ ?   (= (7c–d))
    c.   *Which* student should**n't** ___ read *which* book?
    d. ? *Which* book should**n't** *which* student read ___ ?

6. This also holds more generally for Inquisitive Semantics, for which, to my knowledge, there is no compatible theory of intervention.

7. It is worth noting that for intervention effects to occur as Beck (2006) theorizes in structures like (16b), the Roothian alternatives used by focus-sensitive operators

and the Hamblin alternatives used for question interpretation must be the same formal objects. This equivalence of focus alternatives and *wh*-interpreting alternatives is therefore an important theoretical claim of Beck's system. This formal equivalence reflects the long-observed similarities between *wh* and focus realization crosslinguistically, including in syntax and prosody (Arregi 2002; Culicover 1992; Horvath 1986; Simpson 2000; Simpson and Bhattacharya 2003; Szendrői 2003; Truckenbrodt 2013; and many others). However, see for example Mayr 2014 for arguments against this approach.

Note that there may also be another problem when interpreting configuration (16b). Standard focus-sensitive operators use both the focus-semantic value and the ordinary semantic value of their prejacent for their interpretation (Rooth 1985, 1992), but the ordinary semantic value for the complement of the intervener in (16b) will be undefined. Thus, two things may go wrong in intervention configurations.

8. Note that the more general schema in (15) predicts intervention effects not only in questions but also in association-with-focus constructions. Beck (2006) discusses this prediction but fails to find intervention effects in these configurations. However, see Erlewine and Kotek 2014, 2018 for discussion and an argument that such effects in fact exist, when covert focus movement is controlled for.

9. Beck uses *C* for the context set. I reserve *C* for the interrogative complementizer and use the term *ALT* instead.

Also, here I follow Beck (2006) in assuming that *only* takes scope over the entire clause. A more standard assumption is that in subject-*only* cases, the operator and its associate form a constituent. These details are not important for the purpose of this illustration.

10. Or perhaps more accurately:

(i) *A two-place semantics for* only
$[\![only]\!](\alpha)(\beta)(w) = 1$ iff for all p such that $p(w) = 1$ and $p \in \alpha, p \to \beta$

This will cover the case of alternatives that are entailed by the prejacent: for example, *Mary only swam*, where *Mary swam* entails *Mary was in the water*. I leave this aside for the moment.

11. Following Beaver and Clark (2008), the $\sim$ operator itself is not necessary for the logic of the argument. All that matters is that a focus-sensitive operator is the first operator c-commanding an in-situ *wh*, instead of a question operator.

12. With the possible exception of Cable's Q-particle (see Cable 2007, 2010, but see also the discussion in section 4.5).

13. See Cheng and Demirdache 2010 for precisely such a mechanism, which I argue should be ruled out. I note that this mechanism incorrectly predicts that the structures it was developed for should be island-insensitive.

Chapter 6

1. This chapter is largely based on data first presented in Kotek 2014a and subsequently published in Kotek 2017a, 2017c.

2. For Pesetsky (2000), the mode of composition used to interpret *wh*-in-situ, which is sensitive to intervention effects, is *feature movement* (contrasted with *phrasal movement*). However, Pesetsky offers no reason for this. Hence, I take his description of the data at face value but do not adopt his explanation of intervention effects.

3. Although the data tested in this chapter and the next are quite complex, they have been tested with over a dozen native speakers of English, who all share the contrasts reported here. Some speakers also struggle to detect the single-pair reading of these questions, but here I will concentrate only on the pair-list reading. Note that I use the notation $*^{PL}$ to indicate a degraded judgment compared with a provided baseline.

4. This is a simplification of a vast literature, but it suffices for present purposes.

5. Alternatively, the *wh*-phrase moves above negation to avoid an intervention effect, but leaves the NPI unlicensed, again leading to ungrammaticality.

6. Of course, *only* can associate with complex phrases and not single words. A more precise wording might therefore be "An operator like *only* must be associated with a lexical constituent in its c-command domain." I leave this detail aside at the moment.

7. Alternatively, we would find a violation of the PLA, again leading to ungrammaticality.

8. This example is slightly modified from Erlewine 2014, through the addition of a context. Erlewine reports that this question retains its single-pair reading but loses its pair-list reading.

9. Thanks to an anonymous reviewer for *The Linguistic Review* for this observation.

10. For example, they prefer an answer such as *Mary gave no boy his least favorite picture*.

11. Thanks to Bob Frank (pers. comm.) for suggesting this example to me.

12. See Pesetsky 2000:64 et seq. for what happens if we attempt to give such wide scope to other interveners. See Krifka 2001 for more on universal quantifiers quantifying into questions.

13. A grammaticality pattern parallel to the one that will be shown in (26)–(30) obtains with the universal quantifier *each*.

14. See Branan 2017a for two additional cases of exceptionally wide scope for *wh*-in-situ in English Superiority-violating questions that is achieved through noninterrogative movement: extraposition and high attachment of a parasitic gap. Branan shows that, just as in the cases I present here, when *wh*-in-situ is given wide scope, intervention effects disappear.

15. For notational convenience, I illustrate the fact that the right node is shared across both conjuncts with a ___ , and the exceptional wide scope (which feeds *wh*-movement) with a *t*(race).

16. At this point, I leave aside extending of this work beyond English and German. Although there is significant overlap in particular interveners and environments that lead to intervention crosslinguistically, the judgments are notoriously subtle. Some remaining issues include contrasts between root and embedded questions in Korean and Japanese (Hagstrom 1998; Tomioka 2007b), as well as the report that Amharic and Shona show no intervention effects at all (Eilam 2008; Zentz 2016), although see Zentz 2016 for a potential explanation of this latter point. In both cases, I believe that a closer

examination is required in order to decide whether the phenomenon is indeed the same as the one in English, and to diagnose the potential presence of covert movement in the structures. Such examination goes beyond the scope of this book.

17. See also Kotek 2017b for a different account of intervention where the in-situ mode of composition is alternatives computation. Briefly, I propose that intervention is the result of movement into regions of alternatives computation; it is known that Predicate Abstraction is not well-defined over nontrivial alternatives (Rooth 1985). I argue that intervention happens precisely when a λ-binder must be introduced in a part of structure where alternatives are projected. For details, see the cited work.

Chapter 7

1. Parts of this chapter are based on data first presented in Kotek 2014a and subsequently published in Kotek 2016.

2. Recall that a pronunciation rule, (8) of chapter 2, determines that, in English, the highest *wh*-phrase in Spec,CP is pronounced at the head of its movement chain and that all other *wh*-phrases are pronounced at the tail of their chains.

3. Or, in some cases, that the intervener has moved out of the way, as shown in chapter 6. These cases will not concern us in this chapter.

See also Erlewine and Kotek 2014 and Kotek and Erlewine 2016 for other arguments motivating the intervention diagnostic.

4. A single-pair reading of the question is also possible, given an appropriate context.

5. In this example, I have replaced the predicate *be offended* with *come*, since native speakers report that it is easier to judge the question with the latter predicate than with the former. I use an *if*-adjunct in the text, but the facts remain the same if a *because*-adjunct is used instead.

6. Although the data tested in this section are quite complex, the over two dozen native speakers I have consulted report that their judgments are very clear: all speakers who accept pair-list readings of baseline examples such as (3) also accept the pair-list reading of the baselines (5)–(6) and the (b) variants of (7)–(10), and they detect a loss of that reading in the critical (a) variants of (7)–(10). Some speakers also struggle to detect the single-pair reading of these questions.

7. Example (7a) is equally ungrammatical under the pair-list reading if *only* follows *come*.

(i) *[PL] *Which* linguist will come **only** [if we invite *which* philosopher]?

A *Glossa* reviewer points out that the question in (7b) degrades if it is embedded under *know*, as in (iia). I agree with this judgment and note that, in fact, the question is degraded under other embeddings such as *want to know* (iib), as well. I suspect that this effect is due to properties of the embedding that are independent of intervention effects, but I leave this as an open issue for future research.

(ii) a. \# John knows *which* linguist will come [if we **only** invite *which* philosopher].

 b. \# John wants to know *which* linguist will come [if we **only** invite *which* philosopher].

I additionally offer the examples in (iii)–(v), where *only*'s associate is clearly distinct from the *wh*-phrase, to eliminate a potential confound (I thank Chris Tancredi for suggesting these examples).

(iii) Context: Some linguists will attend the conference to hear a particular philosopher, if invited, but will refuse to eat dinner with that philosopher. Others will refuse to attend the conference if a particular philosopher is invited but will insist on going to dinner with that philosopher. What I want to know is:

Q: *Which* linguist will **only** come to [dinner]$_F$ (and not attend the conference) if we invite *which* philosopher?

A: *^{PL}Chomsky will only come to dinner if we invite Quine,
Kayne will only come to dinner if we invite Lewis,
Bresnan will only come to dinner if we invite Arendt, ...

This question easily allows a single-pair response, but a pair-list answer is harder. In contrast, the nonisland question in (iv) can have a pair-list answer as in (iii).

(iv) *Which* linguist will **only** come to a [dinner]$_F$ with *which* philosopher?

Likewise, the following examples show a contrast in their ability to have a pair-list answer:

(v) a. *^{PL} *Which* linguist will **everyone** want to invite if *which* philosopher gives a talk?

b. *Which* linguist will **everyone** want to invite to interact with *which* philosopher?

8. Again, it is crucially the pair-list reading that is affected. The judgments I report here are different from judgments for very similar examples found in Dayal 2002. Dayal reports judgments provided by an anonymous *Linguistic Inquiry* reviewer, according to whom both (9a) and (9b) are ungrammatical. I have been unable to find speakers who confirm Dayal's reported judgments. Instead, speakers consistently report the judgments that I note here.

9. I thank David Pesetsky (pers. comm.) for bringing this fact to my attention.

10. Following Fox's (1995, 2000) Scope Economy, I assume that covert movement of the relative clause is blocked in (13a) because it does not affect the semantic interpretation of the question or its linearization. This economy principle is overridden in the case of overt extraposition, where movement has consequences for the pronunciation of the sentence.

11. A similar result is also obtained with high epistemic adverbs such as *fortunately*. Note that here it is the entire extraposed clause containing the *wh* that takes scope above the intervener. The *wh* may not be able to leave the clause, because of freezing effects, making the extraposed clause an island for extraction (e.g., Wexler and Culicover 1980).

12. More precisely, in-situ approaches to question semantics do not require any movement for the interpretation of *wh*-phrases, and—all things being equal—would assume *wh* to occupy its base-generated position. Such theories are compatible with *wh* occupying other positions at LF.

13. Inside the island, *wh* would be interpreted as it is interpreted in other cases of pied-piping—in situ, using in-situ interpretation. See Cable 2007, 2010 and Kotek

and Erlewine 2016 for details on intervention effects in pied-piping constituents and a semantic theory compatible with those facts. Notice that under this view, (16b) would also incorrectly be predicted to be ungrammatical.

14. I assume here that vP and CP are phases. This characterization is certainly true for the island-containing structures discussed in this chapter.

15. As reported in Cheng and Demirdache 2010:474, Ratiu's translation is 'Who knows the student to whom was dedicated what yesterday?', which I find difficult to parse. Ratiu notes that this question has only a single-pair reading, not a pair-list reading.

16. Cheng and Demirdache (2010) propose a choice function semantics for the interpretation of the questions they consider. As noted above, I opt for a focus-alternatives approach to wh-in-situ since there are theories of intervention effects compatible with this approach, but there are no current theories of intervention that assume a choice function semantics for wh-in-situ.

17. However, such approaches have been argued to be computationally intractable, to be too powerful, and to make incorrect empirical predictions. See, in particular, Collins 1996, Frampton and Gutmann 1999, Gärtner 2002, Johnson and Lappin 1999, Potts 2001, and Sternefeld 1996. Compare also Chomsky 1995, 2000, 2001 with earlier Minimalist work in Chomsky 1992, 1993, as discussed in Reinhart 2006:chap. 1. See Graf 2013 for arguments against these objections.

   For another approach that may derive partial movement without the need for transderivational constraints, see Heck and Müller 2000.

18. A longer movement step could be possible but may be ruled out by economy considerations (Chomsky 1995; Fox 1995, 2000).

19. However, nothing hinges on this particular approach. But see Fox and Nissenbaum 1999 for an empirical argument that covert movement operates rightward in this way.

20. For experimental evidence for a reanalysis step in cases of covert movement in questions, universal quantification, and degree constructions, see chapter 8, Hackl, Koster-Hale, and Varvoutis 2012, and Breakstone et al. 2011, respectively.

21. More precisely, Takano (1998) argues that English exhibits obligatory covert object shift. I believe that this is equivalent to short covert scrambling, as I have been referring to this movement, and as argued by the other authors cited here.

22. See Hornstein 1995, Kitahara 1996, and Pica and Snyder 1995 for related discussion and a proposal to model QR in terms of A-movement. See arguments against this approach, specifically against Hornstein 1995 but, I believe, extending to these other proposals as well, in Johnson 2000a and Kennedy 1997.

23. Although the effect can be fairly weak, it is apparent in sentence-processing studies; see Hackl, Koster-Hale, and Varvoutis 2012. See chapter 8 for more discussion of this issue.

24. Although QR is normally clause-bound, that is not always the case. The following is an observation by Moltmann and Szabolcsi (1994), discussed by Fox (2000):

(i) *QR is not always clause-bound*
    a. *One girl* knows that *every boy* bought a present for Mary.

                                                  (one > every, *every > one)
    b. *One girl* knows what *every boy* bought for Mary.   (one > every, every > one)

See further discussion of long-distance scrambling/QR in Wurmbrand 2018 and arguments against long-distance scrambling in Miyagawa 2011.

25. I thank Phil Branigan (pers. comm.) for bringing these data to my attention.

26. Note that the *wh* here and in (26d) can be interpreted as *wh*-indefinites (Martin Hackl and Hagen Blix, pers. comm.).

27. See additional discussion and predictions for the behavior of short vs. long scrambling as A-movement vs. Ā-movement, respectively, in Mahajan 1990.

28. Overt scrambling in German is also possible for other, information-structural reasons. Such parallel movement may occur covertly in English; detecting whether this is in fact the case is left for future work.

Chapter 8

1. This chapter reports findings based on work conducted under the supervision of Martin Hackl; preliminary results were reported in Kotek and Hackl 2013. The research reported in this chapter was supported by National Science Foundation Dissertation Improvement Grant #1251717.

2. As in other parts of the book, these LFs are simplified in some ways that are not relevant to the point at hand. I do not represent vP unless it is relevant to the LF, nor do I show subject raising from vP to TP, successive-cyclic *wh*-movement, or T-to-C movement.

3. How to define identity in the domain of ellipsis is a much-debated question. For example, experiments have shown that voice mismatches are possible in some contexts but not others (e.g., Arregui et al. 2006; Kehler 2001; Kertz 2010; San Pietro, Xiang, and Merchant 2012). It has also been argued that such mismatches are possible in VP-ellipsis but not in sluicing (Merchant 2013). I will not attempt to contribute to the definition of identity here. I simply assume that traces count as identical for the purpose of ellipsis parallelism if they are bound from parallel positions (e.g., Fox 2002).

4. More specifically, for all participants included in the analysis, a regression equation predicting RTs from word length using all items is fit to adjust for differences in word length and differences in participants' natural reading rates. At each word position, the RT predicted by the participant's regression equation is subtracted from the actual measured RT to obtain an RRT. Outlier results for each participant—in this case, beyond two standard deviations from the mean for a given condition and position—are excluded from the analysis (here, accounting for less than 5% of the data).

5. There is a debate in the sentence-processing literature about whether or not the size of the antecedent site affects the processing of the ellipsis site (see Frazier and Clifton 2000, 2001; Martin and McElree 2008, 2009, 2011; Murphy 1985). Note that the results discussed here do not depend on the answer to this question. Although the current thinking in the literature suggests that a larger antecedent does not necessarily incur a larger cost in the processing of ellipsis, it is possible to attribute the increased processing cost that HKV (2012) observe for the nonlocal ACD cases either to the longer covert movement step associated with the *large ellipsis* condition, or to the fact that *large ellipsis* involves a more complex VP and hence a more complex meaning than *small ellipsis*.

6. See HKV's (2012) graphs and discussion showing that this is indeed the case in their experiments. As we will see, this is also the case in the experiments presented here.

7. Extensional types are shown just for the relevant part of the structure. For simplicity, I abstract away from the VP-internal subject hypothesis.

8. Note that I am illustrating movement here as targeting TP, since I am abstracting away from vP and vP-internal subjects. Nothing hinges on this assumption.

9. In fact, this assumption may be made even if we entertain a theory of ACD resolution that does not involve any movement.

10. To simplify the discussion, in what follows I ignore the highest predicate embedding the question. I thus refer to the lower VP inside the embedded question as the *embedded VP* and to the larger VP inside the embedded question as the *matrix VP*.

11. Previous processing work, as well as rating and corpus studies, shows that questions with D-linked *wh*-phrases (Pesetsky 1987) are easier to process than questions with bare *wh*-pronouns (Arnon et al. 2006; Clifton, Fanselow, and Frazier 2006; Fanselow, Lenertova, and Weskott 2008; Featherston 2005a,b; Frazier and Clifton 2002; Hofmeister et al. 2007). In order to make the experimental items as easy to process as possible, the items in Experiments 1–3 all use D-linked *wh*-phrases.

12. Testing on a number of standard monitors showed this method to consistently avoid line breaks inside the region of interest; furthermore, it was found to be the most natural among several other line break options in a pilot study.

13. These sentences are not included in the analysis because the difference in line breaks made them no longer parallel to the target sentences.

14. Ibex: Internet Based Experiments, accessible at http://spellout.net/ibexfarm/.

15. The average completion time for all of the experiments presented here was above 25 minutes. Particularly slow RTs in our experiments tended to reflect long breaks and distracted behavior of participants, introducing extraneous noise into the results. Particularly fast RTs were similarly contributed by distracted participants.

16. Although this exclusion rate is quite high, I take it to be necessary in order to filter the higher noise level that Amazon Mechanical Turk participants exhibit relative to lab participants. This more parsimonious criterion helps ensure the validity of the results I report here.

17. Here and in the other experiments, the results remain statistically unaltered if this step is not performed.

18. RRTs were calculated on the basis of a regression equation that predicted RT from word length using all words from all experimental items, except for the first word and the last word of the sentence.

19. Similar results are obtained for log-transformed RTs in the data. Such a transformation is performed to normalize the data and reduce the effect any outliers have on the results. I report the results for RRTs for convenience.

20. Note, in particular, that the *which-was* condition appears to be slower than the other three conditions. However, the *determiner* × *ellipsis size* interaction is not significant ($p = .344$).

21. As we will see, this effect consistently shows up on the second and third words after the verb. Furthermore, this was confirmed for this experiment in a pilot experiment using the same items presented here. See also the discussion in section 8.2.3.4.

22. A more specified model that includes the effect of *determiner* yielded a false convergence.

23. However, an important difference between these results and HKV's (2012) is that while Experiment 2 yields two main effects, HKV observed an interaction, such that *every-was* and *the-was* did not differ significantly from each other. This played a role in HKV's argument that only local QR facilitates ACD resolution. The results of Experiment 3 will provide the missing evidence for making this claim here as well. I return to this point after introducing that experiment.

24. Although it has not been a major focus of attention in the literature, I argue that *also* acts as an intervener in English, exhibiting the same grammaticality paradigm as better-known interveners such as *only*: a Superiority-obeying question with *also* c-commanding the in-situ *wh*-phrase is grammatical, (iia), but a Superiority-violating question with *also* c-commanding the in-situ *wh*-phrase is ungrammatical (iib).

(i) *Baseline: Superiority-obeying and superiority-violating questions are both grammatical*

I know that the teacher punished some students last week. Do you know …
   a. *which* punishment the teacher gave ____ to *which* student on Friday?
   b. *which* student the teacher gave *which* punishment to ____ on Friday?

(ii) Also *is an intervener in English*

I know that the teacher punished some students on Thursday. Do you know …
   a.   *which* punishment the teacher **also** gave ____ to *which* student on Friday?
   b.   * *which* student the teacher **also** gave *which* punishment to ____ on Friday?

However, see Haida and Repp 2013 for an argument that *auch* 'also' is not an intervener in German.

25. Several other options were entertained as possible interveners in Experiment 3. The use of sentential negation was rejected to avoid confounds due to *neg*-raising. The use of adnominal focus elements such as *only*-DPs was rejected because of the added complexity they would introduce, with the need to accommodate yet another participant in an already rich context. Universal quantifiers such as *every* could not be used because they were a part of the *determiner* manipulation. Other adverbs such as *never* or *always* presented challenges in keeping the items uniform across experiments. On the other hand, *also* allowed for minimal alterations to the items of Experiment 1, while still affording a clear truth-conditional difference between sentences with *also* in different positions. These design considerations eventually led to the choice of *also* as the intervener in Experiment 3.

26. There are several options for what element in (23)–(24) a reader might choose to be the associate of *also*. One natural choice is *protégé*, which contrasts with *soloist* occurring higher in the sentence. Other options native speakers have reported to me include the noun *concerto* and the verb *play*. The actual choice made by readers is immaterial to the predictions for this experiment: all that matters is that *also* acts as a

focus-sensitive operator, forcing movement above it in the case of *which* but not in the case of *every*.

27. A more specified model including the effect of *also* for items did not converge.

28. In one of the two individual iterations of this experiment, the result at this word additionally showed an *ellipsis size* × *also* interaction, driven by slower RTs of large ellipsis (*was*) with *low also* compared to the other three conditions. In the other iteration of the experiment and in the aggregate, this interaction did not rise to the level of significance, and therefore I refrain from overinterpreting it here.

29. I thank Alexandre Cremers (pers. comm.) for suggesting this analysis to me.

30. I thank Alexandre Cremers for suggesting this idea and discussing its implications with me.

31. In fact, the interaction is never even close to significance.

32. Even if a theory of intervention compatible with this view of *wh*-phrases is put forth in the future, the main conclusion about the nature of covert *wh*-movement nonetheless stands: movement need not target interrogative C, but is normally shorter and more limited in scope.

33. This, then, leads to important and interesting questions concerning what other $\langle et, t \rangle$ elements might be included in this set. If, for example, the quantifier *no one* might be included, then the answer *No one* to a question such as *Who came?* would be a straightforward full answer to the question. Under current thinking within the Hamblin semantics tradition, such is not the case, but this remains an open and contested question.

34. I thank Chris Tancredi for proposing this point to me.

Chapter 9

1. In particular, this work suggests that all interveners are focus-sensitive. This may be appropriate for some interveners, such as *only*, *also*, and perhaps focus-sensitive negation, but it is less obviously appropriate for other interveners, such as *every*.

2. Likewise, if a theory of intervention effects based on choice functions as the affected mode of in-situ composition in a question is developed, or a theory couched within Inquisitive Semantics, this will again affect how the data may be interpreted.

3. Another, related point of determinism discussed in Kotek and Erlewine 2016 concerns covert pied-piping in multiple *wh*-questions: the constituent that is covertly pied-piped along with the *wh* is the largest among the options that would be available in overt pied-piping.

References

Abels, Klaus. 2012. *Phases: An essay on cyclicity in syntax.* Berlin. De Gruyter.

Akahane, Hitoshi. 2007. A phase-theoretic analysis of object omission. Ms., Yamaguchi University.

Anderson, Catherine. 2004. The structure and real-time comprehension of quantifier scope ambiguity. Doctoral dissertation, Northwestern University.

Aoun, Joseph, Norbert Hornstein, and Dominique Sportiche. 1981. Some aspects of wide scope quantification. *Journal of Linguistic Research* 1:67–95.

Aoun, Joseph, and Yen-hui Audrey Li. 1993. *Wh*-elements in situ: Syntax or LF? *Linguistic Inquiry* 24:199–238.

Aoun, Joseph, and Yen-hui Audrey Li. 2003. *Essays on the representational and derivational nature of grammar: The diversity of* wh-*constructions.* Cambridge, MA: MIT Press.

Arnon, Inbal, Neal Snider, Philip Hofmeister, Florian T. Jaeger, and Ivan A. Sag. 2006. Cross-linguistic variation in a processing account: The case of multiple *wh*-questions. In *Proceedings of the Thirty-Second Annual Meeting of the Berkeley Linguistics Society: General session,* ed. Zhenya Antić, Charles B. Chang, Emily Cibelli, Jisup Hong, Michael J. Houser, Clare S. Sandy, Maziar Toosarvandani, and Yao Yao, 23–36. http://linguistics.berkeley.edu/bls/previous-proceedings/bls32.pdf.

Arregi, Karlos. 2002. Focus on Basque movements. Doctoral dissertation, MIT.

Arregui, Ana, Charles Clifton Jr., Lyn Frazier, and Keir Moulton. 2006. Processing elided verb phrases with flawed antecedents: The recycling hypothesis. *Journal of Memory and Language* 55:232–246.

Baayen, R. H. 2004. Statistics in psycholinguistics: A critique of some current gold standards. In *Mental lexicon working papers I,* 1–45. University of Edmonton.

Bachrach, Asaf, and Roni Katzir. 2009. Right-node raising and delayed spellout. In *Interphases: Phase-theoretic investigations of linguistic interfaces,* ed. Kleanthes K. Grohmann, 283–316. Oxford: Oxford University Press.

Baker, Carol L. 1970. Notes on the description of English questions: The role of an abstract question morpheme. *Foundations of Language* 6:197–217.

Barr, Dale J., Roger Levy, Christoph Scheepers, and Harry Tily. 2013. Random effects structure for confirmatory hypothesis testing: Keep it maximal. *Journal of Memory and Language* 68:225–278.

Barss, Andrew. 2000. Minimalism and asymmetric *wh*-interpretation. In *Step by step: Essays on Minimalist syntax in honor of Howard Lasnik*, ed. Roger Martin, David Michaels, and Juan Uriagereka, 31–52. Cambridge, MA: MIT Press.

Bates, Douglas M., and Deepayan Sarkar. 2007. Ime4: Linear mixed-effects models using S4 classes. R package version 0.9975-12, http://CRAN.R-project.org/.

Beaver, David, and Brady Clark. 2008. *Sense and sensitivity: How focus determines meaning*. Oxford: Wiley-Blackwell.

Beck, Sigrid. 1996a. Quantified structures as barriers for LF movement. *Natural Language Semantics* 4:1–56.

Beck, Sigrid. 1996b. *Wh*-construction and transparent Logical Form. Doctoral dissertation, Universität Tübingen.

Beck, Sigrid. 2006. Intervention effects follow from focus interpretation. *Natural Language Semantics* 14:1–56.

Beck, Sigrid, and Shin-Sook Kim. 1997. On *wh*- and operator scope in Korean. *Journal of East Asian Linguistics* 6:339–384.

Beck, Sigrid, and Shin-Sook Kim. 2006. Intervention effects in alternative questions. *Journal of Comparative German Linguistics* 9:165–208.

Bennett, Ryan. 2009. Two subject asymmetries in Defaka focus extraction. Qualifying paper, Rutgers University.

Bennett, Ryan, Akinbiyi Akinlabi, and Bruce Connell. 2012. Two subject asymmetries in Defaka focus constructions. In *WCCFL 29: Proceedings of the 29th West Coast Conference on Formal Linguistics*, ed. Jaehoon Choi, E. Alan Hogue, Jeffrey Punske, Deniz Tat, Jessamyn Schertz, and Alex Trueman, 294–302. Somerville, MA: Cascadilla.

Bever, Tom. 1970. The cognitive basis for linguistic structure. In *Cognition and the development of language*, ed. John R. Hayes, 279–362. New York: Wiley.

Bobaljik, Jonathan David. 1995. Morphosyntax: The syntax of verbal inflection. Doctoral dissertation, MIT.

Bolinger, Dwight. 1978. Asking more than one thing at a time. In *Questions*, ed, Henry Hiz, 107–150. Dordrecht: Reidel.

Bošković, Željko. 2000. Sometimes in [Spec,CP], sometimes in situ. In *Step by step: Essays on Minimalist syntax in honor of Howard Lasnik*, ed. Roger Martin, David Michaels, and Juan Uriagereka, 53–87. Cambridge, MA: MIT Press.

Bošković, Željko. 2002. On multiple *wh*-fronting. *Linguistic Inquiry* 33:351–383.

Bošković, Željko. 2003. On the interpretation of multiple questions. *Linguistic Variation Yearbook* 1:1–15.

Bošković, Željko. 2007. A note on *wh* typology. In *Linguistic investigations into formal description of Slavic languages*, ed. Peter Kosta and Lilia Schürcks, 159–170. Frankfurt am Main: Peter Lang.

Bouton, Lawrence F. 1970. Antecedent-contained pro-forms. In *Papers from the Sixth regional meeting, Chicago Linguistic Society*, 154–167. Chicago: University of Chicago, Chicago Linguistic society.

Branan, Kenyon. 2017a. In-situ *wh*-phrases in Superiority violating contexts don't have to be in-situ. In *A pesky set: Papers for David Pesetsky*, ed. Claire Halpert, Hadas Kotek, and Coppe van Urk, 353–359. MIT Working Papers in Linguistics 80. Cambridge, MA: MIT, MIT Working Papers in Linguistics.

Branan, Kenyon. 2017b. Prosodic intervention. Ms., MIT.

Breakstone, Micha, Alexandre Cremers, Danny Fox, and Martin Hackl. 2011. On the analysis of scope ambiguities in comparative constructions: Converging evidence from real-time sentence processing and offline data. In *Proceedings of SALT 21*, ed. Neil Ashton, Anca Chereches, and David Lutz, 712–731. https://journals.linguisticsociety .org/proceedings/index.php/SALT/issue/view/88.

Brody, Michael. 1990. Some remarks on the focus field in Hungarian. In *UCl working papers in linguistics 2*, ed. John Harris, 201–225. London: University College London, UCL Division of Psychology and Language Sciences.

Bruening, Benjamin. 2001. Syntax at the edge: Cross-clausal phenomena and the syntax of Passamaquoddy. Doctoral dissertation, MIT.

Buccola, Brian, and Benjamin Spector. 2016. Modified numerals and maximality. *Linguistics and Philosophy* 39:151–199.

Büring, Daniel. 1996. Drinking, accents, and negation. In *Proceedings of Workshop on Focus*, ed. Elena Benedicto, Maribel Romero, and Satoshi Tomioka, 37–50. Amherst: University of Massachusetts, Graduate Linguistic Student Association.

Büring, Daniel. 2003. On D-trees, beans, and B-accents. *Linguistics and Philosophy* 26:511–545.

Butler, Alastair. 2001. Intervention effects in English questions. In *Proceedings of Szklarska Poreba Workshop 2*. http://citeseerx.ist.psu.edu/viewdoc/download?doi=10.1.1 .21.5072&rep=rep1&type=pdf.

Cable, Seth. 2007. The grammar of Q. Doctoral dissertation, MIT.

Cable, Seth. 2010. *The grammar of Q: Q-particles,* wh-*movement, and pied-piping*. Oxford: Oxford University Press.

Chang, Lisa. 1997. *Wh*-in-situ phenomena in French. Master's thesis, University of British Columbia.

Charlow, Simon. 2017. The scope of alternatives: Indefiniteness and islands. Ms., Rutgers University.

Cheng, Lisa Lai-Shen. 1991. On the typology of *wh*-questions. Doctoral dissertation, MIT.

Cheng, Lisa Lai-Shen, and Hamida Demirdache. 2010. Trapped at the edge: On long-distance pair-list readings. *Lingua* 120:463–480.

Chierchia, Gennaro. 1993. Questions with quantifiers. *Natural Language Semantics* 1:181–234.

Chomsky, Noam. 1973. Conditions on transformations. In *A festschrift for Morris Halle*, ed Stephen R. Anderson and Paul Kiparsky, 232–286. New York: Holt, Rinehart and Winston.

Chomsky, Noam. 1981. *Lectures on government and binding*. Dordrecht: Foris.

Chomsky, Noam. 1992. A minimalist program for linguistic theory. MIT Occasional Papers in Linguistics 1. Cambridge, MA: MIT, MIT Working Papers in Linguistics.

Chomsky, Noam. 1993. A minimalist program for linguistic theory. In *The view from Building 20*, ed. Kenneth Hale and Samuel Jay Keyser, 1–52. Cambridge, MA: MIT Press.

Chomsky, Noam. 1995. *The Minimalist Program*. Cambridge, MA: MIT Press.

Chomsky, Noam. 1998. Minimalist inquiries: The framework. MIT Occasional Papers in Linguistics 15. Cambridge, MA: MIT, MIT Working Papers in Linguistics.

Chomsky, Noam. 1999. Derivation by phase. MIT Occasional Papers in Linguistics 18. Cambridge, MA: MIT, MIT Working Papers in Linguistics.

Chomsky, Noam. 2000. Minimalist inquiries: The framework. In *Step by step: Essays on Minimalist syntax in honor of Howard Lasnik*, ed. Roger Martin, David Michaels, and Juan Uriagereka, 89–155. Cambridge, MA: MIT Press.

Chomsky, Noam. 2001. Derivation by phase. In *Ken Hale: A life in language*, ed. Michael Kenstowicz, 1–52. Cambridge, MA: MIT Press.

Chomsky, Noam. 2008. On phases. In *Foundational issues in linguistic theory*, ed. Robert Freidin, Carlos Otero, and Maria Luisa Zubizarreta, 133–166. Cambridge, MA: MIT Press.

Ciardelli, Ivano, Jeroen Groenendijk, and Floris Roelofsen. 2017. Inquisitive Semantics: A new notion of meaning. Ms., University of Amsterdam.

Ciardelli, Ivano, Floris Roelofsen, and Nadine Theiler. 2017. Composing alternatives. *Linguistics and Philosophy* 40:1–36.

Clifton, Charles, Jr., Gisbert Fanselow, and Lyn Frazier. 2006. Amnestying Superiority violations: Processing multiple questions. *Linguistic Inquiry* 37:51–68.

Clifton, Charles, Jr., Lyn Frazier, and Patricia Deevy. 1999. Feature manipulation in sentence comprehension. *Rivista di Linguistica* 11:11–39.

Cole, Peter, and Gabriella Hermon. 1998. The typology of *wh*-movement: *Wh*-questions in Malay. *Syntax* 1:221–258.

Collins, Chris. 1996. *Local economy*. Cambridge, MA: MIT Press.

Collins, Chris. 2001. Economy conditions in syntax. In *Handbook of syntactic theory*, ed. Chris Collins and Mark R. Baltin, 45–61. Oxford: Blackwell.

Comorovski, Ileana. 1989. Discourse and the syntax of multiple constituent questions. Doctoral dissertation, Cornell University.

Constant, Noah. 2014. Contrastive topic: Meanings and realizations. Doctoral dissertation, University of Massachusetts, Amherst.

Culicover, Peter W. 1992. Topicalization, inversion, and complementizers in English. In *Going Romance and Beyond: Fifth Symposium on Comparative Grammar*, ed. Denis Delfitto, Martin Everaert, Arnold Evers, and Frits Stuurman, 1–43. Utrecht: OTS.

Dayal, Veneeta. 1996. *Locality in* wh *quantification*. Dordrecht Kluwer.

Dayal, Veneeta. 2002. Single-pair versus multiple-pair answers: *Wh*-in-situ and scope. *Linguistic Inquiry* 33:512–520.

Dayal, Veneeta. 2016. *Questions*. Oxford: Oxford University Press.

Diesing, Molly. 1992. *Indefinites*. Cambridge, MA: MIT Press.

Dornisch, Ewa. 2000. Overt quantifier raising in Polish. In *Proceedings of Generative Linguistics in Poland (GLiP 1)*, ed. Piotr Bański and Adam Przepiórkowski, 47–58. Warsaw: Polish Academy of Sciences, Institute of Computer Science.

É. Kiss, Katalin. 1986. Against the LF-movement of *wh*-phrases. Ms., Hungarian Academy of Sciences, Budapest.

É. Kiss, Katalin. 1987. *Configurationality in Hungarian*. Dordrecht: Reidel.

É Kiss, Katalin. 2002. *The syntax of Hungarian*. Cambridge: Cambridge University Press.

Eilam, Aviad. 2008. Intervention effects: Why Amharic patterns differently. In *WCCFL 27*, ed. Natasha Abner and Jason Bishop, 141–149. Somerville, MA: Cascadilla Proceedings Project.

Elliott, Patrick. 2015. Nested *wh*-questions and the locality of scope-taking. Slides from the workshop Questions at the Syntax-Semantics Interface, University College London.

Engdahl, Elisabet. 1986. *Constituent questions: With special reference to Swedish*. Dordrecht: Reidel.

Epstein, Samuel David. 1992. Derivational constraints on $\bar{A}$-chain formation. *Linguistic Inquiry* 23:235–259.

Erlewine, Michael Yoshitaka. 2014. Movement out of focus. Doctoral dissertation, MIT.

Erlewine, Michael Yoshitaka, and Hadas Kotek. 2014. Intervention in focus pied-piping. In *NELS 43*, ed. Hsin-Lun Huang, Ethan Poole, and Amanda Rysling, 1:117–130. Amherst: University of Massachusetts, Graduate Linguistic Student Association.

Erlewine, Michael Yoshitaka, and Hadas Kotek. 2016. Even-NPIs in Dharamsala Tibetan. In *Introduction to formal syntax, semantics, and morphology of South Asian languages*, ed. Emily Manetta and Ayesha Kidwai, special issue, *Linguistic Analysis* 40(3–4):129–165.

Erlewine, Michael Yoshitaka, and Hadas Kotek. 2018. Focus association through movement: Evidence from Tanglewood. *Linguistic Inquiry* 49:441–463.

Erteschik-Shir, Nomi. 1973. On the nature of island constraints. Doctoral dissertation, MIT.

Fanselow, Gisbert, Denisa Lenertova, and Thomas Weskott. 2008. Studies on the acceptability of object movement to Spec,CP. In *The discourse potential of underspecified structures*, ed. Anita Steube, 413–438. Berlin:Water de Gruyter.

Featherston, Sam. 2005a. Magnitude estimation and what it can do for your syntax: Some *wh*-constraints in German. *Lingua* 115:1525–1550.

Featherston, Sam. 2005b. Universals and grammaticality: *Wh*-constraints in German and English. *Linguistics* 43:667–711.

von Fintel, Kai, Danny Fox, and Sabine Iatridou. 2014. Definiteness as maximal informativeness. In *The art and craft of semantics: A festschrift for Irene Heim*, ed. Luka Crnič and Uli Sauerland, 1:165–174. Cambridge, MA: MIT, MIT Working Papers in Linguistics.

Ford, Marilyn, Joan Bresnan, and Ron Kaplan. 1982. A competence-based theory of syntactic closure. In *The mental representation of grammatical relations*, ed. Joan Bresnan, 727–796. Cambridge, MA: MIT Press.

Fox, Danny. 1995. Economy and scope. *Natural Language Semantics* 3:283–341.

Fox, Danny. 2000. *Economy and semantic interpretation*. Cambridge, MA: MIT Press.

Fox, Danny. 2002. Antecedent-Contained Deletion and the copy theory of movement. *Linguistic Inquiry* 33:63–96.

Fox, Danny. 2003. On Logical Form, In *Minimalist syntax*, ed. Randall Hendrick, 82–123. Oxford: Blackwell.

Fox, Danny. 2012a. The semantics of questions: Introductory remarks. Handout, MIT. http://lingphil.mit.edu/papers/fox/firstclass.pdf.

Fox, Danny. 2012b. Multiple *wh*-questions: Uniqueness, pair-list and second-order questions. Handout, MIT. http://lingphil.mit.edu/papers/fox/uniqueness-pair-list.pdf.

Fox, Danny. 2012c. Possible ramifications for superiority. Handout, MIT. http://lingphil.mit.edu/papers/fox/Superiority.pdf.

Fox, Danny, and Martin Hackl. 2006. The universal density of measurement. *Linguistics and Philosophy* 29:537–586.

Fox, Danny, and Jon Nissenbaum. 1999. Extraposition and the nature of covert movement. In *WCCFL 18*, ed. Sonya Bird, Andrew Carnie, Jason D. Haugen, and Peter Norquest, 132–144. Somerville, MA: Cascadilla Press.

Frampton, John. 1991. Relativized Minimality: A review. *The Linguistic Review* 8:1–46.

Frampton, John, and Sam Gutmann. 1999. Cyclic computation. *Syntax* 2:1–27.

Frazier, Lyn. 1999. *On sentence interpretation*. Dordrecht: Kluwer.

Frazier, Lyn, and Charles Clifton. Jr. 2000. On bound variable interpretations: The LF-only hypothesis. *Journal of Psycholinguistic Research* 29:125–139.

Frazier, Lyn, and Charles Clifton. Jr. 2001. Parsing coordinates and ellipsis: Copy α. *Syntax* 4:1–22.

Frazier, Lyn, and Charles Clifton. Jr. 2002. Processing D-linked phrases. *Journal of Psycholinguistic Research* 31:633–660.

Frazier, Lyn, and Janet D. Fodor. 1978. The sausage machine: A new two-stage parsing model. *Cognition* 6:291–325.

Frazier, Lyn, and Keith Rayner. 1982. Making and correcting errors during sentence comprehension: Eye movements in the analysis of structurally ambiguous sentences. *Cognitive Psychology* 14:178–210.

Gärtner, Hans-Martin. 2002. *Generalized transformations and beyond: Reflections on Minimalist syntax.* Berlin: Akademie Verlag.

George, Benjamin R. 2011. Question embedding and the semantics of answers. Doctoral dissertation, UCLA.

Giannakidou, Anastasia. 1997. The landscape of polarity items. Doctoral dissertation, University of Groningen.

Gibson, Edward. 1998. Linguistic complexity: Locality of syntactic dependencies. *Cognition* 68:1–76.

Golan, Yael. 1993. Node crossing economy, superiority and D-linking. Ms., Tel Aviv University.

Gordon, Peter C., Randall Hendrick, and Marcus Johnson. 2004. Effects of noun phrase type on sentence complexity. *Journal of Memory and Language* 51:97–114.

Graf, Thomas. 2013. Local and transderivational constraints in syntax and semantics. Doctoral dissertation, UCLA.

Groat, Erich, and John O'Neil. 1996. Spell-out at the LF-interface. In *Minimal ideas*, ed. Werner Abraham, Samuel David Epstein, Höskuldur Thráinsson, and C. Jan-Wouter Zwart, 113–139. Amsterdam: John Benjamins.

Groenendijk, Jeroen. 2009. Inquisitive Semantics: Two possibilities for disjunction. In *Seventh International Tbilisi Symposium on Language, Logic, and Computation*, ed. Peter Bosch, David Gabelaia, and Jérôme Lang, 80–94. Berlin: Springer-Verlag.

Groenendijk, Jeroen, and Floris Roelofsen. 2009. Inquisitive Semantics and pragmatics. *In Meaning, content and argument: Proceedings of the ILCLI International Workshop on Semantics, Pragmatics and Rhetoric (SPR-09)*, ed. Jesús M. Larrazabal and Larraitz Zubeldia, 41–72. San Sebastián: Universidad del País Vasco, Servicio Editorial.

Groenendijk, Jeroen, and Martin Stokhof. 1984. Studies on the semantics of questions and the pragmatics of answers. Doctoral dissertation, University of Amsterdam.

Hackl, Martin, Jorie Koster-Hale, and Jason Varvoutis. 2012. Quantification and ACD: Evidence from real-time sentence processing. *Journal of Semantics* 29:145–206.

Hagstrom, Paul. 1998. Decomposing questions. Doctoral dissertation, MIT.

Haida, Andreas, and Sophie Repp. 2013. Focus alternatives or indefinite alternatives? Experimental evidence. In *Proceedings of the 19th Amsterdam Colloquium*, ed. Maria Aloni, Michael Franke, and Floris Roelofsen, 131–138. Berlin: Humboldt University, Department of English and American Studies.

Hallman, Peter J. 1997. Reiterative syntax. Master's thesis, UCLA.

Hamblin, Charles. 1973. Questions in Montague English. *Foundations of Language* 10:41–53.

Heck, Fabian. 2008. *On pied-piping: wh-movement and beyond.* Berlin: Mouton de Gruyter.

Heck, Fabian, and Gereon Müller. 2000. Repair-driven movement and the local optimization of derivations. Ms., University of Stuttgart and IDS Mannheim.

Heim, Irene. 1994. Interrogative semantics and Karttunen's semantics for *know*. In *IATL 1: The Proceedings of the Ninth Annual Conference (Ben Gurion University of the Negev) and of the Workshop on Discourse (Hebrew University of Jerusalem)*, ed. Rhonna Buchalla and Anita Mittwoch, 128–144. The Israel Association for Theoretical Linguistics.

Heim, Irene, and Angelika Kratzer. 1998. *Semantics in generative grammar*. Oxford: Blackwell.

Hofmeister, Philip, Florian T. Jaeger, Ivan A. Sag, Inbal Arnon, and Neal Snider. 2007. Locality and accessibility in *wh*-questions. In *Roots: Linguistics in search of its evidential base*, ed. Sam Featherston and Wolfgang Sternefeld, 185–206. Berlin: Mouton de Gruyter.

Hoji, Hajime. 1985. Logical Form constraints and configurational structures in Japanese. Doctoral dissertation, University of Washington.

Hornstein, Norbert. 1995. *Logical Form: From GB to Minimalism*. Cambridge, MA: Blackwell.

Horvath, Julia. 1986. *FOCUS in the theory of grammar and the syntax of Hungarian*. Dordrecht: Foris.

Huang, C.-T. James. 1982a. Logical relations in Chinese and the theory of grammar. Doctoral dissertation, MIT.

Huang, C.-T. James. 1982b. Move *wh* in a language without *wh* movement. *The Linguistic Review* 1:369–416.

Huang, C.-T. James. 1995. Logical Form. In *Government and Binding Theory and the Minimalist Program*, ed. Gert Webelhuth, 127–173. Oxford: Blackwell.

Jackendoff, Ray. 1972. *Semantic interpretation in generative grammar*. Cambridge, MA: MIT Press.

Johnson, David, and Shalom Lappin. 1999. *Local constraints vs. economy*. Stanford, CA: CSLI Publications.

Johnson, Kyle. 2000a. How far will quantifiers go? In *Step by step: Essays on Minimalist syntax in honor of Howard Lasnik*, ed. Roger Martin, David Michaels, and Juan Uriagereka, 187–210. Cambridge, MA: MIT Press.

Johnson, Kyle. 2000b. When verb phrases go missing. In *The first GLOT International state-of-the-article book*, ed. Lisa Lai-Shen Cheng and Rint P. E. Sybesma, 3–9. Berlin: Mouton de Gruyter.

Johnson, Kyle, and Satoshi Tomioka. 1997. Lowering and mid-size clauses. In *Proceedings of the 1997 Tübingen Workshop on Reconstruction*, ed. Graham Katz, Shin-Sook Kim, and Winhart Haike, 185–206. Universität Stuttgart and Universität Tübingen.

Just, Marcel A., Patricia A. Carpenter, and Jacqueline D. Wooley. 1982. Paradigms and processes in reading comprehension. *Journal of Experimental Psychology: General* 111:228–238.

Karttunen, Lauri. 1977. Syntax and semantics of questions. *Linguistics and Philosophy* 1:3–44.

Kazanina, Nina, and Colin Phillips. 2000. Differential effects of constraints in the processing of Russian cataphora. *Quarterly Journal of Experimental Psychology* 63:371–400.

Kehler, Andrew. 2001. *Coherence, reference, and the theory of grammar.* Stanford, CA: CSLI Publications.

Kennedy, Christopher. 1997. Antecedent-Contained Deletion and the syntax of quantification. *Linguistic Inquiry* 28:662–688.

Kertz, Laura. 2010. Ellipsis reconsidered. Doctoral dissertation, University of California, Davis.

Kim, Shin-Sook. 2002a. Focus matters: Two types of intervention effect. Paper presented at WCCFL 21. http://www-users.york.ac.uk/~sk899/talks/kim-WCCFL21HO.pdf.

Kim, Shin-Sook. 2002b. Intervention effects are focus effects. In *Japanese/Korean Linguistics, vol. 10*, ed. Noriko Akatsuka, Susan Strauss, and Bernard Comrie, 615–628. Stanford, CA: CSLI Publications.

Kim, Soowon. 1991. Chain scope and quantification structure. Doctoral dissertation, Brandeis University.

Kishimoto, Hideki. 2005. *Wh*-in-situ and movement in Sinhala questions. *Natural Language and Linguistic Theory* 23:1–51.

Kitahara, Hisatsugu. 1996. Raising Q without QR. In *Minimal ideas*, ed. Werner Abraham, Samuel David Epstein, Höskuldur Thráinsson, and C. Jan-Wouter Zwart, 189–198. Amsterdam: John Benjamins.

Kitahara, Hisatsugu. 1997. *Elementary operations and optimal derivations.* Cambridge, MA: MIT Press.

Kobele, Gregory, and Harold Torrence. 2006. Intervention and focus in Asante Twi. *ZAS Papers in Linguistics* 46:161–184.

Kotek, Hadas. 2012. Readings of Hebrew multiple questions. In *WCCFL 30*, ed. Nathan Arnett and Ryan Bennett, 216–225. Somerville, MA: Cascadilla Proceedings Project.

Kotek, Hadas. 2014a. Composing questions. Doctoral dissertation, MIT.

Kotek, Hadas. 2014b. *Wh*-fronting in a two-probe system. *Natural Language and Linguistic Theory* 32:1105–1143.

Kotek, Hadas. 2016. Covert partial *wh*-movement and the nature of derivations. *Glossa* 1(1):25, 1–19.

Kotek, Hadas. 2017a. Dissociating intervention effects from superiority in English *wh*-questions. *The Linguistic Review* 34:397–417.

Kotek, Hadas. 2017b. Intervention effects arise from scope-taking over alternatives. In *proceedings of NELS 47*, ed. Andrew Lamont and Katerina Tetzloff, 2:153–166. Amherst: University of Massachusetts, Graduate Linguistic Student Association.

Kotek, Hadas. 2017c. Questioning superiority. In *A pesky set: Papers for David Pesetsky*, ed. Claire Halpert, Hadas Kotek, and Coppe van Urk, 457–466. MIT Working Papers in Linguistics 80. Cambridge, MA: MIT, MIT Working Papers in Linguistics.

Kotek, Hadas, and Michael Yoshitaka Erlewine. 2016. Covert pied-piping in English multiple *wh*-questions. *Linguistic Inquiry* 47:669–693.

Kotek, Hadas, and Martin Hackl. 2013. An experimental investigation of interrogative syntax/semantics. In *Proceedings of the 19th Amsterdam Colloquium*, ed. Maria Aloni, Michael Franke, and Floris Roelofsen, 147–154. http://maloni.humanities.uva.nl/AC2013/AC_proceedings.pdf.

Kratzer, Angelika. 1991. The representation of focus. In *Semantik/Semantics: An international handbook of contemporary research*, ed. Arnim von Stechow and Dieter Wunderlich, 825–834. Berlin: Mouton de Gruyter.

Kratzer, Angelika. 1995. Stage-level vs. individual-level predicates. In *The generic book*, ed. Gregory Carlson and Francis Jeffry Pelletier, 125–175. Chicago: University of Chicago Press.

Kratzer, Angelika, and Junko Shimoyama. 2002. Indeterminate pronouns: The view from Japanese. In *The Proceedings of the Third Tokyo Conference on Psycholinguistics (TCP 2002)*, ed. Yukio Otsu, 1–25. Tokyo: Hituzi Syobo.

Krifka, Manfred. 2001. Quantifying into question acts. *Natural Language Semantics* 9:1–40.

Krifka, Manfred. 2006. Association with focus phrases. In *The architecture of focus*, ed. Valéria Moinár and Susanne Winkler, 105–136. Berlin: Mouton de Gruyter.

Kuno, Susumu, and Jane J. Robinson. 1972. Multiple *wh* questions. *Linguistic Inquiry* 3:463–487.

Kuroda, S.-Y. 1965. Generative grammatical studies in the Japanese language. Doctoral dissertation, MIT.

Ladusaw, William A. 1980. *Polarity sensitivity as inherent scope relations*. New York: Garland.

Larson, Richard K., and Robert May. 1990. Antecedent containment or vacuous movement: Reply to Baltin. *Linguistic Inquiry* 21:103–122.

Lasnik, Howard, and Mamoru Saito. 1984. On the nature of proper government. *Linguistic Inquiry* 15:235–290.

Lasnik, Howard, and Mamoru Saito. 1992. *Move α: Conditions on its application and output*. Cambridge, MA: MIT Press.

Lebeaux, David. 2009. *Where does binding theory apply?* Cambridge, MA: MIT Press.

Lechner, Winfried. 2013. The syntax-semantics interface. In *Syntax: An international handbook*, ed. Tibor Kiss and Artemis Alexiadou, 1199–1256. 2nd ed. Berlin: Mouton de Gruyter.

Li, Haoze, and Jess Law. 2014a. Focus intervention: A quantificational domain approach. In *NELS 44: Proceedings of the Forty-Fourth Annual Meeting of the North East Linguistic Society*, ed. Jyoti Iyer and Leland Kusmer, 1:273–287. Amherst: University of Massachusetts, Graduate Linguistic Student Association.

Li, Haoze, and Jess Law. 2014b. Generalized focus intervention. In *Proceedings of SALT 24*, ed. Todd Snider, Sarah D'Antonio, and Mia Weigand, 473–493. https://journals.linguisticsociety.org/proceedings/index.php/SALT/issue/view/54.

Li, Haoze, and Jess Law. 2016. Alternatives in different dimensions: A case study of focus intervention. *Linguistics and Philosophy* 39:201–245.

Lipták, Anikó. 2000. On the difference between focus movement and *wh*-movement. *GLOW Newsletter* 44:78–79.

MacDonald, Maryellen C., Neal J. Perlmutter, and Mark S. Seidenberg. 1994. Lexical nature of syntactic ambiguity resolution. *Psychological Review* 101:676–703.

Mahajan, Anoop K. 1990. The A/A-bar distinction and movement theory. Doctoral dissertation, MIT.

Martin, Andrea E., and Brian McElree. 2008. A content-addressable pointer underlies comprehension of verb-phrase ellipsis. *Journal of Memory and Language* 58:879–906.

Martin, Andrea E., and Brian McElree. 2009. Memory operations that support language comprehension: Evidence from verb-phrase ellipsis. *Journal of Experimental Psychology: Learning, Memory, and Cognition* 35:1231–1239.

Martin, Andrea E., and Brian McElree. 2011. Direct-access retrieval during sentence comprehension: Evidence from sluicing. *Journal of Memory and Language* 64:327–343.

Mathieu, Eric. 1999. *Wh* in situ and the intervention effect. In *UCL working papers in linguistics 11,* ed. Corinne Iten and Ad Neeleman, 441–472. London: University College London, UCL Division of Psychology and Language Sciences.

Mathieu, Eric. 2002. The syntax of non-canonical quantification: A comparative study. Doctoral dissertation, University College London.

May, Robert. 1985. *Logical Form: Its structure and derivation.* Cambridge, MA: MIT Press.

Mayr, Clemens. 2010. The role of alternatives and strength in grammar. Doctoral dissertation, Harvard University.

Mayr, Clemens. 2014. Intervention effects and additivity. *Journal of Semantics* 31:513–554.

Merchant, Jason. 2001. *The syntax of silence.* Oxford: Oxford University Press.

Merchant, Jason. 2013. Voice and ellipsis. *Linguistic Inquiry* 44:77–108.

Miyagawa, Shigeru. 2001. EPP, scrambling, and *wh*-in-situ. In *Ken Hale: A life in language*, ed. Michael Kenstowicz, 293–338. Cambridge, MA: MIT Press.

Miyagawa, Shigeru. 2011. Optionality. In *The Oxford handbook of linguistic Minimalism*, ed. Cedric Boeckx, 354–376. Oxford: Oxford University Press.

Moltmann, Friederike, and Anna Szabolcsi. 1994. Scope interaction with pair-list quantifiers. In *Proceedings of NELS 24*, ed. Mercè Gonzàlez, 381–395. Amherst: University of Massachusetts, Graduate Linguistic Student Association.

Murphy, Gregory. 1985. Processes of understanding anaphora. *Journal of Memory and Language* 24:290–303.

Nicolae, Andreea. 2013. Any questions? Doctoral dissertation, Harvard University.

Nishigauchi, Taisuke. 1986. Quantification in syntax. Doctoral dissertation, University of Massachusetts, Amherst.

Nishigauchi, Taisuke. 1990. *Quantification in the theory of grammar*. Dordrecht: Kluwer.

Nissenbaum, Jon. 2000. Investigations of covert phrase movement. Doctoral dissertation, MIT.

Novel, Marc, and Maribel Romero. 2009. Movement, variables, and Hamblin alternatives. In *Proceedings of Sinn und Bedeutung 14*, 322–338. https://www.univie.ac.at /sub14/proc/novel-romero.pdf.

Partee, Barbara Hall. 1986. Noun phrase interpretation and type-shifting principles. In *Studies in Discourse Representation Theory and the theory of generalized quantifiers*, ed. Jeroen Groenendijk, Dick de Jongh, and Martin Stokhof, 115–143. Dordrecht: Foris.

Partee, Barbara Hall, and Mats Rooth. 1983. Generalized conjunction and type ambiguity. In *Meaning, use and interpretation*, ed. Rainer Bäuerle, Christoph Schwarze, and Arnim von Stechow, 334–356. Berlin: de Gruyter.

Pesetsky, David. 1987. *Wh*-in-situ: Movement and unselective binding. In *The representation of (in)definiteness*, ed. Eric Reuland and Alice G. B. ter Meulen, 98–129. Cambridge, MA: MIT Press.

Pesetsky, David. 1998. Some optimality principles of sentence pronunciation. In *Is the best good enough?*, ed. Pilar Barbosa, Danny Fox, Paul Hagstrom, Martha McGinnis, and David Pesetsky, 337–383. Cambridge, MA: MIT Press.

Pesetsky, David. 2000. *Phrasal movement and its kin*. Cambridge, MA: MIT Press.

Phillips, Colin. 1996. Order and structure. Doctoral dissertation, MIT.

Phillips, Colin. 2003. Linear order and constituency. *Linguistic Inquiry* 34:37–90.

Pica, Pierre, and William Snyder. 1995. Weak crossover, scope, and agreement in a Minimalist framework. In *WCCFL 13: The Proceedings of the Thirteenth West Conference on Formal Linguistics,* ed. Raul Aranovich, William Byrne, Susanne Preuss, and Martha Senturia, 334–349. Stanford, CA: CSLI Publications.

Polinsky, Maria, Carlos Gomez Gallo, Peter Graff, and Ekaterina Kravtchenko. 2012. Subject preference and ergativity. *Lingua* 122:267–277.

Polinsky, Maria, and Eric Potsdam. 2014. Left edge topics in Russian and the processing of anaphoric dependencies. *Journal of Linguistics* 50:629–669.

Pope, Emily N. 1976. *Questions and answers in English*. The Hague: Mouton.

Potts, Christopher. 2001. Three kinds of transderivational constraints. In *Syntax and semantics at Santa Cruz, vol. 3*, ed. Séamas Mac Bhloscaidh, 21–40. Santa Cruz: University of California, Linguistics Department.

Preminger, Omer. 2011. Agreement as a fallible operation. Doctoral dissertation, MIT.

Pritchett, Bradley L. 1992. *Grammatical competence and parsing performance*. Chicago: University of Chicago Press.

Ramchand, Gillian. 1997. Questions, polarity and alternative semantics. In *Proceedings of NELS 27*, ed. Kiyomi Kusumoto, 383–396. Amherst: University of Massachusetts, Graduate Linguistic Student Association.

Ratiu, Dafina. 2005. Questions multiples en roumain. Master's thesis, Université de Nantes.

Ratiu, Dafina. 2007. Evidence for (counter) cyclic movement from Romanian. Paper presented at the 37th Linguistics Symposium on Romance Languages.

Reinhart, Tanya. 1997. Quantifier scope: How labor is divided between QR and choice functions. *Linguistics and Philosophy* 20:335–397.

Reinhart, Tanya. 1998. *Wh*-in-situ in the framework of the Minimalist Program. *Natural Language Semantics* 6:29–56.

Reinhart, Tanya. 2006. *Interface strategies: Optimal and costly computations*. Cambridge, MA: MIT Press.

Richards, Marc D. 2004. Object shift and scrambling in North and West Germanic: A case study in symmetrical syntax. Doctoral dissertation, University of Cambridge.

Richards, Norvin. 1997. What moves where when in which language? Doctoral dissertation, MIT.

Richards, Norvin. 2000. An island effect in Japanese. *Journal of East Asian Linguistics* 9:187–205.

Richards, Norvin. 2001. *Movement in language: Interactions and architectures*. Oxford: Oxford University Press.

Richards, Norvin. 2010. *Uttering trees*. Cambridge, MA: MIT Press.

Richards, Norvin. 2016. *Contiguity theory*. Cambridge, MA: MIT Press.

Rizzi, Luigi. 1990. *Relativized Minimality*. Cambridge, MA: MIT Press.

Rizzi, Luigi. 2001. Relativized Minimality effects. In *The handbook of contemporary syntactic theory*, ed. Mark R. Baltin and Chris Collins, 89–110. Oxford: Blackwell.

Roberts, Craige. 1996. Information structure: Towards an integrated formal theory of pragmatics. In *Papers in semantics*, ed. Jae-Hak Yoon and Andreas Kathol, 91–136. OSU Working Papers in Linguistics 49. Columbus: The Ohio State University, Department of Linguistics.

Roelofsen, Floris. 2011. Algebraic foundations for Inquisitive Semantics. In *Proceedings of the Third International Conference on Logic, Rationality, and Interaction*, ed. Hans van Ditmarsch, Jerome Lang, and Shier Ju, 233–243. Berlin: Springer-Verlag.

Rooth, Mats. 1985. Association with focus. Doctoral dissertation, University of Massachusetts, Amherst.

Rooth, Mats. 1992. A theory of focus interpretation. *Natural Language Semantics* 1:75–116.

Rooth, Mats, and Barbara Hall Partee. 1982. Conjunction, type ambiguity, and wide scope *or*. In *Proceedings of the First West Coast Conference on Formal Linguistics*, ed. Daniel P. Flickinger, Marlys Macken, and Nancy Wiegand, 353–362. Stanford, CA: Stanford University, Linguistics Department.

Ross, John Robert. 1967. Constraints on variables in syntax. Doctoral dissertation, MIT.

Ross, John Robert. 1969. Guess who? In *Papers from the Fifth Regional Meeting, Chicago Linguistic Society*, ed. Robert I. Binnick, Alice Davison, Georgia M. Green, and Jerry L. Morgan, 252–286. Chicago: University of Chicago, Chicago Linguistic Society.

Rudin, Catherine. 1985. *Aspects of Bulgarian syntax: Complementizers and* wh *constructions*. Columbus, OH: Slavica.

Rudin, Catherine. 1988. On multiple questions and multiple *wh* fronting. *Natural Language and Linguistic Theory* 6:445–501.

Rullmann, Hotze, and Sigrid Beck. 1998. Reconstruction and the interpretation of *which*-phrases. In *Proceedings of the 1997 Tübingen Workshop*, ed. Graham Katz, Shin-Sook Kim, and Haike Winhart, 223–256. Universität Stuttgart and Universität Tübingen.

Sabel, Joachim. 2003. Malagasy as an optional multiple *wh*-fronting language. In *Multiple* wh-*fronting*, ed. Cedric Boeckx and Kleanthes Grohmann, 229–254. Amsterdam: John Benjamins.

Sag, Ivan. 1976. Deletion and Logical Form. Doctoral dissertation, MIT.

San Pietro, Steven A., Ming Xiang, and Jason Merchant. 2012. Accounting for voice mismatches in ellipsis. In *WCCFL 30*, ed. Nathan Arnett and Ryan Bennett, 303–312. Somerville, MA: Cascadilla Proceedings Project.

Shan, Chung-chieh. 2004. Binding alongside Hamblin alternatives calls for variable-free semantics. In *Proceedings of SALT 14,* ed. Robert B. Young, 289–304. https://journals.linguisticsociety.org/proceedings/index.php/SALT/issue/view/95.

Shimoyama, Junko. 2001. *Wh*-constructions in Japanese. Doctoral dissertation, University of Massachusetts, Amherst.

Shimoyama, Junko. 2006. Indeterminate quantification in Japanese. *Natural Language Semantics* 14:139–173.

Simpson, Andrew. 2000. Wh-*movement and the theory of feature-checking*. Amsterdam: John Benjamins.

Simpson, Andrew, and Tanmoy Bhattacharya. 2003. Obligatory overt *wh*-movement in a *wh*-in-situ language. *Linguistic Inquiry* 34:127–142.

Soh, Hooi Ling. 2005. *Wh*-in-situ in Mandarin Chinese. *Linguistic Inquiry* 36:143–155.

Sternefeld, Wolfgang. 1996. Comparing reference-sets. In *The role of economy principles in linguistic theory*, ed. Chris Wilder, Hans-Martin Gärtner, and Manfred Bierwisch, 81–114. Berlin: Akademie Verlag.

Sulemana, Abdul-Razak. 2017. Q-particles and the nature of covert movement: Evidence from Bùlì. Ms., MIT.

Szabolcsi, Anna. 1981. The semantics of topic-focus articulation. In *Formal methods in the study of language*. ed. J. A. G. Groenendijk, T. M. V. Hanssen, and M. B. J. Stokhof, 513–541. Amsterdam: Mathematisch Centrum.

Szendrői, Kriszta. 2003. A stress-based approach to the syntax of Hungarian focus. *The Linguistic Review* 20:37–78.

Takano, Yuji. 1998. Object shift and scrambling. *Natural Language and Linguistic Theory* 16:817–889.

Tancredi, Chris. 1990. Not only EVEN, but even ONLY. Ms., MIT.

Tancredi, Chris. 1992. Deletion, deaccenting and presupposition. Doctoral dissertation, MIT.

Tanenhaus, Michael K., and John C. Trueswell. 1995. Sentence comprehension. In *Speech, language, and communication*, ed. Joanne L. Miller and Peter D. Eimas, 217–262. 2nd ed. San Diego, CA: Academic Press.

Tomioka, Satoshi. 2007a. Intervention effects in focus: From a Japanese point of view. In *Proceedings of the 2nd Workshop on Prosody, Syntax, and Information Structure (WPSI 2)*, ed. Shinichiro Ishihara, 97–117. Potsdam: Potsdam University Press.

Tomioka, Satoshi. 2007b. Pragmatics of LF intervention effects: Japanese and Korean interrogatives. *Journal of Pragmatics* 39:1570–1590.

Toosarvandani, Maziar. 2008. *Wh*-movement and the syntax of sluicing. *Journal of Linguistics* 44:677–722.

Toosarvandani, Maziar. 2009. Ellipsis in Farsi complex predicates. *Syntax* 12:60–92.

Truckenbrodt, Hubert. 2013. An analysis of prosodic F-effects in interrogatives: Prosody, syntax, and semantics. *Lingua* 124:131–175.

Tsai, Wei-tien Dylan. 1994. On nominal islands and LF extractions in Chinese. *Natural Language and Linguistic Theory* 12:121–175.

Tunstall, Susanne L. 1998. The interpretation of quantifiers: Semantics and processing. Doctoral dissertation, University of Massachusetts, Amherst.

Uegaki, Wataru. 2015. Interpreting questions under attitudes. Doctoral dissertation, MIT.

Uegaki, Wataru. 2018. A unified semantics for the Japanese Q-particle *ka* in indefinites, questions and disjunctions. *Glossa* 3(1):14.

Van Dyke, Julie A., and Brian McElree. 2006. Retrieval interference in sentence comprehension. *Journal of Memory and Language* 55:157–166.

Wachowicz, Krystyna. 1974. On the syntax and semantics of multiple questions. Doctoral dissertation, University of Texas.

Wagers, Matthew W., and Colin Phillips. 2009. Multiple dependencies and the role of the grammar in real-time comprehension. *Journal of Linguistics* 45:395–433.

Warren, Tessa, and Edward Gibson. 2002. The influence of referential processing on sentence complexity. *Cognition* 85:79–112.

Wexler, Kenneth, and Peter Culicover. 1980. *Formal principles of language acquisition*. Cambridge, MA: MIT Press.

Williams, Edwin. 1974. Rule ordering in grammar. Doctoral dissertation, MIT.

Williams, Edwin. 1977. Discourse and Logical Form. *Linguistic Inquiry* 8:101–139.

Willis, Paul. 2008. The role of topic-hood in multiple-*wh* question semantics. In *WCCFL 27: Proceedings of the 27th West Coast Conference on Formal Linguistics*, ed. Natasha Abner and Jason Bishop, 87–95. Somerville, MA: Cascadilla Proceedings Project.

Wiltschko, Martina. 1997. D-linking, scrambling and superiority in German. In *Groninger Arbeiten zur germanistischen Linguistik*, ed. Werner Abraham, 107–142. Groningen: Germanistisch Institut.

Wold, Dag. 1996. Long distance selective binding: The case of focus. In *Proceedings of SALT 6*, ed. Teresa Galloway and Justin Spence, 311–328. https://journals.linguisticsociety.org/proceedings/index.php/SALT/issue/view/103.

Wurmbrand, Susi. 2018. The cost of raising quantifiers. *Glossa* 3(1):19.

Xiang, Ming, Boris Harizanov, Maria Polinsky, and Ekaterina Kravtchenko. 2011. Processing morphological ambiguity: An experimental investigation of Russian numerical phrases. *Lingua* 121:548–560.

Yang, Barry Chung-Yu. 2008. Intervention effects and the covert component of grammar. Doctoral dissertation, National Tsing Hua University.

Yang, Barry Chung-Yu. 2011. Intervention effects and *wh*-construals. *Journal of East Asian Linguistics* 21:43–87.

Zentz, Jason. 2016. Forming *wh*-questions in Shona: A comparative Bantu perspective. Doctoral dissertation, Yale University.

Zwicky, Arnold M. 1971. In a manner of speaking. *Linguistic Inquiry* 2:223–233.

Index

Linguistic Inquiry Monographs

Samuel Jay Keyser, general editor